David Laing, Alexander Craig

The Poetical Works of Alexander Craig of Rose-Craig

1604-1631

David Laing, Alexander Craig

The Poetical Works of Alexander Craig of Rose-Craig
1604-1631

ISBN/EAN: 9783744677608

Printed in Europe, USA, Canada, Australia, Japan

Cover: Foto ©Thomas Meinert / pixelio.de

More available books at **www.hansebooks.com**

THE
POETICAL WORKS
OF
ALEXANDER CRAIG
OF ROSE-CRAIG

THE
POETICAL WORKS

OF

ALEXANDER CRAIG

OF ROSE-CRAIG

1604-1631

NOW FIRST COLLECTED

PRINTED FOR THE HUNTERIAN CLUB
MDCCCLXXIII

NOTE.

For this reprint of ALEXANDER CRAIG'S WORKS—the firſt collected edition—Mr. DAVID LAING, of Edinburgh, has been kind enough to write the accompanying Introduction, and the Council, on behalf of the Members, begs here to expreſs its ſenſe of his kindneſs. Thanks are alſo due to the Right Hon. the EARL OF ELLESMERE, to Mr. S. CHRISTIE-MILLER, Britwell, Buckinghamſhire, and to Mr. JAMES MAIDMENT, Edinburgh, for their liberality in lending their copies of the very rare original editions.

Each work has been given as in the original, page for page, line for line, and word for word. Miſprints have conſequently been reproduced; but all diſcovered are pointed out and corrected in the Regiſter of Errata.

Only Two hundred copies have been reprinted, excluſively for Members of THE HUNTERIAN CLUB, with ten additional copies for preſentation by the Council.

GLASGOW, *November*, 1873.

CONTENTS.

TITLE-PAGE, NOTE, AND CONTENTS. - - - 4 leaves.

INTRODUCTORY NOTICE by DAVID LAING, LL.D., Edinburgh. - - - - - - 16 leaves.

THE POETICALL ESSAYES OF Alexander Craige SCOTO-BRITANE. Seene and allowed. Imprinted at London by William *White*, dwelling in Cow-lane, neere Holborne Conduit. - - 1604. 4to. 23 leaves.

    Two copies known: one in the British Museum, and the other in the poffeffion of Mr. S. CHRISTIE-MILLER, Britwell, Buckinghamfhire.

THE AMOROSE Songes, Sonets, and Elegies: Of M. ALEXANDER CRAIGE, *Scoto - Britaine.* Imprinted at London by *William White.* - 1606. 8vo. 84 leaves.

    Two copies known: one in the Library of the Right Hon. the EARL OF ELLESMERE, Bridgewater Houfe, London, and the other in the poffeffion of Sir CHARLES E. ISHAM, Bart., Lamport Hall, Northamptonfhire.

THE POETICAL RECREATIONS OF Mr. ALEXANDER CRAIG *OF ROSECRAIG. AT EDINBVRGH* Printed by *Thomas Finlafon.* WITH LICENCE. 1609. 4to. 16 leaves.

    Three copies known: one in the poffeffion of Mr. JAMES MAIDMENT, Advocate, Edinburgh; another in the Library of the Writers to the Signet, Edinburgh; and a third in the Library of the Univerfity of Edinburgh.

CONTENTS

THE POETICALL RECREATIONS OF Mr. ALEXANDER CRAIG, of Rofe-Craig, *Scoto Britan. Otium fine literis mors eft, & vivi hominis Sepultura. ABERDENE*, Printed by Edward Raban, For David Melvill. *CVM PRIVILEGIO.* - - 1623. 4to. 18 leaves.

> Three copies known: one in the Library of Mr. S. CHRISTIE-MILLER, Britwell; another in the Library of Marifchal College, Aberdeen; and a third, which belonged to the late Mr. ROBERT PITCAIRN, W.S., Edinburgh. This work is entirely different from the preceding one of 1609, with a fimilar title.

THE PILGRIME AND HEREMITE, In forme of a Dialogue, *By Master Alexander Craig. Imprinted in ABERDENE, By* EDWARD RABAN, *for David Melvill.* - - - - - 1631. 4to. 18 leaves.

> Unique, but wanting Sig. B, 4 leaves. 𝔅lack 𝔏etter. In the poffeffion of Mr. S. CHRISTIE-MILLER, Britwell.

MISCELLANEOUS POEMS. - - - - - 5 leaves.

INDEXES, REGISTER OF ERRATA, AND GLOSSARY. - 16 leaves.

ALEXANDER CRAIG, A.M.,
OF ROSE CRAIG.

HE Author, with his fine founding title, Craig of Rofe Craig, whofe POETICAL REMAINS are now for the firft time collected, has, fince his own day, never received any great fhare of attention. The events of his life are not well afcertained, nor had Rofe Craig been identified with any place or property in Scotland. Neither have the volumes of poetry which he iffued ever before been acceffible, owing to their remarkable rarity. In the Prefbytery of Brechin there is a fmall parifh of Craig, and his delivering a poetical addrefs at Kinnaird to the King, during his progrefs northwards in 1617, at firft fuggefted that he might have belonged to that diftrict. On the other hand, in the abfence of more direct claims, the number of his Aberdeen friends furnifhed an apparent connexion with that county. Indeed, Mr. George Chalmers, in his MS. collections (chiefly made by his Nephew) for a Hiftory of the Scottifh Poets, exprefsly calls Craig a native of Aberdeenfhire.[1] On one occafion, however, Craig himfelf, in 1606, inftead of his ufual fignature of SCOTO-BRITANE, having fubftituted at the end of one of his dedications "A. C. Scoto-Banfa," this feemed at once to folve the difficulty, as it afforded a fatisfactory proof that the place of Craig's nativity was the town of Banff, which, it is unneceffary to add, borders on the north-weft part of

---

[1] MS. Collections, in my own poffeffion.

A

INTRODUCTION.

Aberdeenſhire. Some circumſtances, to be afterwards noticed, render this conjecture indiſputable.

ALEXANDER CRAIG was born at Banff about the year 1567, and received a good claſſical education in the Pariſh School of the county town. At the uſual age of fifteen or ſixteen he was ſent to complete his ſtudies at the Univerſity of St. Andrews; and in the *Nomina Incorporatorum*, in St. Leonard's College, we find ALEX. CRAIGE among the ſtudents who ſubſcribed the Articles of Religion (or the King's Confeſſion) in the year 1582. Among the Univerſity Records, there is preſerved the duplicate volume with the original ſignatures of the Students at that time, from which the following facſimile has been obtained from the "Nomina Incorporatorum qui Articulos Relligionis ſubſcribunt Anno 1582:"—

In 1586 Craig received his degree of Maſter of Arts. Among his fellow-ſtudents that year was Sir James Sempill (1566-1626); and two years later, Robert Aytoun (1570-1638), whom Craig addreſſed as his old friend and college companion. What courſe of life he was deſigned to follow has not been aſcertained.[1] He may have attracted the notice of the youthful King, and if not connected with the Royal Houſehold, he may have been otherwiſe employed: he makes at leaſt a vague alluſion to having been abroad; but it is of no uſe to indulge in mere conjecture.

On the acceſſion of King James to the throne of England, Craig, like many of his countrymen, haſtened to follow their royal maſter to the South in the hope of preferment:

---

[1] Maſter Alexander Craig's name occurs as a witneſs to an Aſſedation of the Teyndis of the Parochine of Turriff, 15 February, 1587-8. If he ſigned as a Notary Public, this might have been the Poet's Father. (Spalding Club Collections, Shires of Aberdeen and Banff, vol. ii. p. 349.)

INTRODUCTION.

"He followed King James to London, in 1603, and continued there several years, endeavouring to gain both fame and money by his poetry, and he was not successful. He wrote encomiastic poems, in a high strain of flattery, on the King and Queen; and he gained the favour of some of the courtiers by the same means."—*Chalmers.*

His first publication of "Poeticall Essayes," printed at London in 1604, has an Epistle directed "To my dread Soveraigne JAMES, by the grace of God, of *Britaine, Fraunce* and *Ireland,* King." It displays, as usual, much pedantic learning.

"I haue," he says, "(accomplished Archi-Monarch) with the rest of these *Boreo-Britan* Poets, been ingrately silent; and with the cold ashes of Feare, haue couered the coales of my Loue: Becaufe as *Archileonida* sayd to the Thracian Legates, There were many moe more valiant citizens in Sparta, then her sonne Brasidas. I find myself but a doltish Cheril among so many delicate Homers: I write not to enlarge thy fame, which is boundles; nor to begge reward, which I merit not; nor to purchase prayse, which I craue not; but in few lines to shew the infinitie of my Loue to your Grace."

The Poet had not thought himself bound to adhere to such lofty professions, for while he takes every occasion to celebrate the King's fame in flattering terms, and promises on receiving due encouragement to continue to sing his Majesty's praises, he evinces a sufficiently ardent desire to obtain praise and fame for himself, although his necessities obliged him to beg plainly and rather importunately for reward.

In allusion to the King's juvenile work, *The Essayes of a Prentise in the Diuine Art of Poesie,* printed at Edinburgh in 1584, he says:—

> "Thou art the swete Musæus of our dayes,
> And I thy Prentise, and must give thee praise."

INTRODUCTION.

Craig, at leaſt in his ſolicitations, was not unſucceſsful; having obtained the following grant of an annual penſion of 600 merks, or £400 Scots money, dated at Whitehall, December 9th, 1605. The warrant does not ſtate what good, true and thankful ſervice his "belouit ſervitour" had rendered to his Majeſty:—

"OURE Souerane Lord ordanis ane letter, &c., makand mentioun that his Hienes for the guid trew and thankfull ſervice done and to be done to his Grace be his belouit ſervitour Maiſter ALEX^R CRAIGE and to giue him better courage and habilitie faythfullie to continew thairin with adwyse and confent of his Hienes right truſtie couſing and familiar counſallour George Erle of Dunbar Lord Home of Berwick Great Theſaurar of Scotland hath gevin grantit and difponit, and by the tennor heirof doith giue grant and difpone To the ſaid MR. ALEX^R CRAIG during all the dayis and fpace of his lyff ane zeirlie fie and penſioun of ſex hundereth merkis money of Scotland to be zeirlie vpliftit and reſſauit be him furth of the reddieſt and beſt caſualities dew and proper to his Maieſties Theſaurar within the Kingdome of Scotland at tua termes in the zeir Witfonday and Martemes be equall portionis the firſt termes payment to haue bene and began at the terme of Witfonday laſt by paſt in this prefent zeir of God J^m vj^c and fyue zeiris and ſua furth zeirlie and termalie in tyme cuming during his lyff, Commanding his Hienes Theſaurar, prefent and to cum, &c. . . . .

"At Quhythall the nynt day of December the zeir of God J^m vj^c and fyue zeiris.

"*Sic fuprafcribitur* JAMES REX.
et fubfcribitur, CANCELLARIUS . DUMBAR .
BALMERINOCH. COMPTROLLER."[1]

At the next meeting of the Scottiſh Parliament an Aƈt of Ratification of this Penſion was paſſed, Auguſt 11th, 1607, in the following terms:—

[1] Regiſter of Prefentations to Benefices, &c., vol. iii., fol. 117^b.

INTRODUCTION.

"Ratification in favouris of Mr. Alexander Craig of his penfioun of fex hundreth merkis.[1]

Oure Souerane Lord upoun Confideratioun of the gude trew and thankfull fervice done to his hienes by his servito͛ mr. alexander Craig and to Inhable his faithfull cōtinuance thairin with confent and advyfe of the eftaittis of this pn̄t parliamēt hath ratefeit approvin and confermed and by the tenno͛ of this pn̄t act Ratefeis appreves and confermes ane yeirlie penfioun of fex hundreth merkis money of scotland to be yeirlie upliftit by him during all the dayes of his lyfetyme, ffurth of the reddieft and beft cafualiteis due and propir to his ma^teis thefaurar pn̄t and to come of the faid kingdome of Scotland. As at lenth cōtenit in his gift of penfioun of the date At Whythall the nynt day of december the yeir of god J^m vj^c and fyve yeiris granted by o͛ fouerane Lord with advyfe and confent of George erle of dunbar Lord home and berwick great thefaurar of scotland And with advyfe and cōfent foirfaid Decernis & ordanis the faid gift of penfioun to have full ftrenth and effect in all tymes cūmīng In all and findrie heidis claufs' and circumftances thairoff no͛tw'ftanding whatfumevir other act of parliamēt or law |civill| canoun or municipall which may in ony forte prejudge And decernis and declaris that the faid gift of penfiouñ fall be a fufficient richt and titill to the faid m͛ alex͛ for uplifting the faid yearlie fie and penfioun during his lyfetyme as faid is | So that frome hence furth | no generall nor particular difcharges fhall be powerfull to prevaill Aganis the faid m͛ alexanderis penfioun during his lyffe And with cōfent foirfaid ordains l͛res to be directit heirupon on ane fingle charge of ten dayes alanerly alf' oft as neid beis."

Mr. Chalmers, in his Manufcript Notes, continues,—

"Craige afterwards retired to Scotland, and enjoyed his penfion. He appears to have fettled at a place named *Rofe Craig*, which cannot be traced on any of the maps old or modern. Perhaps the name was given by himfelf."

[1] Acts of the Parliament of Scotland, vol. iv. p. 389.

INTRODUCTION.

Extracts from the Lord High Treasurer's Accounts.

1606
July   Item to Mr Alex^r Craig for his penſioun of the termes of Witſonday and Mertymes termes J^m vj^c and fyve, and for the Witſonday terme J^m vj^c and ſex yeirs takand zeirlie iiij^c li   *Jnde* vj^c li[1]

1610–May.   Item to Mr Alex^r Craig for his penſioun of this terme (Witſonday 1610)   -   ij^c li

Similar entries occur under the dates, Feb. 1611, Nov. 1611, May 1612, June and Nov. 1614, May and Nov. 1615, Nov. 1616, June and Nov. 1617, June 1618.

Under the head of "Feallis and Penſiones off termes preceding" we find,

1621–March.   Item to Mr Alex^r Craig his penſioun for the terms of Witſonday and Mertimes 1620, as his acquittance producit upon compt beris   iiij^c li

That, latterly, there had been delays, or even the non-payment of this penſion at the time, appears from ſeveral copies of verſes addreſſed by him to the Earl of Mar and others, in his volume printed at Aberdeen in 1623.

To return to Craig's poetical career: Pinkerton in 1786 mentions his name among the Poets of Scotland who, after King James ſucceeding to the crown of England, "wrote in Engliſh, as the court and polite language," but ſays,—"Of this writer nothing is known, ſave that he publiſhed in 1606 'The Amoroſe Songs,' &c."

This little volume, dedicated to the Queen, was firſt brought into ſpecial notice by the Rev. Henry John Todd, in his Notes to Milton's Poetical Works, London, 1801. In reference to Milton being indebted to the concluding lines of *The Paſſionate Shepherd to his Love*, which had

[1] The Accounts from 1606 to 1610 are not preſerved.

INTRODUCTION.

ufually been afcribed to Shakefpeare, but which Bifhop Percy proved was by Marlowe, and the *Nymph's Reply* by Sir Walter Raleigh, the induftrious and learned Archdeacon Todd fays,—

"But there is a poet, little known, I apprehend to fame; whofe early imitation both of *The Paffionate Shepherd*, and *The Reply*, deferves notice. It may not feem foreign to the fubject of this note, and I flatter myfelf I fhall oblige the lovers of ancient poetry, if I exhibit fome of thefe forgotten ftanzas: From '*The Amorofe Songes, Sonets, and Elegies of* M. Alexander Craige, Scoto-Britaine. *Imprinted at London by William White*, 1606, 12mo.'"

Thefe extracts need not be quoted. The volume itfelf was fo rare that no other copy than one in the Bridgewater Collection was then known to exift.

The fame volume was more fully and very accurately defcribed by John Payne Collier, Efq., in his privately printed "Catalogue, Bibliographical and Critical, of Early Englifh Literature, forming a portion of the Library at Bridgewater Houfe, &c., London, 1837," 4to. Alfo, in its republication as "A Bibliographical and Critical Account of the rareft Books in the Englifh Language, &c.," 1865, 2 vols., 8vo. Mr. Collier juftly remarks, that Craig's verfes in 1604 as well as in 1606 "are more remarkable for their adulation than their poetry." Well! there is no denying the truth that Craig has not increafed his claims as a Poet by his continual claffical allufions and comparifons, whether from Ancient Hiftory, or in reference to the Gods and Goddeffes of Heathen Mythology.

In this volume of 1606, befides the dedication to the Queen, he has an "Epiftle generall to Idea, Cynthia, Lithocardia, Kala, Erantina, Lais, Pandora, Penelopæ," to all of whom he alfo adds feparate epiftles and feveral fonnets, and his reputation would not have fuffered had feveral of them been fuppreffed. He exhibits a want of all delicacy or propriety in having preferved and fwelled out the volume,

INTRODUCTION.

inscribed and presented to her Majesty, with verses such as those which he addressed to the "inconstant" and "lascivious" Lais. But he evidently had an overweening conceit of his own verses.

In his farewell Elegie to Kala, he furnishes a fresh proof of his estimate of his own effusions. He wishes, he says, this had been the first, as it would be the last of numerous verses that he had sent to his "sweet Kala," but it was not in his power, even

> . . . . "if now I could,
> My publisht Rymes recall;
> But they are gone abrod
> Vpon the winges of Fame."

In one of his Poems, as Mr. Collier says,—

"He [Craig] refers to his youth, and promises to present the lady he calls Lithocardia with 'some better poem.' These names probably have all an individual application, and in one of his sonnets Craige unequivocally tells us that Penelope is Lady Rich. Although he here and there speaks diffidently of his own powers, it is evident that he thought he was destined to immortality, and to give immortality to those whom he celebrates: a 'Sonnet to Idea,' begins,—

> ' My Muse shal make thy boundles fame to flie
> In bounds where yet thy selfe was never seene;
> And were not for my songs thy name had beene
> Obscurelie cast into the graue with thee.'"

In the same strain he writes to "Idea:"—

> "My flowing Songs I consecrate to thee,
> Good reason were, that they should all be thine.
> Thy presence creats all those thoughts in mee,
> Which mee Immortall, and maks thee Diuine."

At the end of this volume of 1606 Craig has added his imitation of the poems of Marlowe and Raleigh, with a separate dedication—"To my Honorable good Lord and

INTRODUCTION.

Maifter (the true Mæcenas of my Mufe) George Earle of Dunbar, Lord Barwick, high Trefurar of Scotland"—ending with thefe words:—"What I haue heere fet downe, is for your follace; and fo I befeech your Honor to accept from the Table of my Chamber, at your liberall charge and allowance, the . 5 . day of Nouember 1606."

There can be little doubt that, befides thus partaking of his bounty, it was through the good offices of the Earl of Dunbar that Craig had obtained his penfion. Thefe additional poems are written in the names of Alexis and Lefbia, and the firft contains an allufion which confirms the conjecture refpecting the author's birth-place, when he makes Alexis fay,—

> "Come be my Loue, and liue with mee.
> . . . . .
> And wee fhall fee the Riuers rin,
> With delicat and daintie din:
> And how my DOUERN night and day,
> With fweet Meanders flides away
> To pay her debts vnto the Sea."

The Dovern, the only river in Banffshire, takes its rife on the confines of that county and of Aberdeenfhire. The town of Banff is fituated on a hill, overlooking the weftern bank of the river and its confluence with the fea, as it flows into the German Ocean. Befides this allufion, it appears that the ftately building of the old Caftle of Banff, demolifhed by General Munro in Auguft, 1640,[1] was within the town; and that towards the northern extremity of the Caftle grounds, there was a fpot that was called the Rofe Craig, which is fuppofed to have been the fite of the Chapel of the Holy Rood prior to the Reformation; and which afterwards became the Poet's refidence.[2]

In his next publication, at Edinburgh, 1609, Craig evinces

---

[1] Gordon's Hiftory of the Gordons, vol. ii. p. 339.
[2] New Statiftical Account (Banff), vol. xiii. p. 29.

B

INTRODUCTION.

his gratitude by a fpecial dedication—"To the moft Honorable my fingvlar good Lord and Patron G. E. of Dvnbar," &c. In this volume "the Author bemoneth his hard fortunes in England," and fays,—

> "Beyond the Mountains of the froftie North,
> I fome-time feru'd a *Caledonian* Dame."

A confiderable interval having elapfed between this and his next volume, which was iffued with a fimilar title at Aberdeen in 1623, a few incidental notices of his literary friends, at this period of his life, may be added.

Of all Craig's poetical brethren, the one who firft deferves notice is Sir ROBERT AYTOUN. He was a native of Fife, born at Kinaldie about the year 1570, and was educated at St. Leonard's College, St. Andrews, where for a time they were fellow-ftudents. In Craig's "Poeticall Effayes, 1604," his name is attached to the concluding fonnet, "Why thought fond *Grece*," &c. In 1609, Craig addreffed a fonnet "To his dear friend, and *fellow ftudent* M*r*. Robert AEton"—

> "Sing fwift hoof'd *Æthon* to thy matchles felfe,
> And be not filent in this pleafant fpring:
> . . . .
> Ah, fhall thy Mufe no further frutes forth-bring,
> But *Bafia* bare, and wilt thou write no more
> To higher notes?"

The allufion here is to his Latin poem, "Bafia, five Strena ad Jacobum Hayum Eq. Illuftr.," publifhed in 1605; and it called forth the reply,—

> "AETHON CRAGIO SVO.
> Fane wold I fing, if Songs my thoghts culd eafe."

Aytoun, who received the honour of knighthood, Auguft 30, 1612, was made Private Secretary to the Queen Anna, as well as Gentleman of the Bedchamber to the King. He died at Whitehall in February, 1638, in the fixty-ninth

INTRODUCTION.

year of his age, and was interred in Weſtminſter Abbey, where his monument ſtill exiſts. The moſt complete edition of his Poetical Remains, with a memoir by the Rev. Charles Rogers, LL.D., was publiſhed in 1871, 8vo.

In his volume of 1609 Craig has ſome lines "Againſt the Sellers of Tobacco." When his friend, Dr. WILLIAM BARCLAY, printed a ſmall tract with this title, "Nepenthes, or the Vertues of Tabacco: by William Barclay, Mr. of Art, and Doctor of Phyſicke. Edinburgh: Printed by Andro Hart, A.D. 1614." at the end of the tract, Barclay added ſix ſhort poems to ſome of his friends and kinſmen.

"*To the fauourable Lector, health.*

"There were ſome pages which I thought not meet to leaue emptie, good Lector, either for thy ſake, or for Tabaccoes ſake, or for mine owne ſake: for thy ſake, becauſe I wearie not to talke with thee: for *Tabaccoes* ſake, becauſe the worth of it deſerueth ſome verſes: for mine owne ſake, becauſe I neuer hauing ſleeped in *Parnaſſus*, but beeing a valley Poete, I perſuade myſelfe that my verſes ſhall be read more for the merites of the matter, then for the value of the Workeman. Therefore I addreſſe myſelfe firſt to gaze againſt a Craig, from whence ſome muſicall influence may bedew my braine.

Vt ſic repente Poeta prodeam.

The firſt accordingly is addreſſed,

To his good and olde friend, M. Alexander Craig.

> CRAIG, if thou knowes the vertues of this plant,
> Why doſt thou dye thy quill in inke of blame?
> If thou knowes not, for to ſupplie thy want,
> Why followes thou the voice of faining fame?
>   Is it not ſlander to this plant and thee,
>   To ſpeake of it ſo poëticallie?"

The next author to be mentioned is ALEXANDER GARDYNE or GARDEN, whoſe earlieſt performance has

INTRODUCTION.

this title:—"A Garden of Graue and Godlie Flovvres: Sonets, Elegies, and Epitaphs. Planted, polifhed, and perfected by Mr. Alexander Gardyne. Edinburgh: Printed by Thomas Finlafon. 1609." 4to. Reprinted for the Abbotsford Club, 1845, 4to. It contains the following lines:—

Alex. Rupeo, Suo, S.

" Kind cunning CRAG, I can nought bot commend,
Thy wondrous wit, thy Judgement, thy Ingyne,
For thy attempts, brought to fo braue an end,
Bewrayes thee for, none worldly, bot divine,
And if thou lift, from Men to lead thy Line,
Or brwik, that they, thy firft for-Beares ware
Then 'cording too, this Judgement meane of mine,
Thee to no *Craig*, nor *Petra*, I compare,
Bot I avow, proclame, and does declare,
Thee (th' only he, that fol' deferues the fame,)
That learned old, the great *Petrarchas* heare,
He was the *Craig*, of whom, thou (Sandie) came.
   For with thy works, that worthie thou reuiu's
   And by thy lines, his Ladie *Laura* liues."

This fuggefts that the firft of "Certaine Encomiaftick Poefies to the Author," although anonymous, may have been contributed by Craig. It is as follows:—

" I feeme like *Cynthia* while thou fhines I fweare,
I am miftun'd whairas Thou fweetly fings,
And barren too, whair Thou begins to beare,
Whofe Ruftick Mufe bot Baftard brats forth brings:
   Yet what I can, Ile doe it in thy fight,
   War't but to len, a lufter to thy light.

I will not preafe, to pratle of thy praife,
Thy worke bears witneffe of thy wondrous worth,
Bot while I liue and when I end my daies
I muft intreat thy fauour this farre forth:
   About thy *Garden* place me neere hand by,
   That I may fmell thy floures whair eu'r I lye.

Introduction.

> So fhall I reft contented in thy fauor,
> Grac'd while I grow, In fuch a glorious Ground,
> Whair Vertue, Wit, and worth fo fweetly fauour,
> Whair Eloquence and Art fo much Abound:
> Whair I fhall proue part of thy fweet Repofes
> Surpaffing fugred Myrrh and mufced Rofes."

Another poetical work by this Alexander Garden or Gardyne, Advocate, Aberdeen, is "The Theatre of the Scotifh Kings," firft publifhed at Edinburgh, 1709, 4to. On the title the Advocate is, by miftake, ftyled Profeffor of Philofophy at Aberdeen. When reprinted in the Abbotsford Club volume, 1845, I was enabled to fhow that the father and fon of the fame name had been confounded; and alfo, that on collating the 1709 volume with the MS. preferved in the Advocates' Library, the commendatory verfes had been omitted, including the following:—

> "To A. G., Author of the Theatre of the Scotifh Kinges.
>
> Braue Pedaret, pretended to haue bene,
> Firft Senator, and cheefe in Sparta chofen:
> When Rols were red, yit was his Name onfene
> He fund his friendis, in their affectiounes frozen:
>   Yea, when hee thought his dooingis fhuld decore him,
>   He fund Three hundred Spartans plac'd before him.
>
> Yit wes he glaide, to fie the Citie floorifh,
> Thought many, many, wer prefer'd to him:
> So when I fie the facred Nymphs doo nowrifh
> Thy fpirit braue, (thogh whilft I fink, thou fwim,)
>   I greatlie joy, and Thow may'ft greatlie glorie,
>   In litill bounds, to bind fo large a ftorie.
>
>   Al. Craige."

In the Extracts from the Hawthornden Manufcripts belonging to the Society of Antiquaries of Scotland, and printed in the Archæologia Scotica, vol. iv. p. iii., the following *Sextain* was given as a juvenile production of Drummond. I fuggefted that it referred to Craig, but not

INTRODUCTION.

having feen his volume of 1606, I could not explain the reference to "Kala," one of the eight damfels whom Craig addreffed under fictitious names. Although by no means complimentary, the lines need not be overlooked :—

"SEXTAIN.

" With elegies, fad fongs, and murning layes,
 Quhill CRAIG his Kala wald to pitie move,
 Poore braine-ficke Man ! he fpends his deareft dayes ;
 Such fillie rime can not make women love !
  Morice, quho fight of neuer faw a booke
  With a rude ftanza this faire Virgine tooke."

It is unneceffary to enlarge on his lady-loves—his "matchleffe Idea," to whom he engaged to be her "euer obleged and vnmanumifable flaue,"—or "Cynthia" or "Lithocardia," being "their Ladyfhips owne," while he vowed to his fweet Kala, "I, both at home and abrod, fhall continue Thine till death," befides his lefs creditable intercourfe with a lady of eafy virtue, named "Lais;" all which may furnifh a fufficient comment on Drummond's words.

We now come to PATRICK GORDON, who ftyled himfelf "Gentleman." He is fuppofed to have been a younger fon of Sir Alexander Gordon of Cluny; and is defcribed as having acted as the King's Political Agent in Poland. He was inftrumental in procuring the arreft and execution of an unfortunate Pole, called Stercovius, who had written a violent fatire on the Scots nation, which had reached the ears of "his moft facred Majefty;" and the expenfe attending this tragedy is faid to have been not lefs than fix hundred pounds fterling.[1]

Gordon had a more afpiring fpirit than either Craig, Garden, or Barclay, as inftead of Songs, Sonnets, or occafional verfes, he "fet forth" two works "done in Heroick verfe." His encouragement, however, could not

---
[1] See Pitcairn's Criminal Trials, vol. iii. p. 448.

INTRODUCTION.

have been great, as only a Firft Book of either work ever appeared. Craig, at leaft, promifed the author a fufficient leafe of immortality, in his copy of verfes prefixed to "The Famous Hiftorie of the Renouned and Valiant Prince Robert, furnamed The Bruce, King of Scotland, &c. By Patrick Gordon, Gentleman. At Dort, Printed by George Waters, 1615," 4to. This volume is very rare, but it was reprinted at Edinburgh in 1718, 12mo, and again in 1758.[1]

> "*In Prais of the Prais-worthie Author.*
>
> " Wife *Virgil* wrote AEneades long, to prais
> Anchifes Sone, whome he did not behold;
> *Octavian* lykd his heigh and loftie Phrafe,
> And gave the *Mantuan*, Money, Moyne, Gold:
>   The Prais of *Bruce* (no queftione) thou proclames,
>   To pleas and prais the *Faith's Defender* Iames."
>
> " If *Maroes* figments leive in frefh requeft,
> Which be of *Stiks*, *Cocitus*, *Serber* penn'd,
> Of *Charon*, *Hell*, *Elyfium* and the reft,
> Thy Storie trew fhall with the World take End:
>   And, to thy prais, I dar be bold to fay,
>   No Lines prophaine can live a longer Day.
>   CRAGE."

Another work by Patrick Gordon, of equal rarity and less known, as it was never reprinted, bears this title, "The Firft Booke of the Famous Hyftorye of Penardo and Laiffa, other-ways callid the warres of Love and Ambitione." This alfo was printed "at Dort, by George Waters," 1615, 12mo.

King James the Sixth having at length revifited his native kingdom in May, 1617, all claffes vied with each other to teftify their loyalty, of which a permanent Memorial exifts in the collection publifhed by John Adamfon, Minifter

---

[1] A metrical Hiftory of King Robert the Bruce, of the fame period and in a fimilar ftyle, ftill exifts in MS. The author has not been identified.

INTRODUCTION.

of Liberton, and afterwards Principal of the Univerſity of Edinburgh, under the following title:—

"ΤΑ ΤΩΝ ΜΟΥΣΩΝ 'ΕΙΣΟΔΙΑ. The Mvſes Welcome to the High and Mightie Prince IAMES, by the Grace of God, King of Great Britaine France and Ireland, Defender of the Faith &c. At his Majeſties happie Returne to his olde and natiue Kingdome of Scotland, after xiiii Yeeres Abſence, In Anno 1617. Digeſted according to the order of his Majeſties Progreſſe. By J. A. *Soli ſic pervius orbis.*

"Printed at Edinburgh, by Thomas Finlaſon, Printer to his moſt excellent Maieſtie. 1618."[1]

From this volume we find, as might be expected, that the King, during his royal progreſs was everywhere received with the greateſt and moſt enthuſiaſtic gratulations, in the form of Speeches and Verſes in Latin, Greek, Hebrew, and Engliſh (but not one in the Scottiſh dialect), delivered or preſented by profeſſors, miniſters, ſchoolmaſters, provoſts, bailies, and town-clerks. The moſt remarkable of all theſe welcomes was the FORTH FEASTING, by the Poet of Hawthornden.

The King entered Edinburgh at the Weſt Port, on the 16th of May, when Mr. John Hay, as their Clerk-Deputie, in the name of the Town, delivered a Speech, in which he expreſſes how "wee are refreſhed, yea revived with the heat and bright beames of our Sunne (the powerfull Adamant of our Wealth), by whoſe removing from our Hemiſphære we were darkned, . . . the verie Hilles and Groves . . . with pale lookes repreſenting their miſerie for the departure of their Royal King."

On Thurſday the 22nd of May the King's Majeſty came to Kinaird when there was preſented to his Majeſty a "Poëme" (in Latin), entitled "Nemo," extending to 474 lines, ſigned JOANNES LEOCHAEUS. Alſo, "This ſubſequent

---

[1] In ſome copies the Printer's name is omitted.

INTRODUCTION.

welcome was alfo prefented to his M. at Kinaird," figned ALEXANDER CRAIG, of Rofe-Craig, and is included in the prefent feries of his Poetical Remains.

It begins:—

> " Great man of God, whom God doeth call and choofe
> On Earth his great Lieutenents place to ufe,
> Wee bleffe the tyme," &c.

Might not the laft two lines of his Welcome have fuggefted or forefhadowed the National Anthem?—

> " And let each true, and faithfull fubject fing
> With heart and woyce conjoynd, GOD SAUE THE KING."

He no doubt knew his Royal mafter would not go to Banff, and vifit the banks of the Dovern and their rofes, otherwife we might be at fome lofs to affign any good reafon for Craig's appearance on that occafion, except the natural defire to attract His Majefty's notice and favour.

The parifh of Kinnaird lies about half-way between Perth and Dundee, to the fouth of the fertile ftrath known as the Carfe of Gowrie. The old Caftle was built on a height, of which fome remains ftill exift, in walls of "an enormous thicknefs, and the different ftoreys floored by ftone arches." It belonged to Sir David Carnegie of Kinnaird, who fucceeded his father of the fame name, in 1598, and was raifed to the peerage by the title of Lord Carnegie of Kinnaird, 14th April, 1616. At the coronation of Charles the Firft, at Holyrood, he was created Earl of Southesk, 22nd June, 1633.

In a well-known work, "The Staggering State of Scots Statefmen," the following lines by Craig are preferved. The author, Sir John Scot of Scotftarvet, in his notice of Colin, Earl of Argyll, Lord Chancellor, who died in 1584, refers to his fon Archibald, feventh Earl of Argyll, who was frequently employed againft the Popifh Earls, and

C

INTRODUCTION.

in keeping in order the powerful and warlike tribes in fome of the Highland diftricts. The Earl of Argyll made his laft public appearance in this country in carrying the Crown at the opening of Parliament, 17th June, 1617. In the following year, on pretence of going to the Spa for the benefit of his health, he received from the King permiffion to go abroad; but, as the news came that he had gone to Spain, and had made defection from the Proteftant religion, this licence was recalled, and he himfelf fummoned to appear before the Privy Council, under the pain of treafon. Scotftarvet fays,— "He went to ferve the King of Spain, and became papift, of whofe flight the poet CRAIG wrote thefe lines:—

> '*Now Earl of Guile, and Lord ForLorn thou goes,*
> *Quitting thy Prince, to ferve his Spanifh foes,*
> *No faith in plaids, no truft in Highland trews,*
> *Camelion-like, they change to many hues.*'"

The Earl did not return to England until 1638, and he died at London in that year, aged about fixty-two.

From the Acts of Parliament we find the Poet acting in a public capacity. He was returned as Commiffioner for the Burgh of Banff, and his name appears in the Sederunt, 25th July and 4th Auguft, 1621. The chief object in the King fummoning this Parliament to meet at Edinburgh was to carry out his favourite fcheme of eftablifhing a uniformity of worfhip in the Churches of England and Scotland; and the firft Act paffed was the Ratification of the Five obnoxious Articles of Perth.

The "Poetical Recreations," printed at Aberdeen in 1623, was Craig's lateft publication. It is dedicated to George, Earl of Enyie, &c., the eldeft fon and fucceffor of George, firft Marquefs of Huntly, in 1636; whofe active fhare with the royalifts in the North is well-known, till he was taken prifoner, fent to Edinburgh, and tried, where he was beheaded at the Market Crofs, March 22, 1649.

This volume contains two ftanzas which Craig addreffed,

INTRODUCTION.

in 1621, to Abakuk Biffet, a fcribe in Edinburgh, who had been clerk to Sir John Skene of Curriehill, Clerk-Regifter; and author of a work which ftill remains unpublifhed.[1] But the chief portion of his Recreations is occupied with various fets of verfes, complaining that his penfion, if not ultimately withdrawn, had been very irregularly paid. It concludes, however, with his *"Satyra Volans,"*—

> "Goe, Swift-wing'd SATYRE,"

which, if not altogether original, is perhaps the moft ftriking of his poetical compofitions. Its ftrain may have been fuggefted by the well-known poem ufually attributed to Sir Walter Raleigh,—

> "Go, Soule, the bodies gueft,
> Vpon a thankleffe arrant."

The Latin verfes fubjoined in 1623 are also worthy of notice as defcriptive of his place of refidence at Rofe-Craig in Banff—its name being Latinized to *Rofipetra.* The title is,—

> "*Rofipetræ meæ ad Imitationem Pfophidii Arcadienfis defcriptio.*"

Who this Pfophidius was, whether a Greek poet or philofopher, he does not fay; but the name was no doubt derived from Pfophis a town in Arcadia, founded, according to Paufanius, by Pfophis the daughter of Eryx, who reigned in Sicania. The learned reader may confult on this point his "Defcription of Greece," (B. viii. chap. xxiv.)

In the fecond Quatrain the Poet fays, His houfe was fmall, not unfuitably furnifhed, and a field well cultivated, the little bank of the river (Dovern) covered profufely with

---

[1] Two copies of this ftrange farrago, both written in his own hand, have Craig's and other commendatory verfes prefixed. The earlieft, addreffed to Charles the Firft, as Prince, in 1622, formerly in the library of the author of "Caledonia," is now in my own poffeffion. The other, addreffed to Charles after he afcended the throne in 1625, is preferved in the Library of the Faculty of Advocates, Edinburgh.

INTRODUCTION.

roses; and here, as on the summit of Parnassus, with the streams of Helicon, and repose, he sung to himself his own pleasant verses.[1]

In this happy and contented spirit, Craig seems to have spent the later years of his life. From the Retours, or Services of Heirs, it appears he died at Banff, when he had reached, we may suppose, the sixtieth year of his age: James Craig having been served heir of Mr. ALEXANDER CRAIG of Rose-Craig, his father, 20 December 1627.[2]

On referring to the original Register, we find the service took place within the Sheriff Court or Town Hall of Banff. Had the Register of Confirmed Testaments of that date for the Commissariat of the district been preserved, it might likely have thrown new light on Craig's personal history and family.

Wishing to ascertain if any additional information respecting the Poet or his place of residence could be obtained from the local registers, I applied to my friend James Gordon, Esq., Sheriff-Substitute, Banffshire, who

---

[1] The following translation of Craig's Latin verses, for which I have been indebted to Mr. Alexander Gibb, the translator of Buchanan's *Jepthah, and Baptistes, &c.*, may be not unacceptable to some readers.

    Description of my Rose Craig in Imitation of Psophidius
        the Arcadian.

    In a fair nook, great store of fruit that yields
    Psophidius lives, and tills his humble fields:
    Content with little, blest in few desires,
    He seeks no less, he to no more aspires.

        Another.

    A cot, not badly furnished, humble fields
    Well till'd, a bank that countless roses yields:
    Here my Parnassus, and Aonian spring,
    So do I live, and smooth songs love to sing.

[2] Inquisitiones Generales. No. 1372. Decr. 20, 1627. Jacobus Craig *hæres* Mag. Alexandri Craig de Rosecraig *patris*. Lib. x. No. 46.

INTRODUCTION.

kindly made all the neceffary inquiries and fearches. Although not fuccefsful in the immediate object of inquiry, Mr. Gordon's letter is fubjoined in the Appendix, as it traces the proprietors of Rofe-Craig in later times. I have alfo fearched in vain for any autograph letter or fignature of Craig, to have ferved for a facfimile.

A pofthumous poem, "The Pilgrime and Heremite," in form of a dialogue, was printed at Aberdeen in 1631. In the dedication to William Forbes of Tolquhon, the editor, Robert Skene, fays:—

"Having collected the difperfed, and long neglected Papers, of this fubfequent Poëfie, the Pofthumes of a worthie Penne, for preferving them from perifhing, for the Perfections of the Departed, maker [or poet] of immortall memorie."

But for all this pious care, the poem ran no fmall rifk of utter oblivion, as only one copy of it has been difcovered, and that one deficient of four leaves.

DAVID LAING.

EDINBURGH.

APPENDIX.

Letter from Mr. Sheriff Gordon, of Banff, to Mr. Laing, respecting Craig of Rose-Craig. (See page 20.)

Banff, *July*, 1873.

. . . Safine, dated 19th Auguft, 1699, in favor of Alexander Lefly of Kininvie, Provoft of Banff, following upon Difpofition by William Scott younger, goldfmith, burgefs of Banff, and Margaret Mortimer his fpoufe, with confent of William Scott elder, burgefs of Banff, in favor of the faid Alexander Lefly, dated 18th Auguft, 1699, conveying *inter alia* " All and haill that croft of Land called Rofehaugh, Rofecraig," &c.

From Valuation Roll of Burgh of Banff, 1708.

	Scots
" Mr. James Joas and Janet Fentoun's in Rofecraig	£ 10 . 00 . 00
Haill Rofecraig	132 . 00 . 00

From Valuation Roll for 1712.

"James Lauries houfe and yeard of Rofecraig and the old ruinous fleat houfe rentalled at twelve pounds Scots   12 . 00 . 00
"The haill field Lands of Rofecraig Coldholme and Cillfcroft now pertaining to the faid Alexander Ogilvy inclofed in part with fton dykes rentalled at thirty one bolls three firlots bear pryce forefaid, extending to One hundred thirty two pounds fiue fhillings and ten pennies 132 . 05 . 10"

How the Lands came into Ogilvy's poffeffion appears from a Charter dated 27th February, 1730, in favour of Lord James Defkford, granted by the Provoft and Magiftrates of Banff, with confent of Alexander Hay of Montblarie, W.S., and Sir William

APPENDIX.

Ogilvy, by adjudication obtained at Ogilvy's inſtance againſt Alexander Leſly, dated 13th February, 1713. There ſeems to have been a competition between Hay and Ogilvy, which being arranged, they obtained a Decree of Roup and Sale from the Court of Seſſion, who diſponed the crofts to Lord Deſkford, upon which the above-mentioned Charter of Confirmation was granted. This Charter confirms the following :—

"The Crofts of Land called Roſecraig &c. with the houſes of Roſecraig and haill yards thereof."

The boundaries are as follows :—

"Having the higher Lands belonging to William Duff of Braco deſcending lineally till it come to the Seagate that leads to the fiſhers crofts at the Weſt, the Seagate at the Eaſt and North, and the common Highgate that leads Eaſt and Weſt at the back of the Caſtle Hill at the South parts of the ſame."

In a Saſine recorded on 9th September, 1850, part of the deſcription is "the Crofts of Land called Roſecraig Roſehaugh Leils Crofts Killingyard with the houſes of Roſecraig and haill yards thereof," and then follows the boundaries as in Charter in Lord Deſkford's favour. From this it appears that Roſecraig is in Earl Seafield's poſſeſſion, and is traced back to William Scott in 1699. Farther back I cannot get. I think that all the titles previous to that will be found in Lord Seafield's Charter Room. Theſe titles would probably ſhow the whole progreſs from Craig to Scott.

As to the family of Craig, I fear little can be made out. It is ſaid, that long ago Craig was a North country name, now it is very rare. There is only one Craig in Banff, a widow, whoſe husband came from the South. I had this from herſelf.

I find a Charter in favour of James Craig, Shoemaker in Banff, of Lots No. 83 and 84 of the Seaton Lands of Banff, dated 20th December, 1797. He built two houſes. He was an old man, and died about the year 1819. Of this man Mr. Alexander Ramſay, aged eighty, tells me he knew him well, having lived near him. He ſays,—"Craig had no family, and I know he had no ſon, becauſe one day I found him ſitting at his door very tired, and he remarked to me, 'It wad hae been weel for me had I had a ſon.'"

APPENDIX.

Craig's widow liferented his property. She lived in one of the houfes, and I have feen an old woman, a Mrs. Harvey, who life-rented the other houfe under her, and who confirms Ramfay. On the widow's death Craig's property paffed to his nephew, and is now the property of Daws Smith. I have feen a relative of Widow Craig, but he cannot tell me anything about the nephew.

In the Old Churchyard I cannot find any graveftone bearing the name of "Craig." It is faid the Craigs are from the North. They may have been fo; they have, however, difappeared from this quarter.

I looked over fome of the Burgh Minutes, as far back as 1624, but the name of Craig is not mentioned as either a Magiftrate or Councillor.

From your letter I obferve that Alex. Craig was fent to the Scots Parliament for the Burgh of Banff in 1621; but was it neceffary that he fhould refide in Banff to qualify him? I apprehend not. He may have gone fouth, retaining his property qualification, and been returned from mere convenience.

A friend of mine has very kindly taken a photograph of the "Rofecraig" as it now is, which I enclofe. When the harbour was formed a road was cut right through the rock, excavations made, and the prefent buildings erected upon it. You will fee that part of the rock ftill appears; and fince that road was made, the rocks on the oppofite fide of the road are laid down in a plan made in 1823 as "Rofe Rocks." In the late Ordnance Survey, however, the old name, "Rofecraig," is reftored. I believe this was done upon the authority of the late Mr. Forbes, Town-Clerk, whofe knowledge of the antiquities of the Burgh was very great.

I am, my Dear Sir,

Very truly yours,

JAMES GORDON.

DAVID LAING, Efq., LL.D.

Since receiving the above letter, I obtained accefs to an Inventory of old title deeds connected with property in Banff, from which I have fubjoined various Extracts, as they

APPENDIX.

throw fome light both on Rofe-Craig and on the Poet's immediate defcendants.

The following is a brief abftract of what appears to relate to the Craigs of the Seventeenth Century:—

Mr. Alexander Craig, burgefs of Banff, June 1609; and apparently the fame perfon is called fon of William Craig, burgefs of Banff, at the fame date.

James Craig and Mary Douglas, his wife, December 1625, June 1630, November 1650, September 1675.

Alexander Craig of Rofecraig, his fon, 1670-1683.

Walter Craig, another fon, and two daughters, Agnes and Ifobel, 1675.

Mr. James Craig, fon of Alexander Craig, 1675.

D. L.

INVENTARY OF THE WRITES OF SEVERAL CROFTS AND TENEMENTS IN BANFF ACQUIRED FROM TIME TO TIME BY JAMES, EARL OF FINDLATER.

Bundle 1ft.

Writes of the Crofts or Common Lands of Banff called Caldhame, afterwards joined in the Titles of James Craig, heir to Alex. Craig, who was fon to James Craig of Rofecraig.

Charter by the Provoft and Baillies of Banff to James Curror of the Common Lands of Banff called Caldhame, lying upon the Eaft part of Banff, in the Territory of Banff, 2 July, 1543.

Safine following thereupon in favours of Mr. James Curror, dated 3 July, 1543.

Feu Charter of Alienation by James Curror, Burgefs of Banff, to George Ogilvie of Dunlugas of the faid Common Lands of Banff called Caldhame, 1574.

Safine in favours of Patrick Chalmers and his wife of a piece

D

APPENDIX.

of Land called Snappiecroft, lying in Banff, proceeding upon the Refignation of James Curror, 10 Auguft, 1591.

Charter of Alienation by Sir George Ogilvie of Dunlugas to Mr. Alex. Craig of a Tenement in Banff, fometime pertaining to Andrew Paterfon, 8 June, 1609.

Inftrument of Safine following thereupon, of fame date.

Charter by Sir George Ogilvie of Dunlugas to Alex^r· Craig, fon of William Craig, Burgefs of Banff, of a Tenement, houfes, and yard in Banff, then poffeft by the faid William, dated 8 June, 1609. Safine following thereon to the faid Alex^r· Craig, 8 June, 1609.

Feu Charter The Provoft and Baillies of Banff to Robert Ogilvie, Burgefs of Banff, of the Common Lands called Caldhame, lying in Banff, proceeding on the Refignation of the Daughters and Heirs Portioners of James Curror, Burgefs of Banff, 25 Auguft, 1631.

Safine following thereon in favours of the faid Robert Ogilvie, dated 1 September, 1631.

Difpofition by Robert Ogilvie, Burgefs of Banff, to Alexander Winchefter, Burgefs of Banff, of the Common Land called Caldhame, lying within the Territory of Banff, dated 2 March, 1633.

Safine thereon in favours of the faid Winchefter, dated 10 April, 1633.

Difpofition by the faid Alexander Winchefter to James Craig of the Common Lands of Banff, in the Territory of Banff, 28 November, 1650.

Safine following thereupon to the faid James Craig and Mary Douglas, his wife, 28 November, 1650.

Difpofition by Mr. James Craig, Burgefs of Banff, to Alex. Craig, his fon, of the Common Lands in Banff called Caldhame, dated 22 November, 1675.

Safine following thereon in favours of the faid Alex. Craig, dated 23 November, 1675.

APPENDIX.

The Writs of the Lands in Banff called the head of the Rood Rig, Pyper's croft, Rothies croft, Wellcroft, Seton's Croft, Croft at Greenknow.

Charter by William Duncan, Burgefs of Banff, in favours of Alexander Craig, Burgefs there, of a Croft of Land in Banff, and a piece of Land called the head of the Rood Rig, dated the 22 November, 1609.

Safine to the faid Alexander Craig, Burgefs of Banff, following on the faid Charter, dated 9 December, 1609.

Contract of Wadfet between James Ogilvie of Birnis, whereby he wadfetts for 300 M^s to Allan Adam, Pyper's Croft, Roodrigs, Rothiefcroft, in the territory of Banff, 30 October, 1604.

Safine in favours of faid Allan Adam in Downies of a Croft, which was formerly in two crofts, called Pyper's Croft and the Rood, a croft called Rothiefcroft, all in the Territory of Banff, proceeding upon the Refignation of James Ogilvie of Birnis.

Affignation of James Ogilvie of Birnis To Robert Ogilvie, Burgefs of Banff, for the Redemption of Pyperfcroft and another croft in Banff, which were wadfett to Allan Adam, dated 5 and Reg^d at Banff 17 July, 1608.

Difpofition by Janet Urquhart, Relict of the faid Allan Adam, and Alexander Adam, his Son, to Robert Ogilvie, Burgefs of Banff, of Pyperfcroft, Wadfett by James Ogilvy for 300 M^s by Contract, dated 30 October, 1604.

Precept of Clare conftat by Walter Ogilvie of Redhyth to Alexander Adam, as Heir to Allan Adam, his Father, of Pyperfcroft, the Roodrig, and Rothies croft, in the Territory of Banff, dated 1 April, 1622.

Difpofition by Alex. Adam to Mr. Alex. Craig, Burgefs of Banff, of Pyperfcroft and Roodrig, in Banff, March, 1622.

Difpofition by Robert Ogilvie, Burgefs of Banff, with confent of Janet Baird, his wife, and Sir Thomas Urquhart of Cromarty to Mr. Alexander Craig of Rofecraig, of the Wellcroft, the Peafe- Croft, Pypers Croft, lying in the Burgh of Banff, dated 31 of Auguft, 1623.

APPENDIX.

Safine following thereon to the faid Alexander Craig, 30 September, 1623.

Difpofition by William Gordon, Burgefs of Banff, to Alex. Craig, Burgefs there, of Rothiefcroft, 4 June, 1622.

Safine following thereon to the faid Alexander Craig, 29 January, 1623.

Difpofition by George Ogilvie of Dunlugas to Alexander Craig of Rofecraig, of Craigiecroft, Setons Croft, and another croft called Part of Greenknow, lying within the territory of Banff, 1622.

Safine following thereupon to faid Alexander Craig, 29 January, 1623.

Retour in favours of James Craig as Heir to Mr. Alex. Craig, his father, 20 December, 1627.

Service before the Baillies of Banff of James Craig as Heir to Mr. Alexander Craig of Rofecraig in a Tenement in Banff, and of Rothiefcroft, Hillcroft, The Craigins, Peaferig, Pypercroft, The head of Roodrig, Craigiecroft, Setoncroft, all lying within the Territory of Banff, dated 15 June, 1631.

Safine following thereupon in favours of the faid James Craig, dated 15 June, 1630.

Difpofition by James Craig of Rofecraig to Alexander Craig, his fon, of Rothiefcroft, Peaferig, Duncanfcroft, Roodrig, all lying within the Territory of Banff, dated the 22 November, 1675.

Safine thereon . . . (left blank).

Writes of Silver Croft, Cordiners Croft.

Charter Thomas Earl of Melrofe to George Ogilvie of Dunlugas proceeding upon the above Refignation of the faid Kingfwellcroft, dated 21 March, 1621.

Feu Charter of Alienation, George Ogilvie of Dunlugas to Alexander Craig of the faid Croft, called Kingfwellcroft, dated 29 June, 1622.

Charter of Confirmation thereof by Thomas Earl of Melrofe, dated 29 June, 1622.

APPENDIX.

Difcharge. Walter Gray to Alex. Craig of two Bonds due by Alex. Craig of Rofecraig, 13 February, 1682.

Difpofition by Alexander Craig of Rofecraig to William Fife, Baillie in Banff, of the Temple Land called Kingfwellcroft, in the Territory of Banff, dated 18 April, 1683.

Bundle 2nd.

Bond of Provifion by James Craig to Agnes Craig, his daughter, bearing Infeftment upon the houfes in Banff, Pyperfcroft, Wellcroft, &c., dated the 27 November, 1675.

Safine fame date.

Bond of Provifion by James Craig of Rofecraig to Ifobel, his fecond daughter, bearing Infeftment on the faid Houfes and Crofts in Banff, dated 27 November, 1675.

Safine, 29 November, 1675.

Difpofition by the faid Ifobel Craig to the faid Alex[r.] Craig, her brother, of her Heritable bond of provifion before mentioned, by the faid James Craig to her for 1000 merks, dated 27 Nov., 1675. This Difpofition is dated the 27 January, 1679.

Safine, 29 January, 1679.

Difcharge by Alexander Wallace, Dean of Guild of Banff, To Alex. Craig of Rofecraig of feveral debts and dilligence againft him, dated 12 February, 1683.

General Retour to Alex. Fife, fon and hair to Will[m.] Fife, his Father, 4 December, 1690.

Precept of Clareconftat by the Magiftrates of Banff To the faid Alex. Fife, as Heir to Will[m.] Fife, his Father, of the Common Lands of Banff, Rothiefcroft, Peaferig, Duncanfcroft, Roodrig, Greenknow, Rofecraig, Pyperfcroft, Craigfcroft, Setonfcroft, Sandifon's croft, all lying in Banff, 6 April, 1695.

31

32

MISCELLANEOUS POEMS

I

[From "ΤΑ ΤΩΝ ΜΟΥΣΩΝ 'ΕΙΣΟΔΙΑ. The Mvſes Welcome To The High and Mightie Prince IAMES &c., Edinbvrgh, Printed by Thomas Finlaſon, Printer to his moſt excellent Maieſtie. 1618," folio, p. 99.]

This ſubſequent welcome was alſo preſented to his M. at Kinaird.

GREAT Man of GOD, whom GOD doeth call, and chooſe
On Earth his great Lieutenents place to uſe,
Wee bleſſe the tyme, wherin the threefold Croun
And Diademe with peace, and great renoun
In that ſo long fore-told, and fatal cheare
Thou on thy braue, and royall brow didſt beare:
As from that tym thy abſence bred our bane,
Thy preſence now reſtores our Joy's againe:
Thou went away to SCOTLANDS deip diſpleaſure
But thy return brings mirth beyond all meaſure.

Aſtræa doth pronunce by thy ſueit tong
What ſhuld of right to Kings on earth belong:
Thy myld aſpect doeth realmes and cities nuriſh,
And as thou frouns or faun's they fall & flooriſh:
Theſe ſuords the ſherp, and bloodie tools of warr,
Which peace hath ſheath'd in ruſt, ſhall from a farr,
Bee drawn agane, and when thou thinks it good
Thy angrie brow ſhall bath the world in blood,
                                        Thou

Thou canſt Dethrone, and giue the royall wreathe
And hyd thy fuord, and hold it in the ſheath.
  Yet now thou deign's to viſit our cqld North,
And with thy Court haſt croſt the ſinuoſe *Forth*,
Which with *Meanders* winding heer and there
Great *Britans* KING upon her back did beare,
Whois bouldin billoes (as they did of yore)
Shall fet thee ſure upon there yonder ſhore.   (ches
And ſtatelie *Tay* with ſtryving ſtreams which mar-
And skorns his courſe ſhuld be controld with Arches,
Who with his ſpeats in ſpightfull raige hath dround
The famoſe *Perths* faire Bridge, & broght to groūd,
Shall ſtraine the ſtrenght of his ſtrong ſtreams thow'll
And be at peace with all the world for thee.   (fee,
  T H O W ſhall not looſe thy labors, nor thy loue,
Which in a Prince moſt rare, moſt rare dooth proue:
This bontie ſingular, which thou imparts,
Encounters not with miſ-conceiving hearts
Nor with ingratefull ſubjects, for each One
Aknowledgeth the good which thou haſt done:
Man neuer was more loved by ane other,
Not *David* by kynd *Jonathan* his brother
As thou by vs, thou dwels in each mans heart,
Our Joy, and our felicitie thou art:
  O had our breiſts of ſtuff tranſparent bene,
That all our thoughts might ſo to thee be ſene,
Thy SCOTLAND do'th (thy royall grace wold tell)
For Courage, Truth, and Loue, the World excell:
And wee confeſſe, our Joyes are perfect now,
Iff they could proue perpetuall, heauens allow
A longer ſtay then thou intends, that ſo
Our loue-ſeik hopes might to the full tyd flo.
  To toyll and travell man is borne wee fee,
As ſparks of fire by nature upward flie,

                                                Thy

Thy travell yet fhalbe compenft with pleafure
Thou fhalt haue fports, and pairt of all our treafure:
Wee'll keep that cuftome with thy facred grace
Which *Athenæus* writes was keept in *Thrace*,
,The fubjects gaue their King when euer hee wanted,
'When they wax'd poore, their fuit's by him wer gran
Thus each in loue fupplied an others neid,   (ted:
Both peace, and wealth, this kynd cōmerce did breid.
And *Perfians* when they did prefent their King,
Some rare propyne they alwayes vs'd to bring.

But put the cafe, this forme which *Perfians* ufed
Wer by fome bafe and wretched wormes refufed,
Thy faithfull *Quæstors*, full of loue and paine,
(Whois betters haue not bene, whois lyk againe
Thou canft not find) fhall fuch aboundance bring,
As King nor Court fhall want no kynd of thing:
Not lyk thofe lowns, whom *Athens* old did truft,
They wer but Theiv's vnhoneft, and injuft.
Thefe *Tamij* the treafure ftole by night,
And then they burnd the Citadel by flight,
That by this fire their fraud fhuld not be feene,
Nor they accus'd, that had fo knavifh beene:
Thy *Quæftors* here are honeft, wyfe, and true;
Thy treafure faiff, thy Baftils bvilt of new:

Stay then (dread Leige) O ftay with ws a while
With pleafing fports the pofting tyme begyle:
Thy fyneft Hawks and fleiteft Hounds fhall find
Of fowls and beafts, a pray of euerie kynd.
For morning both and euenyng flight, each day
Each Hawk thou haft, fhall haue her proper pray;
Each fowl that flies fhall meit thee in thy way,
And in their forts fhall *Ave Cæfar* fay.

Throgh forefts, Parks, and feilds hunt ftag, &
It helps the health to haue the natiue air.   (Haire

Hee

Hee that taks pains and travell sleepeth best,
With greidines hee taks refreshing rest,
His meate to him seems savorie, sweet, and fyne,
Hee glaidlie drinks the heart-comforting wyne:
Good blood, quick spirits, travell sweet do'th cherish
And maks offensiue humors for to perish.
And wyse-men write that Colik, Gout, and Gravel,
The woefull fruits of rest, ar cur'd by travel:
Let not thy horses fatt, for standing Idle,
They'll grow stiff neck'd, and disobey the brydle.
    Let faithfull *Turbo* menage thy affaires
And kill himselfe with care, to ease thy caires.
Thou shalt not trauel, throgh hott barren bounds
Of *Arabie*, nor cold, and snowie sounds
Of *Norwa*, nor the Schythian savage montans,
Nor fenni *Flanders* skant of healthfull fontans,
Nor throgh thy *France* so full of fearfull Jarrs,
Where King and subjects waige intestine warrs,
But throgh Braue BRITAN of all realms the best,
With pleasours all, with peace, and plentie blest,
Which God sejoyn's from all the world (wee see)
That none but *Neptune* shuld thy neighbour bee.
    Let not Our Loue infer the least offence,
Thou art our LORD our kyndlie KING, our Prence:
Our int'rest so is such (Dread Leige) in thee
Thogh Earths great Glob wer thyne, ours thou must
From *Jacob* learne to loue *Canaan* best,   (bee,
The native soill : for when his sonnes wer blest,
Hee charged them to take him heame againe,
Him to interre in *Ephrons* flowrie plaine :
Abraam there, and *Sara* sleep, said hee,
There *Isaak*, and *Rebecca* both doe lye,
And there I buried *Lea* : *Joseph* weiped,
In *Ephron Jacob* with his fathers sleiped :

                                            Joseph

Miscellaneous Poems

Joseph waxd chief in *Pharaos* court, and yet
Knowing the Tribs wold out of *Egipt* flitt,
Hee took his brethren, and the people sworne
His bones from thence shuld be to *Ephron* borne,
To keip their oath his brethren, and the rest
Imbalmed him and put him in a chest,
And when they fled from *Egypt* (as they sweare)
Moyses with him good *Josephs* bones did beare:
 Liue *Nestors* dayes King JAMES but liue among vs
By blood and birth thou do'st alone belong vs,
Stay then at home, to *Thames* make no returne,
Sleip with thy fathers in thy fathers vrn.
 But wee'r too bold to beg thy longer stay,
Since GOD sets doun thy Jests, and gyds thy way,
From death in famine GOD deliuereth thee,
From sword in battell thou shalt still be frie,
Destruction thou shalt skorne, and laugh at dearth,
And shall not feare the cruell beasts on earth,
Ston's of the feild shall be in league with thee,
And beasts at peace with great King JAMES shall be,
Yea thou shall know peace dwells thy tents within,
In spight of *Babell* and that Man of sin:
To thy great Joy ô KING thou shall perceaue,
Thy seed as grasse on earth: Thou shall to graue
In fullest aige (like to a rig of Corne
Broght to the Barne in seafon due) be borne.
 And if the Lord hes said that thou must leaue vs,
If *England* must of this our Joy bereaue vs,
If thou wilt go, and leaue vs full of sorrow,
This prayer short from Paynim pen wee borrow.
 Our sacred King, wyfe JAMES the Lord defend,
And royall seed, till all this All tak end,
Heavens grant to him, his faire and verteous wyfe
In peace and plentie, long and happie lyfe.
            Lord

Lord bleſſe, preſerue, and keep him frie from ill,
Of happie Kings let him be happieſt ſtill:
And, whilſt he lives, let him not ſee, nor heare,
The death of one, that to his Grace ſeems deare,
Let his Dominions farr, and long perſeuer,
And (ſtill adornd with Juſtice) laſt for euer:
Tyme ſtay thy haſt, relent thy former furie,
And let King JAMES our childrens children burie.
O touch him not proud *Fortune* but in kyndnes,
Or if thou do'ſt, hee ſtill defyes thy blindnes:
Heavens grant this Ile, with toyls tormoyled long
May be his meanes, be cur'd from ſin and wrong:
GOD grant hee ſaue Religion from decay,
And reeſtabliſh ſuch as runne aſtray:
Lord let this Starr in brightnes ſtill abound,
To light the World ſo long in Darknes dround:
And let each true, and faithfull ſubject ſing
With heart and woyce conjoynd, *God ſaue the King*.

ALEXANDER CRAIG
Of Roſe-craig.

MISCELLANEOUS POEMS

[From "The Theatre of the Scotiſh Kings" by Alexander Garden or Gardyne, a MS. preſerved in the Advocates' Library, Edinburgh. See Mr. Laing's Introduction, ante, p. 13.]

To A. G., Author of the Theatre of the Scotiſh Kinges.

Raue Pedaret, pretended to haue bene,
    Firſt Senator, and cheefe in Sparta choſen:
When Rols were red, yit was his Name onſene
He fund his friendis, in their affectiounes frozen:
    Yea, when hee thought his dooingis ſhuld decore him,
    He fund Three hundred Spartans plac'd before him.

Yit wes he glaide, to ſie the Citie flooriſh,
    Thought many, many, wer prefer'd to him:
So when I ſie the ſacred Nymphs doo nowriſh
    Thy ſpirit braue, (thogh whilſt I ſink, thou ſwim,)
    I greatlie joy, and Thow may'ſt greatlie glorie,
    In litill bounds, to bind ſo large a ſtorie.

Al. Craige.

[On the Earl of Argyll. From "The Staggering State of Scots Stateſmen," by Sir John Scot of Scotſtarvet. Firſt printed Edin. 1754. See Introduction, ante, p. 17.]

Now Earl of Guile, and Lord ForLorn thou goes,
    Quitting thy Prince, to ſerve his Spaniſh foes,
No faith in plaids, no truſt in Highland trews,
Camelion-like, they change to many hues.

[From "The Famous Hiftorie of the Renouned and Valiant Prince Robert, furnamed The Bruce, King of Scotland, &c. By Patrick Gordon, Gentleman. At Dort, Printed by George Waters, 1615." See Introduction, ante, p. 15.]

In Prais of the Prais-worthie Author.

Wife *Virgil* wrote AEneades long, to prais
    Anchifes Sone, whome he did not behold;
Octavian lykd his heigh and loftie Phrafe,
And gave the *Mantuan*, Money, Moyne, Gold:
    The Prais of *Bruce* (no queftione) thou proclames,
    To pleas and prais the *Faith's Defender* Iames.

If *Maroes* figments leive in frefh requeft,
Which he of *Stiks, Cocitus, Serber* penn'd,
Of *Charon, Hell, Elyfium* and the reft,
Thy Storie trew fhall with the World take End:
    And, to thy prais, I dar be bold to fay,
    No Lines prophaine can live a longer Day.

                                                  CRAGE.

II

iv

INDEXES TO TITLES AND FIRST LINES IN CRAIG'S POETICAL WORKS, 1604-31.

INDEX TO TITLES.

POETICALL ESSAYES, 1604.

	Page		Page
Apologie for his Rival	3	To his Maieſtie—	
Appellation to the Lion	32	1 Sonet: When others ceaſe	7
Calidons Complaint	21	2 Sonet: With mutuall loſſe	7
Eliazabeth, late Qveene of England, her Ghoſt	23	3 Sonet: Great Pompey cauſ'd	8
Epiſtle to his Friend	33	To my dread Soveraigne Iames	2
Scotlands Teares	18	To the Author (*Ro. Aytone*)	45
Sonet: From this Abydos	42	To the Kinges moſt excellent Maieſtie—	
Sonet: I ſome time had a Miſtres	36	Epiſtle Congratulatorie & Perœnetic	9
Sonet: To his Maieſtie of the Vnion of the two famous Realmes Scotland and England	25	To the Kings moſt Royall Maieſtie—	
The Avthor to his Booke	2	1 Sonet: Kind Attalus in Annals old	43
The Cvckoe, and Philomel	30	2 Sonet: Anacreon two dayes two nights	44
The moſt vertuous and accompliſhed Prince Anna, Queene of Britane; Complaineth the abſence of her Lord	17	To the Queens moſt Excellent Maieſtie—	
To his anonim Freind and Miſtres Palinode	34	1. Sonet: In Pallas Church	26
To his Calidonian Miſtris	37		
To his Calidonian Miſtris	38		

1

Index to Titles.

	Page		Page
2 Sonet: Of her Highnes Natall day	26	of Inde	28
3 Sonet: new yeir Gift	27	To the Reader	5
4 Sonet: Thofe famous old Gymnofophifts		To the vertuous and accomplifhed Sir Iames Hay	29

AMOROSE SONGES, 1606.

	Page		Page
A letter to Lesbia, fhewing his difcontents	157	Confirmation of his loue to Erantina	133
Alexis to Lesbia	151	Cragio fuo (*Robertus Aytonus*)	167
Amorous Songes and Sonets	25	De Alexandro Rupœo populari, (*Arthurus Gordonus*)	167
Anagram	40		
Anagram	41	Elegie to Kala	121
A new perfwafion to Lesbia	155	Epiftle generall to Idea, Cynthia, Lithocardia, Kala, Erantina, Lais, Pandora, Penelope	9
A fparing farewell to Kala	118		
At Ideas direction, thefe two Sonets were made—			
1 More then I am	55	Farewell to Lais	117
2 With chaft defires	56	His conftant Refolution to Erantina	132
At the newes of Ideas death, Dialogue twixt the Poets Ghoft and Charon	85	His faythfull feruice to Idea	144
		His louing farewell to Pandora	138
Another Dialogue to the fame purpofe	86	His Reconciliation to Lithocardia after abfence	126
A wrathfull farewell to Kala	119		
Codrvs Complaint and Farewell to Kalatibia	161	His Refolution of abfence and farewell to Lithocardia	125
Codrvs his reconciliation to his heart, after he hath abiured Kalatibia	164	His vnwilling Farewell to Penelope	137

2

Index of Titles.

	Page		Page
Idea after long ficknes, becommeth weil;	87	To his Riuall and Lais	116
Lesbia her anfwer to Alexis	154	To Idea	12
		To Idea	25
		To Idea	26
Lesbia her anfwer	160	To Idea	33
Newyeares gift to Idea	96	To Idea	35
Newyeares gift to Penelope	91	To Idea	36
		To Idea	50
Pandora refufeth his Letter	65	To Idea	51
		To Idea	56
Sonet to Lesbia	159	To Idea	73
To abfent Erantina	61	To Idea	108
To abfent Idea	63	To Idea	112
To abfent Pandora	94	To inconftant Lais	69
To Cinthia	34	To Kala	16
To Cinthia	80	To Kala	42
To Cinthia	97	To Kala	59
To Cynthia	14	To Kala	62
To Cynthia	29	To Kala	66
To Cynthia	57	To Kala	83
To Cynthia	88	To Kala	84
To Cynthia	101	To Kala	98
To Erantina	18	To Kala	99
To Erantina	31	To Kala	100
To Erantina	32	To Kala	113
To Erantina	49	To Kala	115
To Erantina	58	To Lais	17
To Erantina	64	To Lais	43
To Erantina	71	To Lais	44
To Erantina	89	To Lais	53
To Erantina	102	To Lais	60
To Erantina	103	To Lais	70
To Erantina	104	To Lais	77
To frowning Cinthia	74	To Lais	82
To his Pandora, from England	142	To Lais	93
		To Lais	110

Index to Titles.

To Lais . . . 111	To Pandora . . . 76
To Lais . . . 131	To Pandora . . . 78
To Lais . . . 136	To Pandora . . . 90
To Lais . . . 143	To Pandora . . . 105
To Lithocardia . . 15	To Pandora . . . 106
To Lithocardia . . 27	To Pandora . . . 107
To Lithocardia . . 28	To Pandora . . . 114
To Lithocardia. by Anagram 40	To Penelope . . . 21
To Lithocardia. Anagram 41	To Penelope . . . 38
To Lithocardia . . 48	To Penelope . . . 39
To Lithocardia . . 52	To Penelope . . . 54
To Lithocardia . . 67	To Penelope . . . 72
To Lithocardia . . 68	To Penelope . . . 79
To Lithocardia . . 81	To Penelope . . . 92
To Lithocardia . . 109	To Penelope feeke . 95
To my Honorable good Lord and Maifter George Earle of Dunbar 145	To Penelope . . . 120
	To the Author . . 166
	To the moft godly, vertvovs, beavtifvll, and accomplifhed Princeffe, Anna, Queene, . . 3
To Pandora . . . 19	
To Pandora . . . 30	
To Pandora . . . 37	
To Pandora . . . 45	To the Queene her moft excellent Maieftie . 23
To Pandora . . . 46	
To Pandora . . . 47	To the Reader . . 11
To Pandora . . . 75	To the Reader . . 148

POETICAL RECREATIONS, 1609.

A Counfell to Courteours 12	Aethon Cragio fvo (by *Robert Aytoun*) . . 16
A defcription of a pardond, yet still vnrepenting proditor Plexirtus 19	Againft drunkards and lichers . . . 28
A difsvvafion to his friend from his intended mariage 18	Againft ignorance and ill example . . . 27
	Againft ingratitude . . 29

Index to Titles.

	Page		Page
Againſt Pryde	26	The Rape of Proſerpina	30
Againſt Sycophants and Paraſits	31	To abſent Idea	23
		To covetovs covrtiers	14
Againſt the ſellers of Tobacco	16	To eloquent Erantina	22
		To G. E. of Dunbar	3
A Prayer for his impriſoned friend	21	To his abſent and loving Lesbia	23
Auream quiſquis mediocritatem	25	To his afflicted friend	20
		To his aſpyring friend	25
Complaint to his Majeſtie	7	To his baniſhed friend	24
Contempt of Death	32	To his cvſning friend	14
Epitaph	13	To his dear friend, and fellow ſtudent Mr. Robert AEton	15
Epitaph	30		
Epitaph of Iohn firſt Marques of Hammilton	19		
Aliud	19	To his dear friend Mr Al. Dickſon	13
Fortvna ſaevo laeta negotio: tranſmutat incertos honores	20	To his fortunate friend	20
		To his friend who ſeemd ſorie when he left Court	26
His contents at his Tugur	27	To his Lord and Mr. George Earle of Dunbar	17
His regrate for the loſe of time at Court	25	To his Lord and Maſter G. E. Dunbar	28
His vnambitious minde	26		
New yeare gift to his Majeſtie	9	To his Lord and Maſter to be ware of envy	29
Nulla dies ſine linea	25	To his Majeſtie in name of his Noble Maſter	10
Of true friendſhip	31		
Perſwaſions of certainties are vnneceſſarie	28	To his moſt excellent Maieſtie	6
That he neither loues to be too glad nor too ſad	27	To his ſingular good Lord and Maſter	24
The praiſe of Gladpovertie	26	To his vnkinde friend	13
		To Idea at her bownes	24
The praiſe of humilitie in his L. and Mr.	31	To Idea for his long abſence	22

Index to Titles.

	Page		Page
To John Earle of Montrofe firſt Vice-Roy of Scotland	30	To my Lord Admiral at his mariage with Ladie Margaret Stewart	11
To John Lord Ramſay Vicunt of Hadington	8	To my Lord Hay, at his legation to France	11
Ad eundem de eodem	9	To my Lord Sarvsbvrie	11
To Ladie Anna Hay Covntes of Winton	17	To the moſt honorable and religious Lord G. Earle Marſchell,	32
To Miſtres Hartſide at Orknay her natall ſoyle	28	To the reader	5
To my Lady Hartfurde at his Majeſties firſt progres to Totnem	12	To vnfortunat and pure Æmilian at Court	27
		To virteovs and noble Cynthia	15
		Vivitur parvo bene	21

POETICALL RECREATIONS, 1623.

	Page		Page
A Counſell to his married Friend	22	Nocumenta, Documenta	12
Ad Lectorem candidvm	32	Of Themiſtocles	12
Ad Qveſtores	25	Of Timæa, Queene of Sparta	27
Amicus magis neceſſarius quam Aqua & Ignis	21	Panvrgvs	18
Apologie for Poets, againſt	20	Philocoſmvs Epitaph	16
Contempt of Fortune	10	Polemoes Reformation	10
Difference betwixt a King, and a Tyrant	11	Pompeys Mercie	10
Herodias and Salome	15	Reply to a Dilatorie Anſwere, ſent by Sir Gedeon, &c. to the Author	25
I. R.	34		
Liberalitie of Phocion	12	Roſipetræ meæ ad Imitationem Pſophidii Arcadienſis deſcriptio	35
Mamertes Anſwere to a Paraſite	27		
Margites	18	Altera	35
Neroes change	11	Satyra Volans	30

Index to Titles.

	Page		Page
Satyrvla in Plebem	33	Alivd.	24
The Authors Confolation	19	Alivd.	24
The Authors Refolution	34	Alivd.	25
The Miferie of Man	9	To Mvfophilvs	21
The Shortnes of Lyfe	9	To Philocofmvs	16
The temperance of Epaminondas, King of Thebes	11	Alivd.	16
		To Sir George Hay, of Kilfawnes, Great Chancellar of Scotland	29
Tigellini Epitaphium	15		
To a difcredited Courteour	13	Ad Eundem	30
Alivd.	14	To States-men	26
To a libidinous Levi	22	Alivd.	27
To a rude and barbarous Boore, vvho vvronged the Author	19	To the Covrt of Parliament 1621	23
To Chremes	17	To the Caufidickes, who were made tributarie in the faid Court	23
Tranflatio liberior	17		
Ad eundem	17	To the Cowfner	28
Alivd.	18	To the Envyous	29
To George, Earle of Enyie, Lord Gordon, &c.	3	To the Frontifpice of Abakuk Bifsets Booke	22
Ad eundem	5	To the ignorant Iudge	13
To his Majefties Queftors, for his Penfion	24	To the Readers	7
		To the Swearer	28

Pilgrime and Heremite, 1631.

Poliphila before Shee writ her Anfvvere, difputeth vvith her ovvne defires	23	The Heremite his Teftament	27
Her Anfwere, to the Heremite	26	The Pilgrime and Heremite, in forme of a Dialogue	5
Polyphila her Complaint, and Teftament	31	The Poëme	34
The Heremite his Complaint	25	To the Right Honovrable William Forbes of Tolqvhon	3

7

INDEX TO TITLES.

MISCELLANEOUS POEMS.

	Page		Page
In Prais of the Praisworthie Author [Patrick Gordon]	10	was alfo prefented to his M. at Kinnaird	3
On the Earl of Argyll	9	To A. G., Author of the Theatre of the Scotifh Kinges	9
This fubfequent welcome			

INDEX TO FIRST LINES.

POETICALL ESSAYES, 1604.

	Page
And fhall no light at all to len vs light be left?	21
Anacreon two dayes two nights did watch,	44
Ceafe louing Subiects, ceafe my death for to deplore,	23
From this *Abydos* where I duyne and die,	42
Great mightie *Ioue* from his imperiall place,	26
Great *Pompey* cauf'd his Heraulds to proclaime	8
In Annals old we read *Ioue* had but daughters two,	34
In *Pallas* Church did wretched *Irus* ftand,	26
I fome time had a Miftres, and a Freind;	36
Kind *Attalus* in Annals old wee reid,	43
Scarfe had my Mufe refpi'd the fmalleft fpace,	9
Scilurus had twice fourtie Children male,	25
The *Cucko* once (fome fay) would *Philomel* affaile,	30
The *Cucko* once (tis trew) in finging, did compare	31
The Lion fome time went abroade to fpy his pray,	32
This Apill round I fend, ô matchles fare!	27
Thofe famous old *Gymnofophifts* of *Inde*,	28
When *Dedal* taught his tender Sonne to flee,	2
When fabling *Æfop* was at fatall *Delphos* tane,	18
When I remember on that time, that place,	38
When others ceafe, now I begin to fing;	7
Where habit was, dwels fad Priuation now,	17
With mutuall loffe, with none or litle gaine,	7
Why thought fond *Grece* to build a folid fame,	45

Index to First Lines.

Amorose Songes, &c., 1606.

	Page
A frind fome time to *Thracian Cotys* fend,	137
Allace that abfence hath fuch force to foyll,	60
Apelles man did all his Wits imploy	23
A fhepheard poore with ftore of pains oppreft	161
As *Marigould* did in her Garden walke,	41
As thou art now, fo was I once in grace,	116
A very World may well be feene in mee,	48
Blind Loue (allace) and Ielofie vndoo .	113
Blind naked loue, who breeds thofe ftormy broyls	71
Braue *Troilus* the *Troian* ftout and true,	111
Canft thou haue eares, & wil not heare my plaint .	90
Come be my Loue, and liue with mee,	151
Come *Charon* come: (*Ch*) Who cals? (*Gh*.) a wandring Ghoft,	85
Come *Charon* come. (*Ch*.) Who cals? (*Gh*.) a martyrd man,	86
Deare to my foule, and wilt thou needs be gone,	76
Deare to my foule once degne,	138
Difordered Haires the types of my difgrace,	103
Downe frõ the Skies for to behold my Dame	26
Driue not deare hart, in dooll the day,	160
Each thing allace, prefents and lets mee fee,	75
Even as a man by darke that goes aftray,	61
Even as a ventering Merchant fkant of fkill,	44
Faine would I goe, and faine would I abide,	78
Faire Dame adue, for whom I dayly die,	125
Faire dame, for whõ my mornfull mufe hath worne	63
Faire *Kala*, fairer then the Wooll moft faire,	42
Faire louelie *Hebe* Queene of pleafant Youth,	51
Faire *Sicil* fertill firft of Cruell Kings,	106
Falfe *Eriphile* fometime did betray	81
Fond *Celius* fome time in a foolifh vaine,	118
Good caufe hadft thou *Euarchus* to repent,	67
Go you o winds that blow from north to fouth,	46

INDEX TO FIRST LINES.

	Page
Great *Alexander* gaue a ſtraight command,	109
Hadſt thou been blacke, or yet had I been blind,	57
Harpaste poore, was blind of either eye,	143
How oft haſt thou with Siuet ſmelling breath,	69
I haue compard my Miſtris many time	77
If all were thine that there I ſee,	154
If *Caſtor* ſhine, the Seaman hoyſeth ſaile,	74
I feare not *Loue* with blind and frowning face,	68
I firſt receiud ſince did ſweet Sainɛt vnfold	98
If *Rodopæ* the loathſome Strumpet vile,	136
In *Arcadie* ſometime (as Sydney ſay's,) .	47
Ingenij ſi verna ſeges primoribus annis,	167
In Golden world, when *Saturne* did vpgiue	25
In ſtately *Troy* which was by force of fire	36
I panſe not on the gold of *Tagus* ſand,	37
I put my hand by hazard in the hat	108
I ſerue a Miſtris infinitely faire,	38
I ſweare (ſweet *Kala*) by my flames, thy eyes,	99
It ſometime chanſt, as Stories tell by chanſe,	34
Laſt yeare I drew (faire Dame) by very chance,	112
Long haue I had long haires vpon my head,	104
Long ſince hath *Cynthia* ſhown her ful fac'd prid	94
Loue now reſolu'd to work ſo rare a wonder,	166
Loue ſet his Bow, his Bag, and Bolts aſide,	28
More then I am, accurſed mought I bee,	55
My Muſe ſhal make thy boundles fame to flie	73
My wandring Verſe hath made thee known all-whare	144
No hart ſo hard, tho wrought of *Vulcans* ſteele,	89
Nor there where as the yoaked reſtles Horſe	31
Now while amid thoſe daintie Douns & Dales	142
O Beautie doomb aſtoniſh'd Maruels chyld	87
Of late the blind, and naked Archer Boy,	27
Oft haue I ment with Muſicke, ſleepe, & wine,	80
Oft haue I pray'd thee be my Loue,	157
Oft haue I ſworne; oft haſt thou pray'd me too	83
O how I long to heare from thee againe,	100

INDEX TO FIRST LINES.

	Page
Olautia poore was glad,	126
Once more I pray thee be my Loue,	155
Ovtthrough the faire and famous *Scythian* land,	64
O watchfull Bird proclaymer of the day,	45
O what a world I suffer of extreames,	105
O Wounder to the world, whō woundering eyne	32
Poore wandring hart, which like the prodig child	164
Proud *Zeuxis* gaue his Pictures all for nought,	88
Reed this, and then no more,	121
See *Deianira*, see how I am shent	53
Shall absence long bring change,	133
Shall absence long, or distance farr of place,	132
Short is the day, but long (allace) to mee,	39
Since *Ioue* him selfe was subiect vnto Loue,	30
Sore is my head and sorie is my hart,	62
Sweet *Lais*, trust me, I can loue no more,	70
That *Colatine* did talke in *Tarquins* tent,	91
The Brethren three whose hot perfut hath brought	50
The chastest Child will oft for mercie cry,	33
The faire faced Woman, and deformed Ape,	131
The Hobbie Haulke can catch at all no pray,	29
The ielous eyes which watch my louing Dame,	102
The Lipper man, whose voyce can not be hard,	35
The *Locrian* King *Zaleucus* made a law,	96
The *Persian* King in danger to be dround,	54
The *Persian* Kings all waters did abiure,	59
The saikles foule *Philoxenus* was slaine	65
The Tyrant *Nero* houering to behold	58
The whitest Siluer drawes the blackest skore,	119
Thou fawns (faire nimph) for frindship at my hand	117
Thou who began by *Menalus* to mone,	52
Threicij quisquis credit modulamine vatis	167
Time and my thoughts Togither spurr the Post,	159
Twixt Fortune, Loue, and most vnhappie mee,	66
Well may I read as on a snowie sheet	49
VVere I as skild in Medecine as hee,	95

Index to First Lines.

	Page
What euer thou be that claimes or courts my deare	43
VVhen *Ædipus* did foolifhly refigne	84
When *Alexander* did fubdue and bring	92
When Churches all of *Afia* les and more,	40
When *Creffid* went from *Troy* to *Calchas* tent,	82
VVhen *Dionife* was fhut from Regall feat,	93
When *Scythian* Lords long frō their lands had bein	107
VVhen filent night had fpred her pitchie vaile	115
When ftately *Troy* by fubtill *Sinons* guile,	72
VVhen thofe which at *Ardea* did remaine	101
VVhen *Tyndaris* was broght from *Troy* againe	120
While fierce *Achilles* at the fiedge of *Troy*,	79
While gathering in the Mufes garden flowrs,	114
VVhy loue I her that loues not mee againe?	110
Why loues thou more (faire dame) thy Dog then mee?	97
VVith chaft defires I ferue and honor thee	56

POETICAL RECREATIONS, 1609.

Æmilian begs with heart half-brok for forrow,	27
A greedie Moufe did by a privat way	14
Ah, whither now fweet Ladie wilt thou go?	17
Ah, whither now (fweet Sant) art thou retired?	24
Alas, that Time fhould be a foe to fame,	28
Alas, why fould *Califthenes* remaine	8
Apelles fome-time came	6
Attilius ruler of the Roman hoft,	22
Athenian Chares promif'd much to many,	14
Beyond the Mountains of the froftie North,	9
Bleft was thy life, and bleffed didft thou die,	19
Braue *Alcibiad* curious once to know	17
Braue *Cincinnatus* from his houfe was broght,	32
Cleombrotus a Heathen man did heare	22
Deare heart, dear heart, dear, dear, dear heart againe,	23
Deepe danger lyes (deare Lord) in fmootheft looks,	29

Index to First Lines.

	Page
Fair famous Ile where *Zoroaſtres* raign'd,	18
Falſe Sycophant that wrongs the virteous name,	31
Fane wold I render thanks for thy good-will:	15
Fane wold I ſing, if ſongs my thoghts culd eaſe,	16
Firſt let me die before I proue ingrate,	29
Here reſts within this Tomb of truth th' vnmatched zeale	19
He that can walk on ground that's fair and plane,	21
If *Rhadamanthus* in th' Eliſian field,	30
In ſhaddie night the glow-worme ſhines like fire,	31
In ſinfull *Sodome* to liue cleane and poore,	28
In wether fair, and in a temperat ſpring,	20
Ioyes come like oxen heauie peaſ'd and ſlo,	27
I ſcorne to liue at Court, becauſe J ſpy	26
It merits praiſe to manage litle well,	25
It ſeems (me think) a thing of ſmall effect,	31
Long mai'ſt thou liue an argument of praiſe,	24
Loue, *Want*, and *Cares*, all contrare me conſpyre,	7
Mars, *Hercules*, and *Iupiter* we finde,	11
Men ſeldome wiſh to die, thogh nev'r ſo old,	32
No greater fools then *Philodoxes* fond,	28
Of all the wounds whereof that Roman great,	13
O how Time ſlips, and ſlelie ſlids away,	25
Proſcribed *Orcas* thogh J hate thy forms,	28
Shall *Ceres* daughter ſtill remane at hell?	30
Since charge and honor march together ſtill	25
Since thou muſt ſail to ſee the *Celtick* ſhore,	11
Sing ſwift hoof'd *Æthon* to thy matchles ſelfe,	15
Strange are the changes of this changing age,	20
Th' ambitious man no greater foe can haue,	26
That *Thracian* forme at birth of friends to weepe,	13
The bibull Spoynge in tepid water ſet,	12
The faithfull heart is ever fraught with feare,	10
The famous *Perſians* had a forme, we reed,	21
The *Fox* and *Kat*, were walking by the way,	20
The law of God is Lanterne full of light,	27
The ſtanding poole will quicklie ſtink and rott,	25

INDEX TO FIRST LINES.

	Page
The tempeſt beat and falling *Farne* (fair Dame)	12
Thou that haſt made of felling fmoak a trade,	16
Three forts of men vnto the market go,	26
Three things there be for which J'ill not contend,	26
To *Creſus* rich ſhall Codrus gifts propyne,	9
Two potent Kings over *Siciles* two Empyre,	11
Two wofull weeds, the mother Church muſt weare,	24
When falſe and proud *Plexirtus* did confpire,	19
When loſe of *Tyme* at Court was all my gane,	27
With puiſſant pow'r when princely *Pompey* went,	23

POETICALL RECREATIONS, 1623.

Angulo in anguſto terræ, fruƈtuſque ferenti	35
Are wyfe Caufidickes brought to fuch a ſtraite,	23
A *Thebane* kinde did fome-time beg and pray,	11
Beloved Friende, I kindlie doe commende	21
Braue *Brutus* begg'd a Loafe, to faue his Lyfe;	24
Envy doth creepe, where as it dare not goe,	29
Experience, long, and deare, hath made mee finde,	33
Giue Cæfar what is Cæfars; *Chriſt* did fo;	23
Goe, Swift-wing'd *Satyre*, through all States, but feare,	30
Hee's good enough, if hee haue Goods anew,	16
I am no fayned *Iebvſite*, for I	24
If Thou with Faſhiones of thy Wife offende,	22
Iohn Baptiſt tolde drunke *Herod*, hee defilde	15
I reade of one *Margites*, yet I kno	18
I fee fonde Luſt, with moſt vnlawfull Heate,	22
Litigat, & multum Plutus Plutona *fatigat*,	17
Mans weaker partes are thrall to Fortunes wrong;	10
Of all thofe Trees which *Veſtaes* Wombe brings foorth,	20
Once more one poore Petition I prefent;	25
One fome-tyme askd *Diogenes*, how long	9
One tolde *Mamertes*, hee was happie thryfe,	27
Ovr *Queſtors* learn'd their Arithmeticke ill:	24

Index to First Lines.

	Page
O what an Age is this, in which wee liue!	25
Panurgus pryes in high and low Effaires;	18
Parva domus, bene cultus ager, nec inepta supellex	35
Raw Meates make Stomackes ficke, and ftill doe lye,	18
Sifamnes was a *Perfian* Iudge, wee finde,	12
Some rude, vnruelie, barbrous Boores there bee,	19
Stay Pilgryme, ftay, if thou fo curious bee,	16
Take Courage, *Craig*, though Thou be wrong'd too farre,	19
The Cowfner lookes with faire, but fraudfull, face,	28
The Forreft Affe vndaunted did beholde	14
The God of Wealth, *Plotvs* and *Plvto* ftroue,	17
The good fucceffe of *Syllaes* great Effaires,	29
The Graffe-hopper hath wings, but cannot flie:	16
The Lyfe of Man is full of Griefe and Sorrow:	9
Themiftocles was wife, and made a Ieft:	12
The Nightingale, when fhee hath ftor'd her Neft,	34
The Partridge ftores her Neft with Eggs all ftowne,	17
There was a Tyme when Thieves had leaue to fteale,	26
The Royall Throne of *Salomon* the Wyfe,	27
The Snayle did once the Eagle faire intreate,	13
The wyfe *Ægyptians* punifh'd him who fware,	28
Timæa faire, was *Lacedæmons* Queene,	27
To Thee, deare Lord, amidft thefe drierie Tymes,	5
Twixt Was, and Is, how various are the Ods!	22
VVell was it faide, A Friende that's kynde and true,	21
VVhen drunke *Polemo* came to heare the fpeaches	10
VVhen *Nero* firft the *Romanes* did command,	11
VVhen *Philips* great vnconquered Sonne had fende	12
VVhen *Tigranes*, the great *Armenian* King,	10
VVhilft *Ignoramvs* on the Bench doth fit,	13
VVho feem'd fo fure, as hee who late departed?	15
VVho thinks dame Fortune blinde, and fpoylde of Eyes,	30
Wyfe *Adrian* was oft-tymes wont to fay,	11
Your Sub-Receiver fhew'd mee, you were forie,	25

INDEX TO FIRST LINES.

PILGRIME AND HEREMITE, 1631.

	Page
As perfect Poets ere-tymes haue tane paine,	34
But now, and not till now, my Swan-lyke Song I fing;	27
How hard it is, none knowes, fo well as I,	23
So manie thinges before haue perfect Poets pende,	25
O endleffe Night of noyfe, which hath no Morrow!	31
Thy loving Lines I rafhlie did receiue,	26
When pale Ladie *Lvna*, with her lent light,	5

[As fheet B, pp. 13-20, in the only known copy of the PILGRIME AND HEREMITE, is wanting, fome titles and firft lines are doubtlefs omitted here.]

MISCELLANEOUS POEMS.

Braue Pedaret, pretended to haue bene,	9
Great Man of God, whom God doeth call and choofe	3
Now Earl of Guile, and Lord ForLorn thou goes,	9
Wife *Virgil* wrote AEneades long, to prais	10

REGISTER OF ERRATA FOUND IN THE ORIGINAL EDITIONS OF CRAIG'S WORKS, 1604-31.

POETICALL ESSAYES, 1604.

Page	Line		
Title	8	*For*	Wllliam *read* William.
3	6	,,	Lactatius *read* Lutatius.
5	25	(	), blank in original.
14	14	*For*	Panfanfius *read* Paufanias.
15	22	,,	Kinkes *read* Kinges.
18	26	,,	N o *read* Now.
19	7	*Read* we [are].	
19	18	*For*	your *read* young.
22	2	,,	Heroit *read* Heroic.
22	16	,,	Archunonarche *read* Archimonarche.
25	4	,,	Englaud *read* England.
27	17	,,	Enbean *read* Eubean.
27	18	,,	Atlanta *read* Atalanta.
29	16	,,	her: anfwered. *read* her, anfwered,
29	19	,,	facidic *read* fatidic.
31	8	,,	Terens *read* Tereus.
31	17	,,	chrils *read* thrils.
32	3	,,	abraode *read* abroade.
32	12	,,	iudocil *read* indocil.
32	26	,,	lyus *read* lyns.
33	14	,,	omnerited *read* onmerited.
33	20	(	), blank in original.
35	11	*For*	online *read* onliue.
37	17	,,	Miftes *read* Miftres.
39	4	,,	accreftis *read* accrefcis.
41	11	,,	Shott *read* Short.
41	29	,,	uiy *read* my.
44	6	,,	faikes *read* faikles.
45	12	,,	ta'ls *read* tales.

Register of Original Errata.

AMOROSE SONGES, SONETS AND ELEGIES, 1606.

Page	Line		
2	2	*For*	Cytharam *read* citharam.
2	3	,,	Leuibus *read* leuibus.
2	5	,,	pluuiæ, vitantur *read* pluuiæ vitantur.
7	5	,,	Lecedemonians *read* Lacedæmonians.
7	17	,,	Flowes *read* Flowers.
9	4	,,	Penelopæ *read* Penelope.
10	3	,,	been. No *read* been, no.
13	15	,,	rapina, Cœlicolum *read* rapina Cœlicolum.
17	19	,,	cenſnriug *read* cenſuring.
18	10	,,	Ptolomey *read* Ptolemy.
18	20	,,	fœnit *read* ſæuit.
19	Sig.	,,	A ii *read* B ii.
21	,,	,,	A iii *read* B iii.
23	4	,,	Lædais *read* Ledais.
23	Sig.		B iiii omitted in original.
30	8	*For*	Daphni *read* Daphne.
30	11	,,	Ænonæ *read* Œnone.
32	17	,,	inheret *read* inhæret.
33	16	,,	audebæm *read* audebam.
34	16	,,	liqour *read* liquor.
36	16	,,	pertore *read* pectore.
37	3	,,	ſhyniug *read* ſhyning.
37	16	,,	ſiue *read* ſine.
37	16	,,	Munera *read* munera.
38	16	,,	paræter *read* paratur.
39	10	,,	Pænelopæ *read* Penelope.
39	15	,,	Creſus *read* Crœſus.
39	Sig.		C iiii omitted in original.
40	18	*For*	ipſe times *read* ipſa timet?
41	13	,,	canging *read* changing.
41	17	,,	ſprenit *read* ſpreuit.
41	17	,,	galatea *read* Galatea.

Register of Original Errata.

Page	Line		
44	4	*For*	recempence *read* recompence.
44	16	,,	candida *read* Candida.
46	7	,,	rceiue *read* receiue.
47	2	,,	Sydne *read* Sydney.
49	16	,,	veneris *read* Veneris.
49	16	,,	falleudo *read* fallendo.
49	16	,,	refefuit *read* ?
50	2	,,	perfut *read* purfuit.
50	8	,,	fight *read* flight.
51	2	,,	Hæbæ *read* Hebe.
52	16	,,	cadis *read* cadit.
53	16	,,	terci *read* tecti.
53	17	,,	folus *read* foliis.
53	17	,,	perbuit *read* præbuit.
56	18	,,	mortalæ *read* mortale.
57	15	,,	wrecke *read* wracke.
58	5	,,	in in *read* in.
60	16	,,	herebas *read* hærebas.
64	16	,,	ventis, Fudimus *read* ventis Fudimus.
65	5	,,	Cornithian *read* Corinthian.
65	7	,,	fight *read* fight.
65	17	,,	notis *read* votis.
68	14	,,	auth *read* aith, *or* truth?
69	17	,,	Aterius *read* Alterius.
71	17	,,	feufibus *read* fenfibus.
71	17	,,	efss *read* efsc.
74	20	,,	Diccte *read* Dicete.
74	20	,,	maæq; *read* meæq;
74	21	,,	Vnita *read* Vnica.
78	3	,,	Hais agene *read* ?
78	17	,,	molle quieffe *read* molli quiefce.
82	2	,,	Calchs *read* Calchas.
83	16	,,	panpertas *read* paupertas.
83	16	,,	neæra *read* Neæra.
86	16	,,	Elefian *read* Elyfian.
86	19	,,	Janua *read* janua.
90	16	,,	horrens, Cantafus *read* horrens Caucafus.

Register of Original Errata.

Page	Line		
90	17	*For*	hircaneq; *read* Hyrcaneq;
91	2	,,	Colatine *read* Collatine.
94	16	,,	locæ *read* loca.
94	17	,,	lenes ods *read* leues odi.
103	16	,,	duſit *read* duxit?
103	17	,,	cepit *read* cœpit.
106	16	,,	graniora *read* grauiora.
109	16	,,	preantis *read* precantis.
109	17	,,	iudere *read* uidere.
110	16	,,	amantum, Iupiter *read* amantum Iupiter,
111	6	,,	Ænonæ *read* Œnone.
111	6	,,	drerd *read* dreid.
111	9	,,	and *read* ane.
111	16	,,	tuneam ignoto tuneo *read* timeam ignoro; timeo.
117	5	,,	met *read* mee.
117	11	,,	Zethius *read* Zethus.
118	2	,,	Celuis *read* Celius.
118	20	,,	amoris, Suauia *read* amoris Suauia.
119	6	,,	fairſ'd *read* fairſ't.
124	14	,,	laſt *read* leaſt.
125	17	,,	igne *read* ignem.
127	16	,,	farſet *read* farfet.
132	10	,,	ſeen'd *read* ſeen't.
132	11	,,	meen'd *read* meen't.
132	17	,,	paris *read* Paris.
132	17	,,	œnone *read* Œnone.
132	18	,,	xanthi *read* Xanthi.
133	16	,,	Mædea *read* Medea.
134	11	,,	Hemon *read* Hæmon.
136	2	,,	Rodopœ *read* Rhodopis.
139	8	,,	unro *read* unto.
142	2	,,	Englaud *read* England.
145	16	,,	Philopæmen *read* Philopœmen.
145	18	,,	aloue *read* alone.
148	9	,,	ezecrable *read* execrable.
149	9	,,	Mecænas *read* Mæcenas.

Register of Original Errata.

Page	Line	
149	20	*For* donwe *read* downe.
151	Sig.	K iiii omitted in original.
152	3	*For* ſhill *read* ſhrill.
152	8	,, buddings *read* buildings.
153	4	,, And *read* Ane.
153	21	,, Lisbia *read* Lesbia.
155	9	,, Caćtalian *read* Caſtalian.
155	10	,, Thithorea *read* Tithorea.
156	7	,, Vlolet *read* Violet.
156	21	,, agaue *read* agane.
156	25	,, Thon *read* Thou.
157	15	,, Diſpeaſure *read* Diſpleaſure.
160	14	,, chauſe *read* chanſe.
161	2	,, Ralatibia *read* Kalatibia.
162	5	,, thy *read* they.
167	4	,, forttibus *read* fortibus.
167	11	,, refsilijſſe *read* reſilijſſe.

POETICAL RECREATIONS, 1609.

Page	Line	
6	17	*For* Appelles *read* Apelles.
7	28	,, rape *read* reap.
15	19	,, writ *read* write.
15	19	,, vain *read* vein.
24	28	,, Bene *read* Auream.*
27	2	,, Emilian *read* Æmilian.
30	10	,, rapt *read* rape.
30	23	,, To *read* Againſt.*

* Theſe wrong catchwords ſuggeſt omitted leaves, but all the three known copies have the ſame peculiarities.

POETICALL RECREATIONS, 1623.

Page	Line	
12	21	*For* Othanes *read* Otanes.
17	11	,, Crhemes *read* Chremes.
17	14	,, Indicioque *read* Iudicioque.
20	8	,, againſt *read* againſt ?

Register of Original Errata.

THE PILGRIME AND HEREMITE, 1631.

Page	Line		
8	4	*For* hoſpe *read* hoſte.
10	35	,,	Orphus *read* Orpheus.
10	35	,,	Protus *read* Proteus.
25	23	,,	nurix *read* murex.
28	4	,,	Soliphermis *read* Soliphernus.
35	21	,,	eaſe. *read* eaſe,

MISCELLANEOUS POEMS.

Page	Line		
4	14	*For* ſtrenght *read* ſtrength.

GLOSSARY
TO THE ORIGINAL EDITIONS OF CRAIG'S WORKS, 1604-31.

[The various Works are here referred to in the order of their dates, as follows:—
- I. POETICAL ESSAYES, 1604.
- II. AMOROSE SONGES, 1606.
- III. POETICALL RECREATIONS, 1609.
- IV. POETICALL RECREATIONS, 1623.
- V. PILGRIME AND HEREMITE, 1631.
- VI. MISCELLANEOUS POEMS, ——

The figures after the Roman numerals refer to the page and line. Words noted in the Regifter of Errata will here be found in their correct form.]

accrefcis, I, 39/4, increafes.
adoes, III, 22/16, labours, occupation.
aggrege, V, 25/12, aggravate.
agnat heyre, I, 9/17, heir by the father's fide.
aire, I, 31/15, early.
airts, I, 20/11, directions, points of the compafs.
airts, V, 5/23, art's.
allaine, II, 138/18, alone.
als, I, 27/16, as.
alternall, II, 45/13, alternative.
anew, I, 13/2, enow, enough.
anonym, I, 33/15, anonymous.
apill, I, 27/15, apple.
apodofis, I, 13/28, the latter part of a fimilitude.

afyll, II, 140/4, afylum.
ather, I, 10/32, either.
auth, II, 68/14, aith, *i.e.* oath?
ay, I, 28/16, always.
backaft, II, 97/9, back-caft, *i.e.* thrown back.
bairne, V, 34/14, child.
baile-bearing bill, V, 24/15, forrow-bearing letter.
bale, I, 19/31; baill, II, 63/5; baile, V, 6/5, forrow, mifery.
balefull, I, 17/10, forrowful.
band, II, 133/9, bound.
Banfa-Britan, II, 10/17, native of Banff.
baftils, VI, 5/25, caftles.
beadman, I, 4/27, bedeman, royal alms-man.

GLOSSARY.

beforne, v, 33/12, before.
berar, i, 40/24, bearer.
befeike, v, 21/3, befeech.
bewrayes, i, 25/8, difclofes.
bibliothek, ii, 15/9, library.
bibull, iii, 12/2, bibulous, abforbent.
bide, ii, 83/15, ftay, remain; biding, i, 19/31.
bill, i, 41/29, billet, letter.
biparted, ii, 84/5, divided in two.
birkes, iv, 20/19, birch trees.
bleads, iii, 16/21, blades, leaves.
blek, iii, 16/22, ftain, blacken.
blent, v, 34/14, glanced, fhone.
blithe, i, 11/7; blith, i, 19/31; blythe, v, 26/23, glad.
boidkene, iii, 4/15, bodkin.
bonie while, ii, 26/12, pretty time, *i.e.* long time.
Boreo-Britan, i, 3/17, Scotifh.
bouldin, vi, 4/8, fwelling.
bounded roares, i, 22/3, ocean.
boure, ii, 135/7, jeft, fcoff.
bout, v, 5/15; but, i, 12/5, without.
braiks, i, 30/13, brakes, thickets.
branfh, i, 23/18, flourifh.
braft, v, 33/19, burft.
bray, ii, 151/8, brae, hill.
breok, i, 9/25; brooke, v, 24/5; bruke, iii, 30/22, enjoy, poffefs.
brocke, iv, 25/21, fragments, refufe.
buite, v, 32/13, compenfation.
burreau, ii, 4/12, executioner.

byde, iv, 19/19, remain, live.
can, ii, 27/6, gan, *i.e.* did.
caufidickes, iv, 23/17, lawyers, advocates.
chatton, i, 19/6, the broadeft part of a ring where the ftone is fet.
chaunged copie, ii, 21/5, changed fides.
cheare, vi, 3/13, chair, *i.e.* throne.
chiragra, iv, 24/23, gout in the hand.
chops, i, 9/15, cuts.
chyrographie, v, 28/35, handwriting.
circumcituate, v, 30/12, placed around.
circumgire, ii, 31/5, roll round.
claife, v, 12/14, clothes.
claw-backs, iii, 10/11, fcratchbacks, fycophants.
cleange, v, 21/35, cleanfe, *i.e.* free from blame.
clenged, iii, 3/17, cleaned.
cleare, v, 33/36, bright one.
cleekes, iv, 14/4, hooks, hauls.
cleif, iii, 16/13, clef, key in mufic.
clookes, iv, 14/4, cleeks, claws.
clowted, iv, 24/13, patched.
cogiate, v, 30/5, conftrained, forced?
cognat, iii, 13/16, kindred.
commoue, ii, 26/6, unfettle.
compeirs, ii, 94/3, makes appearance.

GLOSSARY.

conceyted, I, 5/10, conceived, imagined.
concolor, I, 32/14, agree in colour.
concredit, I, 23/15, intruſt.
contrars, I, 19/30, contraries.
conuoy, II, 27/4, companion.
coode, I, 22/17, cude, a face-cloth for a child at baptiſm.
courtes, II, 65/4, courteous, polite.
cowſner, IV, 28/8, coſener, cheat.
cvſning, III, 14/1, coſening, cheating.
cuit, V, 10/7, cute, a trifle of no value.
cullours, I, 24/7, flags, ſtandards.
currant, III, 25/24, running.
cutted, II, 139/10, cut ſhort.
daffings, II, 43/11, gay and fooliſh talking.
darne, V, 5/27, covertly.
dead-thraw, V, 27/5, laſt agony of nature.
deafe, V, 12/22, deafen; deauis, II, 43/11; deav'd, V, 27/31.
decarted, IV, 15/20, diſcarded.
decore, I, 23/5, decorate, embelliſh.
decreit, I, 30/13; decret, II, 67/15, decree; deciſion.
dee, I, 34/12, die; deed, II, 63/8; deeing, I, 10/23.
deemd, II, 91/5, adjudged.
deſpight, I, 18/11, indignation.
deſuetude, I, 10/6, diſuſe.
detrude, I, 32/18, thruſt down.

deuce, I, 35/28, deux, two, a pair.
difficill, I, 11/3, difficult.
dight, II, 32/8, ſet forth, array.
digne, II, 88/8, deign.
diuall, II, 155/14, flow down, deſcend.
donke, V, 34/15, dank, moiſt.
dooll, II, 62/12; dole, II, 71/3, dule, grief.
dooleful, I, 35/28, grievous.
dow, IV, 19/25, poſſeſs ſtrength for.
draiue, V, 26/2, drift.
dreid, II, 111/6, dread, doubt.
dririe, I, 23/5, dreary.
driue, II, 159/14, paſs.
drouth, II, 34/7, drought, thirſt.
duill, V, 7/39, dule, grief.
dung, V, 31/29, dinged, knocked.
Dutch, III, 28/19, a German.
duyne, I, 42/2, pine, waſte away; dwins, II, 65/12; dwining, II, 123/7.
earſt, I, 21/25, formerly.
ee, I, 10/30, eye; eene, I, 19/34; eyne, I, 38/12.
eeke, II, 73/10, add; eiked, I, 15/29.
elu's, II, 27/10, elves.
empire, II, 36/4, rule, govern.
emplaſters, II, 62/3, plaſters.
engyne, V, 34/24, wit, ability.
eſphearicke, V, 25/37, ſpherical.
eſtray, II, 27/8, ſtray, waif.
euitation, II, 17/17, avoiding.
exponis, II, 133/18, explains.

25

GLOSSARY.

exequial, II, 84/15, pertaining to funerals; exequall, v, 33/2.
fabulator, II, 11/12, fable maker.
facill, I, 36/15, facile, eafily perfuaded.
facund, II, 72/4, eloquent.
fairlie, v, 5/13, ferlie, ftrange event.
fairf'd, II, 119/6, fairf't, *i.e.* fares it?
falte, I, 35/17, fault.
fand, I, 39/32, found.
fang, IV, 26/13, booty.
fang, v, 33/37, grafp.
fare, I, 32/5, proceed, travel.
far-fett, I, 40/5, far fetched; farfet, II, 127/16.
farne, III, 12/16, fern.
fatidic, I, 29/19, foretelling, divining.
feed, II, 68/6; fead, II, 85/16, feud, enmity.
feire, v, 33/37, companion.
feld, II, 140/20, felled.
fell, II, 62/7, cruel.
fells, I, 32/5, wafte or barren uplands.
fett, III, 11/13, fetch, bring.
fimber, II, 105/11, fringe, border.
flatlings, I, 26/7, flat.
flee, I, 35/13, fly.
fleeis, I, 13/22, flies.
flitt, I, 20/8; flit, II, 104/10, remove.
fog, v, 6/30, mofs.
foraine, I, 32/5, foreign.

forked horne, I, 31/20, double horn.
fray, v, 5/12, a terror, marvel.
fremcaft, II, 118/13, eftranged.
fremmit, II, 110/3; fremmed, II, 123/6, ftrange, foreign.
frieke, v, 34/10, fellow.
fuire, v, 34/10, fared, *i.e.* went.
furrs, II, 120/5, furrows.
gar, v, 33/5, to caufe.
garrient, I, 30/6, chattering.
geir, I, 28/6, effects, goods.
ghoft, I, 23,10, fpirit.
girth, I, 27/2, girdle.
gnoms, I, 10/28, precepts.
God faue the King, VI, 8/19.
Goke, I, 30/6, the Cuckoo.
greeing, II, 116/5, agreeing.
greidines, VI, 6/3, greedinefs.
greene, II, 73/7, ardently defire; green'd, II, 72/9.
greete, v, 11/18; greet, v, 29/15, cry, weep.
greyus, I, 22/27, grees, *i.e.* doft agree.
grouie, II, 52/4, woody.
guiftes, I, 8/11, guefts.
gull, III, 14/10, to dupe, trick.
haile, v, 35/23, whole.
hales, II, 28/10, hauls, draws.
hals, III, 19/7, haufe, throat.
hants, I, 11/32, practifeft.
hap, I, 38/14, happen.
heirar, I, 31/20, hearer, liftener.
hight, II, 160/10, promifed.
him fell, I, 34/6, himfelf.

26

GLOSSARY.

hints, v, 12/40, grafps, lays hold of.
Hobbie Haulke, II, 29/2, the Hobby, *Falco Subbuteo*, ufed in falconry.
hog teach Minerue, I, 12/5, "fus Minervam."
hoif'd, II, 126/7; hoyf'd, II, 105/12, raifed, elated.
holline, v, 30/19, holly.
hoore, II, 110/15, whore.
horie, I, 7/19, hoary.
hofte, v, 8/4, hoft.
hoyfeth, II, 74/2, hoifteth.
huerted, II, 134/23, hurtled, ftunned by a blow, dafhed or thrown violently.
hyde, v, 34/14, hied, proceeded.
hyre, II, 92/8, hire.
ingyne, I, 12/20, wit, intellect, ability.
innated, II, 11/8, native.
inftaur'd, IV, 34/18, reftored.
interturb, II, 132/14, intermingle.
iterat, II, 129/19, repeated.
kend, II, 102/6, known.
kirchiff, II, 97/8, kerchief, head-drefs.
kith, I, 19/30; kythe, II, 162/21; kyth, III, 10/15, fhew, appear.
kurre, III, 27/21, cur, dog.
laiks, I, 15/21, laics, laymen.
laigh, v, 5/16, low.
lake, I, 17/19, lack.
lare, v, 5/23, lore, learning.
leare, II, 28/8, learn.

lafure, III, 27/5, leifure.
laue, III, 14/10; leaue, I, 13/16, remainder, reft.
law's, II, 153/11, billows, waves.
lawtie, v, 12/37, loyalty, integrity.
lay, v, 5/16, lea, meadow.
leach, v, 31/5, leech, phyfician.
leaud, I, 32/26, lewd, *i.e.* ignorant.
lector, I, 5/17, reader.
leele, II, 89/4, true hearted, loyal.
leid, v, 31/5, man, perfon; leids, I, 27/6.
leile, v, 9/15, leal, true; lieleft, v, 28/3.
lets, I, 42/9, hindrances.
libanotes, IV, 4/20, drink-offerings, outpourings.
lift, II, 30/3, fky.
lightlies, v, 9/11, flights, undervalues.
lingage, I, 29/18, language.
lipper man, II, 35/2, leper.
lippars clap, II, 35/13, the inftrument carried by lepers to announce their prefence, and thereby warn paffers-by to avoid them.
litures, I, 3/26, daubings, *i.e.* writings.
loame, I, 15/9, clay.
long-fome, I, 28/15, tedious.
lope, I, 21/20, leap.
louk, v, 8/9, lock, clofe.

GLOSSARY.

loun, II, 93/11; lowne, IV, 18/19, rogue, knaue; lowns, VI, 5/18.
lout, V, 28/20, ſtoop, bow down; lowting, II, 34/9.
low, II, 123/14, flame.
lowrs, II, 119/3, lurks.
lubricke, II, 17/13, wanton.
lucrous, IV, 32/19, lucrative.
lug, V, 5/28, ear.
luker, II, 158/2, lucre.
lyns, I, 32/26, lines.
macerat, II, 162/14, grown lean, famiſhed.
maker, V, 3/11, poet.
mancipat, III, 16/7, enſlaved.
marche, I, 22/16, boundary.
march'd, I, 22/22, were bounded, (as applied to land).
mare, II, 52/9; maire, V, 9/21, more.
maues, II, 156/13, mavis, ſong-thruſh.
medicable, I, 13/35, medicative.
meene, II, 58/7, lament, bemoan.
menage, VI, 6/12, manage.
mend, II, 58/7, help, remedy.
mint, V, 9/38, aim, attempt.
miſtane, V, 24/9, miſtaken.
mold, II, 157/10; molde, I, 34/27; mould, I, 11/10, the earth.
Moli, II, 156/9. "Molly" is wild garlic, *Alium Molle*. Can this be meant?
mought, II, 55/3, might.

mowl'd, IV, 24/14, mouldy.
moyane, II, 113/10; moyan, II, 158/4; moyen, III, 9/21, ſubſtance.
murex, V, 25/23, a ſhell-fiſh from which purple dye was obtained.
Muſe-foe Mars, I, 10/12.
naine, I, 34/25, none.
naufrage, V, 26/8, ſhipwreck.
neoterick, III, 3/18, newly recruited, joined.
nipping, II, 5/15, pinching, biting.
niuie nake, II, 108/5, "neivie, neivie, nick nack," a game of chance, played with the ſhut hands or neives.
nyeſt, I, 9/17, neareſt.
nor, I, 35/17, than.
noyes, II, 84/12, annoyance.
numered, I, 32/26, numbered.
obdure, I, 14/20, obdurate, inflexible.
oblectaments, II, 157/12, powers of pleaſing highly.
obumbrate, II, 15/10, darkened.
onkow, I, 19/9, unco, ſtrange.
onliue, I, 35/11; on-life, II, 20/5, alive.
onmanumitted, I, 4/24, unreleaſed from ſlavery.
onſene, VI, 9/8, unſeen.
oſtraciſm'd, IV, 27/20, baniſhed.
palled, II, 86/10, ſtrengthleſs, infirm.
pangues, II, 48/7, pangs.

GLOSSARY.

panfe, II, 34/4, meditate, think.
papyre, I, 41/21, paper.
patrocinie, I, 29/18, patronage.
pedaret, VI, 9/7, one who voted, by walking over to the fide he efpoufed, in the Roman fenate.
pedifeque, II, 158/6, female follower.
pendul, II, 152/11, hanging out of pofition.
perels, I, 33/13, perils.
pererre, IV, 23/2, wander through.
perfeuer, VI, 8/6, perfevere.
peft (the), I, 41/2, the plague of 1603/4.
pheare, V, 9/9, fere, companion.
pind, II, 87/15; pyned, V, 9/17, tortured, pained.
pine, II, 127/13, pin up.
plumeles, I, 31/16, featherlefs.
pore, II, 119/9, interftice.
pofes, II, 151/10, pofies, nofegays.
poffeyds, II, 101/15, poffeffes.
poft, II, 85/9, hafte, fpeed.
pofting, VI, 5/27, fleeting, flying.
powll, II, 104/14, poll, cut, clip.
preafe, I, 30/7; preaffe, V, 21/2, endeavour earneftly.
precellent, I, 13/4, excellent.
predecried, I, 18/21, predicated, foretold.
primo-genit, III, 5/5, firft-born.
proditor, III, 19/2, traitor.

prolixt, I, 20/29, extending to too great a length.
prophetizing, I, 23/10, giving predictions.
propine, I, 2/10, gift, offering.
propine, II, 7/11; propyne, III, 9/18, give, offer.
protege, II, 146/10, protect.
punk, II, 131/11, whore.
pype of loame, I, 40/4, clay pipe.
quent, II, 53/13, accuftomed.
quhefpering, II, 69/8, whifpering.
quhipt, II, 93/9, whipped.
quick, II, 86/9, living.
randring, II, 107/12, furrendering?
raue, II, 43/9, take by violence.
reele, II, 66/3, a Scotifh dance.
reft, I, 21/7, taken away.
regrate, II, 100/6, complain.
reife, I, 14/35, plunder, robbery.
reide, V, 11/4, read.
remead, I, 18/7, alleviation, remedy.
remead, II, 42/14, ameliorate.
repleit, II, 49/4, full.
retex'd, II, 39/11, rewoven.
rhetors, II, 64/12, rhetoricians.
rig of corne, VI, 7/26, breadth of crop in a cornfield from furrow to furrow.
rim's, II, 39/9, rhymes.
riue, II, 62/9; ryue, V, 30/15, rend, tear.
roches, II, 153/9, rocks.

GLOSSARY.

rueth, v, 9/29; ruth, II, 49/8, kindneſs, tenderneſs.
ruſhbuſh keeps the kow, I, 24/3, *i.e.* a frail defence ſecures the cow.
rype, I, 41/16, ſearch.
ſackt, I, 7/24, ſacked, pillaged.
ſafftie, II, 127/8, material for winding thread upon.
ſaikles, I, 44/6, innocent.
ſals, II, 117/14, brine.
ſalt, I, 21/28, ſea, ocean.
ſant, III, 7/27, faint.
ſarke, II, 53/11, ſhirt.
ſawſie, II, 10/10, ſaucy.
ſcalerigs, IV, 31/23, ?
ſchrole, v, 28/32, ſcroll; ſcrowles, II, 12/14; ſcrowls, II, 85/12.
ſecerne, I, 13/5, to ſeparate.
ſeces, I, 12/14, retirement.
ſeemlie, II, 65/11, comely.
ſeik, I, 22/7, ſick.
ſeiuns, I, 30/11; ſejoyns, VI, 6/22, ſeparates.
ſenſine, I, 10/27, ſince ſyne, ſince that time.
ſetling, I, 10/21, ſettlement.
ſhads, II, 52/4, ſhades.
ſhade, II, 61/13, ſhed, ſpent.
ſhaghhaird, II, 30/10, rough haired.
ſhawes, v, 34/15, woodlands.
ſhed, II, 60/12, ſeparated.
ſheene, v, 34/15, ſhining, bright.
ſhent, II, 53/2, injured.
ſherp, VI, 3/23, ſharp.
ſho, v, 11/8, jo, ſweetheart.

ſhrew, III, 14/13, execrate.
ſib, III, 14/22, kin to, like to.
ſine, II, 67/9; ſyne, I, 19/15, ſince.
ſings, II, 36/13, ſigns.
ſinuoſe, VI, 4/5, winding.
ſite, II, 62/11, ſorrow, grief.
ſkarſe, II, 26/15, bandage.
ſkore, II, 119/2, ſcore, line.
ſlake, I, 13/22, ſlacken, abate.
ſlee, v, 11/7, ſly.
ſleuth, v, 9/30, neglect.
ſmore, II, 90/11, ſmother.
ſogers, III, 3/19; ſogeors, II. 23/17, ſoldiers.
ſore, I, 7/14, pain.
ſouke, I, 40/4, ſuck.
ſouleſooke, II, 60/11, ſucked from the ſoul, *i.e.* endearing.
ſound, I, 7/14, ſwoon.
ſouſe, III, 14/24, ſous, ſmall French coin.
ſouter, II, 10/10, cobbler.
ſpaits, I, 18/9; ſpeats, VI, 4/12, floods.
ſpeele, II, 66/6, climb.
ſpeare, I, 8/12, aſk.
ſpheirs, II, 100/5, ſpheres.
ſpurre the poſt, I, 19/21, haſten.
ſtanks, II, 64/9, pools, ponds.
ſtap, v, 21/13, ſtop.
ſtark, II, 133/12, ſtrong, overpowering.
ſtile, I, 13/29, pen.
ſtire, II, 53/8, ?
ſtone of tuch, I, 13/4, touchſtone for aſſaying metals.

GLOSSARY.

stowne, IV, 17/19, stolen.
sturring (but), II, 33/6, without moving.
sturs, I, 35/10, stirs.
sturt, V, 8/33, trouble, vexation.
subscryv'd, V, 26/24, subscribed.
sueit, VI, 3/19, sweet.
suppone, II, 89/6, suppose.
suspect, III, 17/19, suspicion.
swal, III, 12/9, swell.
syle, V, 7/38, blindness.
syndonles, II, 27/9, sinewless, *i.e.* faint?
tane, I, 11/16; taine, II, 66/15, taken.
tent (take), V, 10/26, be attentive.
terce, I, 32/7, third part.
thigs, IV, 18/22, begs, borrows.
thirsel, I, 24/5, thistle.
thol, III, 14/25, bear, endure; thol'st, V, 12/34; thoyld, I, 9/19.
thrall, I, 26/8, slave.
threesome, II, 66/3, three together.
thrils, I, 31/17, trills.
thyrse, I, 27/16, thrice.
thuartring, II, 52/10; thwartering, II, 132/13, opposing, perverse.
tins, I, 19/6, loses; tyne, IV, 23/22; tint, II, 110/14.
toome, IV, 24/14, empty.
towrs of tree, I, 22/3, ships.
travell, VI, 4/34, labour, trouble.
trews, VI, 9/26, trousers.

triparts, I, 32/7, divides into three.
trow, I, 17/11, believe; trowde, IV, 21/13.
tugure, I, 12/10, cottage, hut.
turse, II, 69/12, carry hastily.
twind, I, 38/8, parted, separated.
vmber, II, 86/10, a shade, spirit.
vmbers, II, 151/7, shades, *i.e.* groves.
vmquhyle, I, 21/24, deceased.
vngratly, I, 19/29, ungratefully.
vnhonest, VI, 5/19, dishonest.
vnmanumissible, II, 13/13, unredeemable.
vnpeppered kate, I, 12/11, unseasoned food.
vnpouled, II, 104/8, unpolled, uncut.
vnrased, II, 135/14, unshorn.
vnskard, V, 22/29, not scared or frightened away.
vre, I, 10/28, practice, use.
vaig, II, 140/10; vaige, II, 160/6, roam, wander; vaging, II, 27/5.
vale, II, 62/13, sink, feel despondent?
viue, II, 9/12, lively, to the life.
voces, IV, 26/13, voices.
volier, I, 19/7, aviary.
volted, I, 22/15, vaulted.
voms, III, 11/4, vomits.
wadder, II, 119/8, weather.
waikenes, I, 33/18, weakness.
waine, V, 5/24, weening, opinion; *v.* will.
waird, II, 121/20, expended.

GLOSSARY.

wan-weirds, v, 9/7, unhappy fates.
wands, II, 107/12, rods.
ware, I, 22/10, expend, bestow.
warkes, I, 10/33, works.
wayles, I, 32/5, pathlefs.
wayns, I, 41/13, decreafes.
weire, v, 29/10, hedge.
wearis, I, 41/13, waftes.
weairs, II, 90/6, wars.
weirdes, I, 9/27; weirds, I, 41/22; weerds, II, 87/14, fate, deftiny.
weine, v, 6/23, judge, believe; weind, I, 35/17.
weyre, I, 9/16, wear.

whyls, II, 97/7; whils, II, 99/6, fometimes.
widkaft, II, 74/3, widefpread.
wildfome, I, 32/5; wildefome, I, 39/28, folitary, dreary.
will of waine, v, 5/24, wild of weening, *hence*, at a lofs what to do.
witt's, I, 15/10, judgment.
woofe, II, 47/10,   ?
wrackt, I, 7/22, wrecked, deftroyed.
wracke, I, 21/23, wreck, ruin.
wrake, I, 21/27, difapproval.
wreats, I, 10/33; writes, I, 16/7, writings.
wyte, v, 22/22, blame.

EATI

THE
POETICAL
RECREATIONS
OF Mr. ALEXANDER CRAIG
OF ROSECRAIG.

AT EDINBVRGH
Printed by *Thomas Finlaſon.* 1609.
WITH LICENCE.

TO

THE MOST HO-
NORABLE MY SINGV-
LAR GOOD LORD AND PATRON
G. E. *OF DVNBAR, LORD AND*
GOVERNOVR OF BERWICK, HEIGH

Thefaurer of *Scotland,* great Maifter of the Mi-
nerals there, *Lieutenent of the middle Shyres*
of Great Britane, one of his Majefties honorable privie Counfell, and Knight
of the moſt noble order of the Garter.

HEN Philip OF
Macedon *came to conquere* Corinth, *the carefull Corinthians
did fortifie their ruined walles,
ſome caried ſtones, ſome trees,
ſome lyme, ſome clenged and dreſ-
ſed their armour, ſome taught & trained the neoterick
ſogers;* no man was found idle to withſtand the common enemie ſaue Diogenes, *he vn-able for any ſervice*

A 2

vice in the republick, did roll himselfe in his Tub vp and downe the streets. One of his familiars asked what he did: Al the Corinthians *(answered* Diogenes*) are busie, and I must be doing something: Each man (my honorable good Lord) at this great Court of Parliament is busie, and lest I alone like* Diogenes *be noted as idle, I will roll my selfe in these foolish rymes vp and downe the streetes; that it may be said I am doing something: the goodes and children of the bond-man belong to the master: These passions are my goodes, or rather my children* Minerva-*like borne from their fathers brane, without a mother, and so due to your L. Take then your owne (dear Lord) from this hand, who according to the antient custome hath bored his eare with a boidkene, to shew that he shall still remaine your Honors most faithfully devoted and voluntarie slaue.*

AL. CRAIG.

TO THE READER.

EXcufe me (good Reader) for the methodleffe placing of thefe Paffions: They are my children, you haue them as they were borne: And fo the Primo-genit muft haue the prioritie at the Preffe. Amongft fo many children fome muft mif-thriue and proue naght: Cherifhe (I pray thee) the good, and leaue the faultie to be reformed by their father.

Fair-wel.

TO HIS MOST EX-
CELLENT MAIESTIE
THE HVMBLE PETITION OF
his Heighnes Orator AL. CRAIG
at Chriſtmas in VVhitehall.

A*Pelles* ſome-time came
  To *Ptolomæus* feaſt,
And had well nye return'd againe
  Inglorius and diſgrac't.
For *Ptolomæus* aſk'd,
  Who cald him to that place,
Then with a coale vpon the wall,
  He painted *Planus* face.
The King knew *Planus* well,
  And did at once proteſt
That hee ſhould faſt, and hee would feaſt
  Appelles with the beſt.
So am I come Great King,
  Vnto thy Chriſtmas chere,
And Povertie againſt my will,
  Invit's me to be heere.
You are a greater King
  Then *Lagus* ſonne, altho

                                        With

With *Ægipt*, *Afric*, he vſurpt,
 And was th' *Arabians* ſo.
Let Povertie I pray,
 Receaue his due diſgrace:
And let thy Poet at this feaſt
 Supplie the Painters place.
But *Lacon* ſome-time ſaid
 Vnto a begging ſlaue,
Giue what I will it is thy craft
 To beg, and euer craue.
Be not affrai'd for that,
 (Thogh for this time J cry)
Jf ſuccurd once, nor ſeeke againe
 J rather ſterue and dye.

COMPLAINT TO HIS
Majestie.

Oue, *Want*, and *Cares*, all contrare me conſpyre,
 Firſt, ſecond, laſt, for me too many bee:
Want breakes my heart, and drown's my high defyre,
And makes my Muſe ſo lowe a courſe to flee.
 But were J rich, the cruell fair wold rew,
 Then ſould J ſing and bid my *Cares* adew.

O happie Artiſt, and Mechanick ſlaue,
Thou mai'ſt a price vpon thy paines impoſe:
My wair is ſuch, I know not what to craue,
And ſo but looke both Loue and Lynes I loſe:
 Strange thing betwix my Soueraigne and my ſant,
 I waiſt my wits, and rape but woes and want.

 Yet

Yet might thefe two reward me if they wold,
And purge me both from povertie and paine:
She with good wil, my royall Syre with gold,
And fo preferue, and faue their flaue vn-flane.
 With modeft lookes, and filent fighs J ferue,
 The fhameles begger thriu's, and yet I fterue.

TO JOHN LORD RAMSAY

*Vicunt of Hadington, the Author be-
moneth his hard Fortunes in England.*

Alas, why fould *Califthenes* remaine
 Where *Agis* both and *Cleo* beare the fway,
Thefe Sicophants and Parafites profaine,
Draw *Macedoes* magnific minde aftray:
Jf *Ariftip* in Court make any ftay,
Some Tyran ftraight fhall fpit into his face,
Thus feeling ill, and fearing worfe each day,
A miriad of mif-fortunes I embrace.
How carefull is *Entimeon* poore thy cafe
At home, abrod, fince Fortun is thy foe;
But ere thou turne to Griece with more difgrace,
Jn Perfia die, and there intomb thy woe:
 To him that liues, and muft die Fortunes flaue,
 Jf nothing elfe, good Perfians grant a graue.

AD

AD EVNDEM DE EODEM.

BEyond the Mountains of the froſtie North,
I ſome-time feru'd a *Caledonian* Dame:
The firſt of all for *Vertue, wit,* and *worth,*
That ever yet adorn'd the rols of fame:
She fed my heart on fanſies ſweeteſt flame,
Yet haue I left both heart and her behind,
And to this land ſpoild of my heart I came
To follow Fortune, which J can not find:
Strange is the ſtate wherein I ſtand, J fee
Twix Fortune heere, and my affections there:
I fled from theſe, this flees againe from mee,
Here *Povertie,* and yonder ſprings *Diſpare.*
  Blind *Cupid* thus, blind *Fortune* are againe mee,
  My *Loue* at home, my *Luck* abrod diſdaine mee.

NEW YEARE GIFT TO
his Majeſtie.

TO *Creſus* rich ſhall Codrus gifts propyne,
To *Maro* wiſe muſt *Mevius* ryms preſent:
O pearles Prince, O Poet moſt divyne,
My Muſe is dead, my moyen all is ſpent:
  Wiſe *Maro* writ, weake *Mevius* wonder ay,
  Rich *Creſus* giue, poore *Codrus* beg and pray.

B   TO

TO HIS MAJESTIE IN NAME
of his Noble Master.

THe faithfull heart is ever fraught with feare,
   And jeloufie is ftill conjoind with loue:
How can J then (dread Liege) be frie from care,
Since from thy fight J fee J muft remoue:
     And thou my *Phofphor*, yea my *Phœbus* bright,
     Whofe prefence day, whofe abfence breeds my night

Yet feare J not for that within thy minde,
That ouglie ghaift *vnkindnes* can haue place:
But caufe J know, fome claw-backs are inclinde
With all their force my Fortunes to difgrace:
     Be thou the poynt, and J the circling line,
     Mine be the pangs, and all the pleafurs thine.

J'le kyth a conftant *Palinure* to thee,
A truftie fteirf-man both in ftorme and calme;
That in my works the wondring world fhall fee
The trueft hand, that ever held a helme:
     Thogh (I confeffe) I am not fkild like him,
     Yet let me fink, fo fweet *Æneas* fwim.

Thus will J goe, becaufe thou do'ft command,
Even for thy fake from out thy fight fome fpace:
And after kiffing of thy facred hand,
J pray the Gods protege thy ftate in peace:
     And when J ceafe for to be true to thee,
     Curft be my life, and wretched may J dye.

                                             TO

TO MY LORD SARVSBVRIE.

TWo potent Kings over *Siciles* two Empyre,
That famous Ile where *Siracufa* ftood:
Where gainft the heavens *Encelad* voms his fyre,
King *Philip* bruks with much *Iberian* blood:
    But wife King *Iames* (O bleft and happie cafe)
    Commands a *Cecill* of more price in peace.

TO MY LORD HAY, AT HIS LE-
gation to France.

SInce thou muft fail to fee the *Celtick* fhore,
From titular to him that keeps the Crown:
Which with thy Name thy Nation fhall decore,
And fett more quils to further thy renown:
    My wifhes both, and prayers fhall attend thee,
    At home, abroad, the living Lord defend thee.

TO MY LORD ADMIRALL AT
his mariage with Ladie Margaret Stewart.

MArs, *Hercules*, and *Iupiter* we finde,
With *Venus, Lyda, Leda* were in loue,
And for obedience to the Archer blind,
The *Sword*, the *Club*, and *Scepter* they remoue:
    And *Neptuns* deput leau's the fomie ftrand,
    To pearfe a *Margarit* fet from *Murray* land.

A Counfell to Courteours.

THe bibull Spoynge in tepid water fet,
  Drinks till it fill each fmall and greedie pore:
But if the Barber in his hand it get,
He wrings all out, which it hath drunk a fore:
    You that in Court with Kings and Princes ftay,
    Mark well in minde the water-fpoynge I pray.

For if you ftand on top of Fortunes wheele,
Beware left with the bibull fpoynge you fwal,
Drink not too much as gluttons, govern well,
Clim not too hie, incafe you catch a fall:
    The King makes vp, the King againe makes downe,
    Both wealth and wrack awaits vpon a Crowne.

To my Lady Hartfurde at his Majefties *firft progres to* Totnem.

There the wyld farne fmelled as fweet as perfume, naturaly.

THe tempeft beat and falling *Farne* (fair Dame)
  Receaves new life, new ftrength, new fmell wee fee:
And for thy fake thy Soveraigne weares the fame
Heigh on his head to ferue and honour thee:
    Thefe are the frutes thy bewtie braue brings forth,
    Thy leaft propynes are valued of moft worth.

TO HIS DEAR FRIEND Mʳ. Aʟ.
Dickson Mʳ. of the Art of *Memorie* who dyed at *winchefter* in *England*.

EPITAPH.

THat *Thracian* forme at birth of friends to weepe,
And to be glad when as againe they dye:
My figh-fwolne heart can not content to keepe,
Since J deare friend muft figh, and murne for thee.
Now haue I lof'd my fecond felfe I fee,
To whom fhall J (fince thou art dead) bemone:
Moft rich of all (the *Scythians* fay) is hee
That hath true friends, now I, alas, have none:
No other death of ould the *Hircans* choof'd,
But to be kild by thefe fame dogs they fed:
Difpleafure fo to be ingratlie vf'd,
Hath broght braue *Dickfon* to his cognat bed.
    Thou taught the Art of Memorie to thofe
    That feemd thy friends, yet prou'd in end thy foes.

TO HIS VNKINDE FRIEND.

OF all the wounds whereof that Roman great,
Braue *Iulius Cæfar* in the fenat died:
The wounds from *Brutus* (burreau moft ingrate)
Did grieue him moft, on *Brutus* ftill he cri'd:
    So were my life to take laft leaue of mee,
    Still wold I cry (*vnkinde, vnkinde*) on thee.

TO HIS CVSNING FRIEND.

A *Thenian Chares* promis'd much to many,
Moſt prodigall of ſmooth perſwading words:
And yet perform'd no thing at all to any,
Such are the frutes falſe eloquence affords:
    Like *Larus* leane of fleſh he had no ſtore,
    But multitude of fethers fair, no more.

Since *Chares* thus concludes to play the knaue,
And ſtill perſiſts proud, impius, falſe, profane:
Shall he begyle, and gull me like the laue,
Yes, faith, once more to exerciſe his vane:
    Yet ſince experience *Chares* maks me wife,
    I ſhrew my heart, and thou begyle me thrife.

TO COVETOVS COVRTIERS.

A Greedie Mouſe did by a privat way
Steale to the pantrie of a wealthie man:
VVhere many diſhes were, and wold aſſay
Each diſh of all: but at the laſt began
    To teaſt an Oiſter, when her guts were filled,
    The Oiſter cloſ'd, and thus the Mouſe was killed.

Thou that haſt crept in credit but by ſtealth,
And teaſts each diſh, ſib to the greedie Mouſe:
VVho builds and maks of others wrack thy wealth,
And ſoulles man will not overſee a ſouſe:
    Thogh Prince behold, and privat men muſt thol thee,
    Some ſharp-ſheld oiſter ſome-time ſall controll thee.

TO VIRTEOVS AND NOBLE
Cynthia.

FAne wold J render thanks for thy good-will:
But thanks are words, and words compenfe no deeds,
And thus muft J remain thy debter ftill,
For which my heart within my bofome bleeds:
    But if it chance that in thy debt I die,
    My froward Fortune hath the fault, not I.

TO HIS DEAR FRIEND, AND
fellow ftudent M^r. Robert AEton.

SIng fwift hoof'd *Æthon* to thy matchles felfe,
And be not filent in this pleafant fpring:
I am thy Echo, and thy Aerie elf,
The latter ftrains of thy fweet tunes I'll fing:
Ah, fhall thy Mufe no further frutes forth-bring,
But *Bafia* bare, and wilt thou write no more
To higher notes, J pray thee tune thy ftring:
Be ftill admir'd as thou haft bene of yore,
Write *Æthon* writ, let not thy vain decay,
Leaft we become *Cymerians* dark, or worfe.
If *Æthon* faill, the Sun his courfe muft ftay,
For, *Phœbus* Chariot laks the cheefeft horfe:
    Thogh Fortun frown, ah, why fhould vertue die,
    Sing *Æthon* fing, and J fhall Echo thee.

                                    AE-

AETHON
Cragio Svo.

FAne wold I sing, if songs my thoghts culd eafe,
Or calme the tempeft of my troubled mynde:
Fane wold J force my filent Mufe to pleafe,
The gallant humor of thy wanton vane:
But O a mifer mancipat to paine,
Sould flaue to forrow, wedded to mifchief,
By mirth of fongs, perhaps more greefe might gane,
Jn vane of them J fhould expect releif:
Then facred *Craig* if thou wold eafe my greef,
Jnvite me not to wantonize with thee:
But tune thy notes vnto my mourning cleif,
And when J weepe, weepe thou to Echo mee.
  Perhaps the teares that from a *Craig* fhall floe,
  May proue a Soveraigne balme to cure my woe.

AGAINST THE SELLERS
of Tobacco.

THou that haft made of felling fmoak a trade,
And Jew and Gentill but remorfe do'ft gull,
And by thefe bafe *Nicotian* bleads are glade
To fpoill, mar, blek, the ftomach, brane, and fkull:
  As thou deferu'ft *Turinus*-like J doome thee,
  By felling fmoak thou liv'ft, let fmoak confume thee.

TO HIS LORD AND M^r. George
Earle of Dunbar.

BRaue *Alcibiad* curious once to know
Jf all were frinds, that fo appeard to bee,
To each of all in fecret he did fhow,
The purtrate of a new-flane-man, faid hee:
    This is a friend whom J haue kild, J pray
    Jn quiet forme come cary him away.

Yet none of all that Crew wold giue confent,
Nor help to put the painted tree a part:
Saue *Kallias* kinde, who only was content,
Hap what might hap, to help with hand and hart:
    Such is my luck (moft loving Lord) I fee,
    J haue not found a *Kallias* kinde, but thee.

Thou art the great *Mæccnas* of my Mufe,
My patron, Lord, my Mafter, and my All:
Whom (whil J liue) but change in me I chufe,
To loue, to ferue, and to attend as thrall:
    Thogh time and abfence breed fufpect, what than?
    J am in fpight of Fortuns nofe thy man:

TO LADIE ANNA HAY COVNTES OF
Winton, one of the Ladies of her Majefties moft
royall bed chalmer, at her return from England.

AH, whither now fweet Ladie wilt thou go?
From Court to Cuntrie, what new change is this?
And wilt thou needft (fweet Sant) be gone? and fo
Bereaue fouth-Britan of fo rare a blis,
    Yes thou muft go, J fee there is no ftay,
    And take ten thoufand Thoufand hearts away.

Take then my heart, my better part with thee,
My wifhes, vow's, my prayers, all thefe all:
For J am thine devoted till J die,
And ftill fhall beare the bloodie yock as thrall:
    And when my head fhall turne to hoạrie gray,
    The world fhall fee that I fhall ferue *An Hay*.

A DISSVVASION TO HIS
friend from his intended mariage.

FAir famous Ile where *Zoroaſtres* raign'd,
  Where *Bactrum* once the ftatelie cittie ftood:
VVhich (when th'ould name *Ariaspe*) was difdain'd,
VVas *Bactria* cal'd from fertill *Bactrus* flood;
VVhere fome-time *Ceter*, *Arams* fonne began,
Of thoufand citties the foundation fure.
In thee the wyues abufe the maried man,
And both with flaue and ftranger play the whoore,
The Dame with Diftaff beats her yeelding Lord,
And for her pryde but punifhment skaips free:
And poore *Actcon* dare not fpeak one word,
From *Bactrian* wyues the Lord deliver thee:
    Nor lead a life infamous, heart-brock, thrall,
    Far better were to wed no wife at all.

A DESCRIPTION OF A PAR-
dond, yet still vnrepenting proditor Plexirtus.

WHen falfe and proud *Plexirtus* did confpire,
His King and Lord *Leonat* to dethrone:
He found the fates were foes to his defire,
At laft when all his baftard-hopes were gone,
    A halter fair about his hals he tyes,
    And on the Prince for pardon ftill he cryes.

The Clement King *Leonat* was contented
To pardon all his faults and foull offences:
And yet we read the Rebell noght repented,
Saue that he could not practize his pretenfes:
    It's pittie then the Prince can not perceaue,
    Plexirtus was, and will be ftill a knaue.

EPITAPH OF IOHN FIRST MAR-
ques of Hammilton.

BLeft was thy life, and bleffed didft thou die,
Thy Oyle was burning, and thy Lamp gaue light,
VVhen lifes prowd foe, pale death did fummond thee
To render earth her due, and heavens their right:
    Thogh death did then thy foule and bodie fever,
    Once thou fhalt be conjoind, and liue for ever.

Aliud.

HEre *refts within this Tomb of truth th' vnmatched zeale*
The father, & the faithful frieđ, of Church & cōmon wel:
In ftorme and calme inclind to doe his Kings command,
Of peace the parent, child of Mars, *cheef glorie of the land.*

                         Fortuna

FORTVNA SAEVO LAETA NEGO-
tio: tranfmutat incertos honores.

STrange are the changes of this changing age,
The cloun turns knight, the knight again turns cloun:
Now is he Lord, who, was of late a page,
And he that threatned all, is now thrown doun:
   Thrife happie he, whofe heart can be content,
   To ferue his God in peace with fober rent.

To his afflicted friend.

IN wether fair, and in a temperat fpring,
The waikeft bird with warbling fongs will foare,
But in a ftorme, or winters rage to fing
With mirrie notes, deferues a praife much more:
   Thy fpring is gone, thy winter growes, O than
   Sing fweetlie now, and fhew thy felfe a man.

To his fortunate friend.

THe *Fox* and *Kat*, were walking by the way,
(As *Æfop* fains) and lo for all his wits
The *Fox* became to hungrie hounds a pray,
Whilft in a trie the *Kat* fecurlie fits.
   Since *Foxes* falfe (dear friend) muft fall, and die,
   Climb with the *Kat*, and make the truth thy trie.
                                                  Vivitur

Vivitur parvo bene.

HE that can walk on ground that's fair and plane,
Shall feldome fall, or if he chance to fall,
He meafures but his lenth, he'ill rife agane,
And haue no harme, nor any hurt at all:
    But he muft fall of force that climbs too hie,
    And if he fall, it's ten to one he'ill die.

Heigh hoifed failes giue vantage to the ftorme,
And if thy ftate be ftately, large, and fair,
The farer mark for mifchief to deforme,
With fpightfull fport proud Fortun play's her there:
    Fair marks are hit with fhots and fhafts mifchivous,
    Which make the wounds more deep & much more
                                      grievous.

Contented *Codrus* with his Cuntrie Dame,
Suppofe his Farme were fet on fire he fear's not,
His wife and he will warme them with the flame,
Come what can come, his compts are caft, he cares not:
    Jf want and wealth were alwaies at my will,
    Away with wealth, let me be *Codrus* still.

A Prayer for his imprifoned friend.

THe famous *Perfians* had a forme, we reed,
That if a Noble were condemd to dee,
They fpar'd himfelfe, and hang'd his cloaths with fpeed,
Poore prifoner, God grant the like to thee:
    Vcalegon his houfe is fet on fire,
    A neighbor kinde wold quench left it burne nyer.

When *Pollio* proud did to his feaft requyre
Auguftus Cæfar, at a folemne time:

                                                     He

He needs wold kill a feruing flaue in yre,
For breaking of a banquet glaffe, fmall crime:
  But *Cæfar* faid, poore flaue, thou fhalt not dee,
  Th'offence is naght, feare is eneugh for thee.

To Idea *for his long abfence.*

A*Ttilius* ruler of the Roman hoft,
 Beg'd leaue his wife and children deare, to fee
His poore effairs he did performe with poft,
And made returne with all the haft might bee,
  He was for this no run-away, but rather
  A loving hufband, and a faithfull father.

I haue like him (wife Dame) at home a wife,
With whom in peace the poafting hours I fpend,
Yet will J loue thee, whill J haue a life,
And till J die my loue fhall never end:
  My poore Adoes withdraw me oft from thee,
  Yet where thou art, my heart fhall ever bee.

To eloquent Erantina.

C*Leombrotus* a Heathen man did heare
 Wife *Plato*, with fuch reverence and refpeck:
As for the loue he to his leffons beare,
He went abrod (kinde man) and brok his neck:
  Thy charming words inchant me fo that J
  Doe nothing now, but mourne, figh, weep, and die.

To his absent and loving Lesbia.

DEare heart, dear heart, dear, dear, dear heart againe,
More dear then writ can shew, or waxe can seale:
O! if thou knew the care, the woe, the paine
I felt since last I tooke from thee fair-well:
    The night in black chimerick thoghts I spend,
    Ere *Phlegon* rise, I wish the day to end.

The dark is lothsome, and the day semes long,
Because, alas, J am not where thou art:
This is not mine, but frowning Fortunes wrong,
Yet hope (deare heart) vp-holds my dying heart:
    Look then for me, before few dayes take end,
    Till when my thoghts to thine, I doe commend.

To absent Idea.

WIth puissant pow'r when princely *Pompey* went,
And made him for *Pharsalic* battell bowne:
With heavie hearts his sogeors did lament,
And oft look'd back to Rome their natiue towne:
    Each in him selfe a civil combat felt,
    To leaue the place wher friends, wiues, childrē dwelt.

I may for this be deem'd a Roman borne,
I am so full of kindnesse and of loue,
In deepest sort (deare heart) I dare be sworne,
My minde from thee no distance may remoue:
    And for thy sake (beare witnesse naked God)
    I loue thy *Bowns* wherein thou mak'st abod.

To Idea *at her bownes.*

AH, whither now (fweet Sant) art thou retired?
Souls-ravifer, alas, where art thou gone?
Thy bewtie now can be no more admired,
Since thou delightft to lurke and liue alone:
    Now *Hermit*-like thou hantft, the more the pittie,
    And for the Farme forbear's the famous Cittie.

Look to thy felfe, thou dwel'ft too neere the fea,
Neptun no doubt will from thofe rocks bereaue thee:
And with his wife divorfe for loue of thee:
Yet am I glade, none but a God muft haue thee:
    VVhen winds and waves, and all are at thy will,
    Proue not vnkinde, J pray thee loue me ftill.

TO HIS BANISHED FRIEND

TWo wofull weeds, the mother Church muft weare,
One Crimfon rid, the other mourning black:
The black betokneth forrow, pane, and care,
The rid bods death, fearce perfecution, wrack:
    It maters not what rags fhe beare abrod,
    Once fhe'll be cloth'd in robs of white with God.

To his *fingular good Lord and Mafter.*

LOng mai'ft thou liue an argument of praife,
A lordlie fubject to my loving pen,
That on thy worth the wondring world may gaife,
A magiftrat admir'd amongft all men.
    Yea, more and more heavens grant thee from aboue,
    The Makers mercie, and the Mafters loue.
                                     Bene

Auream quisquis mediocritatem.

IT merits praise to manage litle well,
A cunning coachman turns in litle roume:
In poore estate a rich content I feell,
And smyle to see a wretches wealth consume:
   J'ill studie then to steward what J haue,
   And not be curious more and more to craue.

His regrate for the lose of time at Court.

O How Time slips, and slelie slids away,
God is forgot, and woe is me therefore:
J waste the night, and weare away the day,
I sleepe, dres, feed, talke, sport, and doe no more:
   Far better were with care to haue redemed,
   Nor sell for noght the thing I most estemed.

To his aspyring friend.

SInce charge and honor march together still
For charge but honour were a toyle too great:
And honor but a charge were ease at will,
To want them both is not the worst estate:
   I loath those loads which lightnesse first pretend,
   But break the neck before the journeys end.

Nulla dies sine linea.

THe standing poole will quicklie stink and rott,
The currant streame is cleanlie both and cleare:
The idle man is Sathans prey, God wott,
A verteous minde the Devill darr not draw neare,
   My fantasies can profit few, and yet
   It hurteth none, but doth me good to writ.

The praise of Glad-povertie.

THree sorts of men vnto the market go,
   One buyes, one selles, an other doth behold,
Great greef and care is in the former two,
Th'expectant waiks secure and vncontrold.
     He liu's (poore man) contented with his lot,
     Vsing the world as if he vs'd it not.

His vnambitious minde.

THree things there be for which J'ill not contend,
   The *way*, the *wall*, and *Tables* highest seat:
What foole is he will frown, or yet offend
For any place, so hee can reach his meat.
     But in good faith, the idlest strife of all,
     Js in my judgement for the way, or wall.

To his friend who seemd sorie when he left Court.

I Scorne to liue at Court, becaufe J spy
   The wicked heaps vp wealth, the foole hath grace:
The wise man weeps, and in disgrace must die,
And vanitie must march in vertues place:
     Far better were on shore secure t' abide,
     Nor saill in vane against both wind and tide.

Against Pryde.

TH' ambitious man no greater foe can haue,
   Then is himselfe, for whilst he still aspires,
He grinds his heart for greef vnto the graue,
With foolish hopes, with fear's, and fond desires:
     God grant my pryde may grow to this degree,
     Jn earth his child, in heaven his Sant to bee.

To vnfortunat and pure Æmilian at Court.

EMilian begs with heart half-brok for forrow,
  Yet finds not frute at all, but long delay:
As leaue me now, or come againe to morrow,
My lafure ferues not yet, I pray thee ftay:
  None pitties thee *Æmilian*, do not griue,
  They get no thing, that haue no thing to giue.

That he neither loues to be too glad nor too fad.

IOyes come like oxen heavie peaf'd and flo,
  But tak their leaue like horfes running poft:
Greifs come at poft, on foot againe they go,
And leaue fad difcontentment with their hoft:
  Both *Ioys* and *Griefs* as paffingers J'il vfe,
  They fhall not be my ghaifts, if J can chufe.

His contents at his Tugur.

WHen lofe of *Tyme* at Court was all my gane,
  To take my leaue, J thoght it was my beft:
And in fome privat manfion to remaine,
Where J might frie from Envyes rage take reft:
  Now bleft be God, no Portar bars my doore
  By day, by night none keeps me but my kurre.

Againft ignorance and ill example.

THe law of God is Lanterne full of light,
  And good example beares this Lantern ftill:
Which fhews the way to walk, and march vpright,
To doe all good, and to decline from ill:
  Without this light who walks, he can'not fee,
  And fuch (will God) fhall be no gyde to thee.

The

To Mistres Hartside *at Orknay her natall soyle.*

PRoscribed *Orcas* thogh J hate thy forms,
   J must commend and praise thy courage still,
I saw thee proue both wise and stout in storms,
And thou art barren sore against my will:
     For had thou sonnes of thy *Amazon* stamp,
     They might be Captains of the Emperors camp.

Perswasions of certainties are vnnecessarie.

NO greater fools then *Philodoxes* fond,
   And such as loue opinions of their own:
Thy wit (wise *Plato*) when I think vpon'd,
Made men to doubt on things that were well known:
     These *Why, How, What,* mad questions of thy schools,
     Wold make the wise men of our age seeme fools.

Against drunkards and lichers.

IN sinfull *Sodome* to liue cleane and poore,
   Jn *Asia* chast amid allurements such:
To hate in Rome the bordell and the whoore,
And to be still abstemius with a Dutch:
     Do'th merit praise, yet this much with correction,
     J find but few can haunt them but infection.

To his Lord and Master G. E. *Dunbar.*

ALas, that Time should be a foe to fame,
   To clip the wings of true report in rage:
Alas, that th'earth should march a noble name:
Like to a bird that's compact with a kage:
     Fame clip'd with time, & hemb'd with earth's embrace
     By Poëts yet out-strips both time and place.
                            Thy

Thy fame (dear Lord) is frie from all difgrace,
(Still be it fo till fire diffolue this frame)
Till when about the worlds broad fpatious face,
My ryms fhall run t'immortalize thy Name:
    Foill to thy fame no time, no place fhall giue,
    So long as *Craig*, or yet his lines can liue.

Againft ingratitude.

FIrft let me die before I proue ingrate,
  No, let the earth devore me ere J die:
Before I liue in fuch a wretched ftate,
To haue no hand but one, no tongue to cry:
    Vnthankfull mouths are graues, then if J take,
    I will at leaft giue praife and prayers back.

To his Lord and Mafter to be ware of envy.

DEepe danger lyes (deare Lord) in fmootheft looks,
  Envy is falfe, and waits thee at thy back:
The poyfning bate is hung at golden hooks,
They ferue as friends that fane wold fee thy wrack.
    Envy awaits on vertue as her flaue,
    Yet ftill delights in digging vertues graue.

O pale Envy, the ouldeft childe of Pryd,
The Dame of Murther, Treafons onely nurfe,
Of glore the ftane, of fquint-ey'd fraud the bryd:
The bleffe of Hell, and Heavens cheefeft curfe.
    God grant my Lord be harmeles from thy hate,
    Thy blood thy drink, thine owne heart be thy meat.

To John EARLE OF MONTROSE
first Vice-Roy of Scotland.

EPITAPH.

IF *Rhadamanthus* in th'Elifian field,
VVith *Æacus* and *Minos* Judges bee.
And Gods over ghofts, they all of due muft yeeld,
For Piëtie, Truth, Juftice, place to thee:
    At leaft *Montroes* for *Minos* muft command,
    And beare his Scepter in the bleffed land.

The Rapt of Proferpina.

SHall *Ceres* daughter ftill remane at hell?
Shall *Pluto* comb her curling loks of amber?
Shall bewtie braue in loathfome bondage dwell?
And be imprifon'd in a pitch-black chamber?
    Ah, fleuthfull *Ceres*, thou art much to blame,
    Thy negligence hath broght thy child to fhame.

Proferpina hath bewtie both and wealth.
A pleafant prey entifeth many a theif:
Of bewtie rapt, of riches muft be ftealth,
And from the hels we heare is no releif:
    Proferpina is *Plutoes* wife it's known,
    The devill is black, yet let him bruke his own.

Against Sycophants and Parasits.

FAlse Sycophant that wrongs the virteous name,
  Proud Parasit thou poysons him that hear's thee:
And brings the absent to disgrace and shame,
Who neither cares for forged lies, nor fear's thee:
    When Titan shyns we see the vermin swarme,
    Thou dwel'st at court becaufe thou know'st it's warm.

False flattering foole, thou art but friendships Ape,
Camelion-like thou changest every hew,
Saue white alone: thou loath's an honest shape.
As cheef companion of the cursed crew:
    Proud Trencher flee thy pansh once fild, thou'ill goe
    And proue to him that feeds thee best a foe.

The praise of humilitie in his L. and M^r.

IT seems (me think) a thing of small effect,
  When Fortun frowns for to be meek and lowlie:
But he that can eies, heart, looks thoghts, deject,
VVhen Fortun fauns is happie both and holie:
    He looks like God, and hath his makers show,
    VVhose pow'r is much, whose sprit is meek and low.

Of true friendship.

IN shaddie night the glow-worme shines like fire,
  And yet no heat to frostie hand she lends:
In calme who swear's he lou's thee, is a lier,
He'ill shrink in storme, and so his friendship ends:
    Let *Pythias* then take *Damon* by the hand,
    VVho for his friend in Fortuns stormes can stand.

                                                    To

TO THE MOST HONORABLE

and religious Lord G. Earle Marſchell, great
Commiſſionar of Scotland for his Majeſtie.

Braue *Cincinnatus* from his houſe was broght,
To be Dictator in the towne of Rome:
Thou in this ſort, (Religious Lord) art ſoght,
Thy Princes place and ſeat for to aſſume:
    He in a month put Rome to reſt and peace,
    And thou haſt done much more in much leſſe ſpace.

Contempt of Death.

MEn ſeldome wiſh to die, thogh nev'r ſo old,
This day of death they doe adjorne till morrow:
And by them all this fond excuſe was told,
(The life is ſweete) ſuppoſe they liue in ſorrow:
    Blind, lame, dumb, deaf, ſick, poore, and more we ſee,
    Men dam'd wold liue, yet know they needs muſt die.

My wofull heart muſt weepe to ſee ſuch fools,
As th' ould, poore, blind, lcame, damd, diſeaſ'd, deaf, dum:
Broght vp and traind in *Epicurus* ſchools,
Can not beleeue there is a life to come.
    God ſaies, I haue a Crown of glore to giue thee,
    Then call, kill, Crown, for Lord I doe beleeue thee.

FINIS.

ESSAYES

THE POETICALL ESSAYEs OF
Alexander Craige
SCOTOBRI-
TANE.

Seene and allowed.

Imprinted at London by WIlliam
White, dwelling in Cow-lane
neere Holborne Conduit.
1604.

THE AVTHOR
TO HIS BOOKE.

WHen *Dedal* taught his tender Sonne to flee,
Out through the fubtile watrie vaults of aire:
Goe not too high, nor yet too low, fayd hee:
Of Floodes beneath, of Fire aboue beware:
   So home-bred Rimes you *Icare*-like muft rife,
   Mid-way betwixt the Vulgar and the Wife.

For you fhall be vnto the vulgar fort
No fit propine, becaufe not vnderftood:
And with the Wife you muft haue fmall refort,
Since they can reape in reading you no good:
   Like *Dedalus* I then direct, thus flie,
   Goe neither low, nor yet I pray too hie.

And though you be directed to a King,
By any meanes approach not Court I pray,
For fome will fay my precepts pricke and fting,
And fome fhall fcorne, fome carpe, fome caft away:
   But (as you muft) if toward Court you goe,
   Since freindes are few, I pray you breed no foe.

   Aerij montes et mollia prata, nemufq;
     et vos carminibus flumina nota meis,
   Quod me tam gracilem voluistis ferre Poetam
     indignor, magnæ laudis amore calens.

TO MY DREAD SO-
VERAIGNE *IAMES*,
by the grace of God, of
Britaine, Fraunce and
Ireland, King.

Atulus Lactatius *hauing done the vtmost of his endeuours to stay his Souldiers that fled before their enemies, put him selfe among the Run-awayes, and dissembled to be a Coward, to beare them companie; That so they might rather seeme to follow their Captaine, then runne away from the Enemie: This was a neglecting of his reputation, to conceale the shame and reproch of others. I haue (accomplished Archi-Monarch) with the rest of these* Boreo-Britan *Poets, been ingrately silent; and with the cold ashes of Feare, haue couered the coales of my Loue: Because (as* Archileonida *sayd to the* Thratian *Legates, There were many moe more valiant Cittizens in* Sparta, *then her Sonne* Brasidas,) *I found my selfe but a doltish* Cheril, *among so many delicate* Homers: *And thus, neither durst I prayse thy Fortunes, nor congratulate thy Greatnes; But now am bold to present to your most sacred eyes these louely litures, both to encourage others, & make sa-*
tisfaction

THE EPISTLE.

tisfaction for my (seeming ingratitude) long silence. I intend not with those Macedonian *Parasites to call* Alexander, *the Sonne of* Iupiter: *nor with* Hermodorus *to make* Antigonus *the sonne of* Phœbus. *I write not to enlarge thy fame, which is boundles; nor to begge reward, which I merit not; nor to purchase prayse, which I craue not; but in few lines to shew the infinitie of my Loue to your Grace. When* Vitellius, *at the Battell of* Cremona *was slaine, the* Parthian *King* Vologesus *sent Embassadours to* Vespasian, *offering him fourtie thousand* Parthian *Horsemen to ayde him, (This was a glorious and ioyfull thing to be sought vnto with offers of so great asistaunce, and yet not to need them): So thankes were giuen to* Vologesus, *and hee at perpetuall peace from thencefoorth with the* Romans. *I haue sent (dread Leige) those Papers Congratulatorie, and Parœnetic, to your Maiestic, not that your Highnes needes them, but with* Vologesus, *to shew my Loue to* Vespasian, *and purchase his thankes. If you like my labours, they come not too late: if you loath them, they come too soone to light. Thus, bold as a true and louing Subiect, fearefull as a blushing and onmanumitted Prentice in Poesie, I remaine your Maiestes,*

Borne Subiect, and bound beadman,

Alexander Craige.

TO THE READER.

HE famous *Grecians* had a Law, (though after mittigated by *Charondas*) that who foeuer for feare did run away from Battle, fhould be punifhed with death. So, leaft I fhould come in the reuerence of that Law, or be called a Cowward, I haue prefumed to publifh thefe my long conceyted Poems to common light: And like that valiant *Bayard* (who feeling himfelfe deadly wounded, and vnable to fit on his Horfe, commaunded his Souldiers to lay him againft a tree, but in fuch fort, as he might die with his face to the Enemie) I refolue, fince I haue alreadie from wifeft cenfors, receiued my death fhot, by printing my papers, to die with my face to the Foe. And fince (louing Lector) *Non omnibus datur adire Corinthum*, I am contented to be poynted at for a foolifh Poet, fo I may be reputed a faythfull Subiect. *Mauricius* forewarned by Dreames, and fundry Prognoftications, that *Phocas* fhould kill him, demaunded of *Philip* his fonne in law who this *Phocas* was? Who anfwered, hee was a faynt and cowardly fellow. The Emperour thereby concluded, hee was both cruell, and a murtherer. I feare no foe (   ) faue faynting *Phocas*, who cowardly concealing his owne, will cruelly murther my Verfes. Thus humbly fubmitting my homely laboures to thy charitable caftigation, I reft.

Thine as thou decerns
and deferues,

Alexander Craige.

1. *SONET*.

TO HIS MAIESTIE.

Hen others ceafe, now I begin to fing;
And now when others hold their peace, I fhout:
(The Lord preferue fweete *Leonatus King*,
That hee may rule great *Britane* round about:)
But if perhaps your Maieftie fhall doubt,
 what makes me fing whē others hold their peace:
My rufticke Mufe when as each one cry'd out,
Could not be heard from fo remote a place,
Dombe Woonder then my Senfe did fo confound,
The greater ftroke aftonifheth the more,
When as I heard thy name fo much renound,
I felt as lying in a found no fore:
   But now reuiu'd, I fing, when others ceafe,
   (In wonted mercie Lord preferue thy Grace.)

2

With mutuall loffe, with none or litle gaine,
   When *Ilion* faire was fully fet on fire,
   Proud *Paris* by his horie riuall flaine,
   And *Tyndaris* brought backe to her Empire:
I know not if the *Phrygians* did require
Melitides, but loe when *Troy* was wrackt,
Kind foole he came (fome fay at their defire)
Yet fayd he nought, but figh'd to fee them fackt:
                                      Hee

POETICALL ESSAYES.

Hee then was kind, I kinder now great Prince:
Hee wept, I fmild, to fee thy *Troy* but blood:
Hee fent for, I vnfought, and had long fince
Been heere, if that my comming could done good:
  Yet in this poynt our kindnes I conione,
  Wee come kind fooles to helpe when all is done.

3

Great *Pompey* cauf'd his Heraulds to proclaime
A publique Feaft to nations farre and neare,
  The young, the old, the rich and poore, all came,
  As welcome guiftes vnto that Princely cheare:
One blind man at a lame began to fpeare,
What fhall we doe? goe fayd the lame, take way,
I fhall be guide, thou on thy backe fhall beare
My lamed limbes; and thus they keepe the day.
Looke peereleffe *Pompey* on my Lines and mee,
They lame, and I without thy fight am blinde:
Wee come from fartheft *Scotifh* coaftes to thee,
Some portion of thy royall Feaft to finde:
  It reftes in thee to welcome vs therefore,
  And make me rich, that I may beg no more.

To

POETICALL ESSAYES.

TO THE KINGES
MOST EXCELLENT
MAIESTIE.

Epistle Congratulatorie & Pèrænetic.

SCarse had my Muse respi'd the smallest space,
From paynting prayses of our ciuill Pace,
Pack'd vp by thee most gratious King of late
In *Calidons* disturb'd vnquiet state,
When loe the Kalendes of this pleasent Spring,
Vnto my eares did ioyfull tydinges bring,
That bles'd *Eliza* had resignd her breath,
And payde the last and hindmost debt to death:
(O fearefull death! the fatall end of all,
With equall Mace thou chops both great and small)
And thou design'd her Diadems to weyre,
Of royall blood her nyest agnat heyre.
  Thou like a *Noah* long has kep't thy Arke,
Thoyld many storme by day, and gloomie darke:
Yet would not breake thy ward till time thy God,
Hath lent thee leaue, and bids thee walke abrode:
But his commaund since thou would nothing do,
Loe he hath ioynd his blessinges therevnto.
Come foorth with Wife and Children, sweete command,
The blessing breok and multiply the land.
  Thus am I solu'd of all my wonted doubt,
Nor wits nor weirdes thy fortunes bringes about,
But that eternall prouidence aboue:
Which thou art bound to serue, with feare and loue.
Those newes of new, haue wak'd my sleeping vaine,
And makes me write vnto your Grace againe

B.   Most

POETICALL ESSAYES.

Moſt harty greetings of thy happy chaunce,
Since thou art King of England, Ireland, Fraunce,
Beſides that famous and vnmatch'd renowne
Of thy vnconquered olde and Scottiſh Crowne.
Long deſuetude hath ruſted ſo my quill,
My wits are weake, but great is my good will.
Though ſcoffing Idiots will my paines depraue,
And *Ariſtarchus* all the credite haue.
I am to thee (dread Leige) thy aerie Elfe:
I borrow but thy words to prayſe thy ſelfe.
   Let Muſe-foe *Mars* elſewhere abroad go dwell,
Of warres and wounds let forraine Fachions ſmell:
Peace dwels with thee, where it hath dwelt ſo long,
Prone to propell, and to permit no wrong.
   Wiſe *Periander* wreates that Crownes of Kings,
On many fearefull fluctuations hings:
And that a Monarch's ſuretie no way ſtood
In victories, in warrie broyles, and blood:
But in the loue of Subiects truſt and true,
Thence ſaid the ſaige did ſetling ſure enſue.
   Graue *Xenophon* thy regiſters records,
That deeing *Cyrus* ſpoke thoſe ſelfe ſame words.
Aratus rare, ſaid ſo to *Philip* great,
That loue and peace confirm's a Kings eſtate:
In ſpeculation Schoolemen beene diuine,
But thou exceeds them Sou'raigne Syre ſenſine:
For thou has put their ſacred gnom's in vre,
Perfection in thy practique makes thee ſure.
   Let forraine lands now looke with enuies ee,
And who would rule, let him come learne at thee:
When ather *Momus* or *Rhamnuſia* barkes,
Thy wits are wondrous both in wreats and warkes.
   Oft times ſaid *Otho* in a rage, that hee
Had rather chuſe nor be a King to die.

                                              And

POETICALL ESSAYES.

And *Diocletian* said, to be a King,
And well to rule, was most difficill thing.
When *Dionise* at *Siracusa* sweare
That *Damocles* some while his Crowne should weare;
But being crownd, he plainely did protest
He neuer could be blithe to be so blest.
Were those on life for to behold thee now,
They could not raigne, nor could they rule as thou.
Thy match on mould nor was, nor yet shall bee:
Thus might they learne for to be Kings at thee.
   Ariston's praise is thine, as I suppose,
Thou keepes thy friends, and reconciles thy foes:
Vespasian-like, whome *Rome* obeyd with loue,
A Shepheard both, and carefull King you proue:
Thy folde bene broke, and lo thou has tane paine
To recollect thy erring flockes againe.
Thy Scepter and thy Sheephooke both are one,
Thou vnder heauen, their Herd and Lord alone.
   And now as *Homer* paynted *Priam* soorth,
Thou has beside thee men of wit and woorth:
Can any harme or strange thing now betide thee,
Vcalegon Antenor are beside thee.
Like *Macedo* the wondering world may doubt thee,
Parmenio and *Philotas* are about thee.
For all these Kingdomes which thou doest command,
A part by hop's, a happy part in hand,
Thou has a Kingdome to thy selfe vnknowne,
Looke rightly too, and *Cecil* is thine owne.
   Were *Plato* now on life, then would he say
That thy republikes blessed are this day:
For thou art wise, and now wise counsell hants,
And with thy wisedome thou supplies their wants.
   Yet this much more I plainely must impart,
A friendly counsel from a faithfull heart:

                                          Though

POETICALL ESSAYES.

Though farre from *Ioue* and thunder-claps I dwell,
My Lines of loue, of truth, and zeale shall smell.
Read then my Rymes most wife and prudent Prince,
And let a Hog, teach *Minerue*, but offence.
Not that I thinke your Grace has any need,
Or know's not els what's heere before you reed.
No, I attest great sacred *Ioue* aboue,
I onely write to manifest my loue:
While in my tugure (such is my estate)
I take repast of poore vnpeppered Kate.
I thanke my God for such as he doth giue,
And pray's withall, that well, and long thou liue:
And in seces at solitarie times,
Thou art remembred in my rusticke Rymes.
Sinetas poore vnto the *Persian* King,
Cold water in his hollow palme did bring:
Which *Artaxerxes* louingly out-dranke,
And gaue *Sinetas* both reward and thanke.
Right so those riuols of my poore Ingyne,
I heere present, from out this palme of mine.
Read then (dread Leige) those trauails of my loue,
Elaborate, and done for thy behoue.

1   Thus I begin, since adulations vaine,
In Courts with Kings and Monarch must remaine:
To assentators thou must giue some eare,
But be no prouder of their prayse a haire:
For *Macedo* would needs be cald a God,
And to this end his Edicts blew abrod:
Which on his head did heape disgrace the rather
Sith he asham'd that *Phillip* was his father.

2   Giue Parasites enough, but not too much,
And be not lauish, least thy lucke be such
As *Timon Coliteus*, who outspent
On *Demeas* and *Gnatonides* his rent;

                                               Of

POETICALL ESSAYES.

Of that vnthankfull numer liue anew,
To promife much, and to performe but few:
Be thou the ftone (precellent Prince) of tuch,
For to fecerne the honeft mindes from fuch.
   3 The faithfull man that once hath done thee good,
And for thy life hath ventered life and blood;
Be thankfull ftill to him, doe not defpite him,
But with thy felfe thinke thou can nee're acquite him:
Proue not vnkinde to caufe true *Phocion* die,
That thus hath fought, and wun the field for thee,
But when fuch friends fo nigh thy fides are feene,
Remember then but them thou had not beene.
   4 *Serapion* who is not taught to fpeike,
Let him not want, fuppofe he fhame to feike;
He is thine owne, and loues thee as the leaue,
His fpeaking lookes will tell when he would haue:
Be (prudent Prince) a *Pompey* in this cafe,
A benefite vnfought hath double grace.
   5 Change not too oft the Rulers of thy ftate,
For that may breed inteftiue ftrange debate:
The Fleeis els full, from fucking more will flake,
But hungry Gnats will make thy woundes to ake:
I pray for them as did *Hymera* old,
For *Dionife*, the tigrifh tyran bold,
(Lord faue fayd fhee, our King from death, difgrace,
For were he gone, a worfe would get his place)
Since in this poynt th'apodofis is plaine,
I turne my ftile vnto your Grace againe.
   6 If any friend in louing forme reueale
Twixt you and him your o'urfights, loue him well:
(Since *Plato* fayes, the braueft mindes bring foorth
Both hatefull vice, and vertue of moft worth.
Wife *Plutarch* writes, in fertill *Egipt* grew
With medicable, enuenomd hearbes anew.)

              B 3.   Doe

POETICALL ESSAYES.

Doe no rebuke, nor publique fhame approue,
But friendly counfaile, which proceedes from loue:
Be not a drunke *Cambifes* in difpeire,
For counfell kind to kill *Prexafpes* heire.
   7 Take *Turinus*, and fmooke him to the death,
Who falfly fels for bribes thy royall breath.
   8 Though *Alexander* in a raging ire,
For prayfing *Philip* his renouned Sire,
Kind *Clitus* kild, be thou more meeke in minde,
And to the prayfers of thy Parents kinde.
   9 Within thy heart let no iniuftice hant,
Let not the wrong'd man weepe for iuftice want:
Panfanias plaintes proud *Philip* did difdaine,
And cruelly for his contempt was flaine.
   10 A Woman old fell downe vpon her knee,
And cryed *Demetrius*, heare my plaints and mee?
I haue no leafure anfwerd he againe.
Hee takes no leafure fayd the wife to reigne.
Doe not thine eares *Demetrius*-like obdure,
With patience heare the fad and plaintiue poore.
   11 Proud *Leo* fpoyld *Iuftinian* his croune,
Deform'd his face, and cut his nofe quite doune:
But when he got his Diadems againe,
He punifht thofe that erft procur'd his paine.
Each gut of rheume that from his nofe did floe,
Gaue argument for to cut off a foe.
O do not thou great Prince delight in blood!
Of crueltie thou know's can come no good;
Be thou *Licurgus*, though thou lackes ane ee.
Forgiue *Alcander*, make him man to thee.
   13 *Vitellius*-like haue not a facill will,
Now to graunt grace, and ftraight commaund to kill.
   13 Great are thy fortunes, farre beyond beleife.
Thou needes no Realmes, nor foraine rentes by reife.

                                      Thy

POETICALL ESSAYES.

Thy minde may well luxuriat in thy wealth,
Thy Crown's are thine but blood or ſtrife or ſtealth:
And ſince thy fortunes are ſo rare: O than!
Each day with *Philip, thinke thou art a man.*

14 Though *Agathocles Sicil* did enioy,
Yet was he ſometime but a Potters Boy:
And that his pride ſhould not become too great,
In veſſels but of Loame he tooke his meate.
Thy witt's the weird's with great promotion tryes,
For woonder few are happy both and wiſe:
Though thou be free from blaſt's of any ſtorme,
Bee humill still, and keepe thy wonted forme.

15 Wreat not thy Law's with blood as *Draco* did,
The God of heau'n ſuch crueltie forbid:
A happie Life, makes ay a happie end,
Be thou a *Solon, Dracois* Law's to mend.

16 *Herodotus* the Hiſtor, and right ſo
The Poet *Pindars* wreats, with many mo,
That Monarch's great, examples good ſhould giue,
Since from their Lords the Laiks learne to liue.
Kinkes be the glas, the verie ſcoole, the booke,
Where priuate men do learne, and read, and looke;
Be thou th'attractiue Adamant to all,
And let no wicked wreſt thy wits to fall.
Goe not to *Delphos* where *Apollo* ſtands,
Licurgus-like with off'rings in thy hands,
By helliſh votes and oracles to ſee
What to thy Law ſhould paird or eiked bee:
From great *Iehouah* counſaile ſeeke, and hee
Shall giue both Gnom's and Oracles to thee,
And ſhall thy ſpir't with prudence ſo inſpire,
As all the world ſhall wonder and admire.

17 From Countries ſarre great King behold and ſee,
With rich Oblations Legates come to thee:

With

POETICALL ESSAYES.

With *Vexores*, and *Tanais* be glaide,
Of fame and honour let it not be faide,
Thou art a greedie *Ninus;* fie for fhame,
That were a ftaine vnto thy Noble name,
18   Laft, fince thou art the child of Peace, I fee
Thy workes, and writes, are witnes both with mee:
(Thy workes I haue no leafure to vnfold;
And though I had, are tedious to be told:
Thy Writes are wond'rous both in profe and ryme)
Let Vertue waxe and flourifh in thy tyme:
Though thou be beft, and greateft both of Kinges,
Mongft Poets all, is none fo fweetely finges.
Thou art the fweete *Mufæus* of our dayes;
And I thy Prentice, and muft giue thee prayfe:
Some other Writer muft thy Woorth proclaime,
Thou fhalt not fing vpon thy felfe for fhame:
Thou haft tranfalpine Poets of thine owne,
Whofe tragique *Cothurus* through the world are knowne:
Thou has likwife of home-bred *Homers* ftore,
Poore *Craige* fhall be thy *Cheryl*, and no more,
Since all my life fuppofe I Poetize,
I fee feauin *Philippeans* muft fuffize:
Not that thou art not liberall at will;
No, no, wife Prince, but caus my Verfe are ill.
Yet fince this furie is but lent to few,
Let vs not want, thou fhalt haue Verfe anew:
If thefe feeme pleafant, I fhall fing againe;
If not, I will from being bold abftaine,
And ceafe to write; but neuer ceafe to pray,
The God of heauen preferue thee night and day.

The

THE MOST VERTVOVS
and accomplifhed Prince *ANNA*, Queene of
Britane, Fraunce, and *Ireland;* Complaineth
the abfence of her Lord and Spous
IAMES, King of the
forefayd Realmes.

WHere habit was, dwels fad Priuation now,
And I am made an Orphane from delight:
To want the fweete fruition of thy fight,
In balefull bed my body when I bow,
Yea neither can I tell, nor can ye trow,
How blacke alace and noyfome is each night,
Nor yet how loathfome is this common light,
Since abfence made diuorfe twixt mee and you.
I am thy *Phœbæ*, thou my *Phœbus* faire:
I haue no light nor life, but lent from thee,
Curft then be abfence, caufer of my care,
Which makes fo long this loath'd eclipfe to bee.
  What woonder I through lake of prefence pine?
  Worm's haue alace their Sunne, and I want mine.

Scotlandes

C.

Scotlands Teares.

WHen fabling *Æsop* was at fatall *Delphos* tane,
And there by doome condem'd to be precipitat & flane
He like a woman weep't, and tooke delight in teaires,
Caufe they alleuiat and made leffe the confcience of his caires.
But *Solon* when he fpi'd his deereft fonne was dead,
He weepd the more, becaufe his teaires to grief gaue no remead:
Yet neither he nor he by teaires could falue his ill,
Though of thofe falt and fruitles flouds impetuus fpaits they fpil
Then maymed *Scotland* thou made Orphane from delight,
Whom all the hofts of heauens abhor with vndeferu'd defpight.
With deeing *Æsop* mourne, or wofull *Solon* weepe:
And tho as they, thou weepe in vaine let not thy forrow fleepe:
With fruftrat *Æfau* fhout, curfe life and wifh to dee,
Since *Iacob* with his mothers helpe thy blefsing fteals from thee:
Now riuall *England* brag, for now, and not till now
Thou has compeld vnconquered harts & fturdy necks to bow.
What neither wits, nor wars, nor force afore could frame,
Is now accomplifht by the death of thy Imperiall Dame.
Eliza faire is gone, into the land of reft,
To that *Elifium* predecried and promis'd to the bleft;
And *England* for her fake now weaires the fabill weede,
But *Scotland* if thou rightly looke thou has more caufe indeede.
They for a *Dian* dead, *Apolloes* beames enioy,
And all their ftraying fteps allace, our *Titan* dooth tonnoy

No

POETICALL ESSAYES.

Now dawn's their glorius day with *Phœbus* rayes befpred,
And we are but *Cymmerian* flaues with gloomy clouds ou'rcled.
Rich neighbour nation then, from thy complayning ceafe:
Not thou, but we fhould figh, & fo to our complaints giue place.
Our Garland lacks the Rofe, our chatton tins the ftone,
Our Volier wants the *Philomel*, we left allace alone.
What art thou *Scotland* then? no Monarchie allace,
A oligarchie defolate, with ftraying and onkow face,
A maymed bodie now, but fhaip fome monftrous thing,
A reconfufed chaos now, a countrey, but a King.
When *Paris* fed his flockes among the *Phrigian* plaines,
Ænone's loue was his delights, his death were her difdaynes.
But when allace he knew that *Priam* was his Sire,
He left *Ænone* fweet, and fyne for *Helene* would afpire.
Proud Pellex *England* fo thou art the adulterat brid,
Who for *Aenone* thinkes no fhame to lye by *Paris* fid.
Who knowes ere it be long, but our your happy King,
With *Belgic, Celtic, Aquitan,* to his Empire may bring?
And he (why fhould he not) your *Troynauant* fhall leaue,
And vnto *Parife* fpurre the poft, his right for to receaue?
Then, then fhall *England* weepe, and fhed abounding teaires,
And we shall to our comfort find companions in our caires.
And till it fo befall, with pitie, not with fcorne,
Vpon this confinde Kingdome looke, as on a land forlorne:
Wife *Plato* would not once admit it in his minde,
He lou'd *Xenocrates* fo well, he could become vnkinde,
And no more can we thinke dread Leige, though thou be gone,
Thou will vngratly leaue vs thus difconfolat allone,
By Contrars Contrars plac'd, no dout moft clearely kith, (blith.
And now thy abfence breedes our bale, whofe biding made vs
O were thou not both wife and good, we fhould not mourne,
We would not for thy abfence weepe, nor wish for thy returne.
Long fleepe made *Rufus* loofe the vfe of both his eene.
O do not thou fweet Prince make ftay, left thou forget vs cleene

Like

POETICALL ESSAYES.

Like *Epimenides* when thou returns againe: (flaine,
The fhapp of al things fhal be chaing't, thine own fheepe fhalbe
Democrit rather choofe no King at all to bee,
Then ouer wicked men to rule, and fuch allace are wee:
Our Iewell *England* ioyes, & yet no way dooth wrong vs; (vs:
The world may fee we were not worth, that thou fhuld be among
But fince it muft be thus, and thou art forc'd to flitt,
Now like a Heart in to the mids of thy great body fitt:
And from thy *Troynauant*, which pleafures ftore impairts,
Behold thy Kingdom's round about thy hand in all the Airts;
Examples old thou taks, and layis before thy face,
The famous *Numids* thoght the midft to be moft honored place
Thus by *Hyempfals* fide *Adherbal Salust* fets,
And fo *Iugurtha* in the midft wee reed no intrance gets.
Graue *Maro* maks likway, the Queene of *Cartage* braue,
Betwix *Afcanius* and the wife *Æneas*, place to haue,
Dooth not *Apollo* too in proudeft pompe appere,
With bright and day-adorning beames in his meridian fphere?
So thou haft choof'd the midft, of all thy Kingdom's knowne;
For looke about thee where thou lift, thou looks but on thine owne
And fince the Gods decree (Great King) that fo fhall bee,
Since Peace muft florifh in thy time, & Wars muft ceafe & die,
But competition too, fince thou has *Englands* Crowne,
Which was a *Heptarchie* of old, of vncontrould renowne,
Let Vs and *Al-bi-on*, that wee with one confent, (tent.
One God, one King, one Law, may be t'adore, ferue, keepe, con-
In *Rome* the *Sabins* grew, with *Tyrians Troians* mixt,
And *Iuda* ioynd with *Ifrael*, but leaft wee feeme prolixt,
And that our louing plaint's, and teares may now take end,
Thee to thy Crowns, thy Crowns to thee, the great good God
(defend.

Calidons

CALIDONS COMPLAINT

At the apparent Voyage to her *England*, of
ANNA Queene of *Great Britaine, France,*
and *Ireland:* with *HENRIE* Prince of
Wales, her moſt gracious Sonne.

AND ſhall no light at all to len vs light be left?
Shal Sunn, Moone, fixed & thoſe ſmal erratic ſtars be reft?
And was it not ynough that *Titan* tooke the flight?
Might not ſweete *Cynthia* yet made ſtay for to haue lent vs light?
Since Sunne and Moone muſt goe, & that bright *Harie* ſtarr,
Let *Pluto* now compare with vs in darknes if he darr,
From darknes was alace our deriuation old
The fatall name ⊠ KOTIA nought but darknes doth vnfold,
Shall our eſtate allace from ſtate be thus downthrowne,
Shal *Scotland* hensforth haue againe no cround K. of their owne?
Shal wee from King, Queene, Prince, & all their brood diſſeuer?
And ſhall not *Scotland* be againe inhabited for euer?
Shall ghaſtly *Ziim* cry, and *Oim* make there ſport,
Within the Palaces where once but Monarch's made reſort?
At libertie alas ſhall *Fauns* and *Satyrs* lope,
And to a helliſh cold diſpare conuert our former hope:
And dare not *Orpheus* looke but once againe abacke?
Or ſhall wee finde no thing at all, but fundamentall wracke?
Would God that vmquhyle Dame (the wiſeſt Dame in deed,
That euer *Britaine* earſt hath borne, or yet againe ſhall breed)
Would God as yet ſhee were to brooke her trident Mace,
Then ſhuld we not bin poynted at for wrake, ſcorne, & diſgrace
Thou ſaild the glaſsie ſalt and conquered endles fame,

C 3.   In

POETICALL ESSAYES.

In prime of loue Heroit Prince, to fee thy *Danish* Dame,
In fleeing towrs of tree thou croc'd the bounded Roares,
And brought our Queene, thy facred Spous to *Calidonian* fhoares
O let not loue wax cold! nor be not now vnkind,   (wind,
Thou need not feare for foamie floods, nor pray for profperous
Since fhee fweet Dame is feik, thy Sonn but young in yeers,
With *Cancer Leo* burns aboue into their torrid Spheers:
Make then a blef'd returne to fee them both againe,
But ô allace! wee ware thofe words vnto the winds in vaine:
For they muft go to thee, more to increas our cairs,
And leaue no thing behind them here, but forow, fighs, & teairs.
Thē wherto ferue thofe plaints? who know's what is appoynted,
Or what the Deftanies decrees to do with their Anoynted.
Nor *Doucir*, nor thofe *Alps*, nor *Tybers* volted Arche,
Vnto that *Archunonarche* great King *Iames* muft be a Marche:
The heauins of the great Prince hade care in to thy Coode,
And kept thee when thou no thing knew of ather bad or good.
How many treafons ftrange, and confpirations great,
Haue bin contriu'd againft thy crowne, & ftanding of thy ftate?
Before thou was, and fince thou has eskaip'd huge fnairs,
Be blithe *Tued* march'd thy kingdoms once, & now muft march
Thy name fhal be enough to conquer feas & lands, (thy cairs.
And manumit afflicted *Grece* from *Turks* and tyrans hands.
When *Rome* fhall be fubdew'd, may thou no go abroad,
And make *Bizantium* old obey the great alguiding God.
But if thou greyus great King our greiued harts to glade,
Of thy triennall vifiting, performe thy promeis made.
Faire gracious Dame, whofe match nor was, nor fhall be feene,
Though fortune fmile, remēber yet that thou was firft our Queene
Accompleifd peereles Prince in body both and mind,
Thinke on thy natiue foyle with loue, and be not cald vnkind:
And fo fince King, Queene, Prince, and all our all muft go,
The Trinitie aboue preferue this Trinitie be-low.
Elizabeth

ELIAZABETH, LATE
QVEENE OF ENGLAND,
HER GHOST.

Eafe louing Subiects, ceafe my death for to deplore,
And do no more with dririe cryes my dolful hearfe decore
Though like *Cynegirus*, when both the hands are gone,
Yee would detaine me with your teeth in my Emperiall throne.
Bee *Thracians* now I pray, and hence-foorth ceafe to mone,
Ere it be long in quiet peace ye fhall finde fiue for one:
For if you can beleeue my prophetizing ghoft,
Æneas gaue *Anchifes* truft, you fhall not thinke me loft.
The death of one (fome fay) the birth of one fhould bee:
Three mails & femels two you haue, moft famous fiue for mee:
For as I feald my Will, my Defignation dew,
And did concredit by the reft to my *Achates* trew:
So now my ghoft is glad, that by my care his paine,   (gaine,
My countries haue their lawfull King, the King his crowns a-
Then branfh imbellif'd foyle, moft pleafant, moft perfite:
The onely earthly *Eden* now for pleafure and delighte.
Rich *England* now reioyce, heaue vp to heauen thy hands,
The bleffed Lord hath bleft thy bounds beyond al other lands.
Since no *Sardanapal* is now become thy King,
No *Dionife* nor *Nero* proud, my death to thee doth bring.
A King vnwoont to giue, or yet to take offence:
A godly *Dauid* ruleth now, a Prophet and a Prince.
                                                      The

POETICALL ESSAYES.

The Pupill now is blith, the Widow weepes not now,
No depredations in thy boundes, the Rushbush keeps the Kow,
The Lyons now agree, and do in Peace delight:
The Thirsel now defends & guards the red Rose & the white.
The british Saints shake hands with crosses ioynd and spred,
Whose cullours on the glassie salt no terror small haue bred:
Those now conioynd in one through *Neptuns* bounded roares,
Shal make the ventring mercheand sail secure to forane shoares:
Flee swift-wingd Fame & tell the best & rarest new's   (hew's,
That time hath yet brought foorth by night or dayes delightfull
For Ships & Swans most rich, most faire, & famous *Thamis,*
Tell *Neptune, Thetis, Triton* too the haps of great king *IAMES*.
Thou murdring *Galliglas,* who long my Laws withstood,
Learne to obey, and bath no more thy blade in british blood:
All you my Subiects deire, do homage dew to him,
And that shal make my blessed ghost in boundles ioyes to swim.

To

SONET,
To his Maieſtie of the
Vnion of the two famous Realmes
Scotland and *Englaud.*

S *Cilurus* had twice fourtie Children male,
And teaching them in peace to paſſe their dayes,
   And that no foe ſhould gainſt their force preuale,
His louing minde hee wiſely thus bewrayes:
A bundle of Darts before their eyes he layes,
And pray'd each Sonne to breake the ſame: at length,
When hee and hee to cruſh thoſe Darts aſſayes,
But all in vaine; hee told them Vnions ſtrength.
You are a Father, and a famous Prence,
Great are the bounds which are great King thine owne,
And like a ſacred *Scilure* in this fence,
Keepes *Britaine* whole, leaſt it ſhould be ouerthrowne.
   The God of heau'n effect what thou intends,
   And bring thy proiects to their happie ends.

To

D.

To the Queens most
Excellent Maiestie,

1. SONET.

IN *Pallas* Church did wretched *Irus* stand,
And saw her paynted on the Chalk-whit wall,
With Booke in one, and Sword in other hand:
And on his face (poore soule) did flatlings fall.
Syne sayd aloud, since I allace am thrall
To pouertie, that I may not propine
Thy Godhead great, with gift nor great nor small,
Yet while I liue, my seruice shall be thine.
So all the pow'rs of this my poore Ingyne,
Shall bee (Faire Dame) employed to pen thy praise,
Thou in Cymmerian gloomie darke shall shyne,
And on thy Vertues, worlds to come shall gaize.
    Thus *Irus*-like wise *Pallas* I adore,
    And honour thee, since I can do no more.

2. SONET.

Of her Highnes Natall; being the shortest day.

GReat mightie *IOVE* from his imperiall place,
And all the *GODS* for blythnes of *Thy Birth*,
Came downe from Heau'n to see thy fairest face,
                      Glad

POETICALL ESSAYES.

Glad to Be guarded by thy beauties girth.
And *Neptune* fet his Flocks out through the Firth,
With all the *Nymphs* in Floods and Seais that dwell:
On *Balens* backs they mounted, made their mirth,
To fee thy fhapp, all leiuing leids excell:
And *Phœbus* father to the Fooll that fell,
In loweft ftate his yocked Horfe did ftay;
But fearing leaft thy beam's fhould burne him fell,
Hee ftole aback, and vpward went away.
    And for thy faik thy Natall day each yeir,
    He vifits yet into his loweft fpheir.

3. SONET.

New yeir Gift.

THis Apill round I fend, ô matchles fare!
    As children do for thyrfe als good agane,
Not fuch as that by which th' *Enbean* rare,
The loue of his *Atlanta* fuift did gane:
Nor that by which *Acontius* did beguile
Cydippe fweet in facred *Dian's Fane.*
My minde abhors all fuch inuention vile,
No fecreit flight doth in my gift remane:
It more refembleth that which *A te* threw
Mongft *Pallas, Iuno, Venus,* Dames diuine.
To thee great *Queene* of all this courtly crew,
I do prefent this paynted Apill mine.
    Were it of Gold, or Paris I, faire Dame,
    It fhould be thine, thou beft deferu's the fame.

POETICALL ESSAYES.

4. SONET.

THose famous old *Gymnosophists* of *Inde*,
 Which *Alexander* did so much admire,
And compted but as churlish and vnkinde,
Cause they refus'd his offred Gold and geir.
Their greatest care and studie was we heir,
To view and marke the motions of the Sunn,
To know his courses in his Zodiac Spheir.
From *Phospor's* rysing till the night begun.
Such is my state, O sacred Saint by thee,
I am a poore Gymnosophist of thine,
Thou art that *Sunn* which I delight to see,
No wealth I wish but that on mee thou shine.
 They long'd for night, so long-some was their day,
 Blithe would I bee for to behold thee ay.

To

TO THE VERTVOVS
AND ACCOMPLISHED
Sir *IAMES HAY* Knight,
one of his Highnes moſt
royall bed-chamber.

*Hen a bad Wreſtler became a knauiſh Phi-ſition, Courage (ſaid* Diogenes *to him) thou has reaſon ſo to doe; for now ſhalt thou helpe to put them in the ground, who heretofore haue layd thee on it. I am from a luckles louer, become an infortunat Poet, and haue determined with Courage, to write Ditties againſt my riuall, that breedes my diſgraces, and with* Archilochus, Iambics, *I minde to make* Lycambes *hang him ſelfe.* Agrippina *foretold by Aſtrologues, that her Sonne* Nero *ſhould kill her: anſwered. Let him kill mee, ſo he may be Emperour, and ſucceed to* Claudius: *all my ſenſes in wofull lingage (which makes me begge thy patrocinie) like facidic Aſtrologs tell me my Pamphlet of the* Cuckoe *and* Philomel, *ſhalbe vnwelcome to many, and receiue ſtrange Commentaries: but if you be content, I care not; my greateſt ambition is to breed your content: my pleaſure to pleaſe you, whoſe Adamantiue vertues haue drawne the Yron of my loue. In publique or priuate, in peaceable negotiations, or warlike occupations to leiue, or die greatly, or glorioyſly, I know no forme or fortune of man, I can admire or regard with ſo much honour, with ſo much loue; yea, at all aduentures of life & death, thou mayeſt command.*

Thine owne poore friend and ſeruient,

D 3. *CRAIGE.*

THE CVCKOE,
AND PHILOMEL.

CRAIGE to his Riuall.

THE *Cucko* once (fome fay) would *Philomel* affaile,
   Arachne-like, if fhee or fhee in finging fhould preuaile:
   The garrient *Goke* would needs with *Prognes* fifter ftriue,
   And proudly preafe poore *Philomel* of dew praife to depriue
Then was the long eard *Afse* made Iudge vnto their Song,
Who with the *Cucko* fentence gaue, & wrought the other wrong.
O Arbiter vnfit to fuch difcording tunes,
Yet iarring notes from *Layis* diuine rude Nature ftill feiuns.
This mak's poore *Philomel* repent, and oft repeit,
In thornie braiks by fabill night th' *Arcadian* beafts decreit.
Such is my carefull cafe, my riuall foe I fee,
For all thefe charming Songs of mine is farr preferd to mee:
For all the Sonnets fweet that I can fing or fay,
Or fend to her, I cum no fpeid, the *Cucko* is my ftay:
And fhee whom ftill I ferue, moft like that long eard beaft,
Maks mee by her decreit to leue inglorious and difgrac't.
But what remeid I reft, content to want reward,
Since *Cuckoes* are in fuch accompt, and *Philomel* debard.
Since *Phœbus* ftoops to *Pan*, and *Minerue* glad to yeild
Vnto th'inuennomd Spiders webb, I gladly loofe the feild,
Yet fhall I ftill complaine, nay fhall fhee heir mee cry,
The *Philomel* fings to her felfe, and hencefoorth fo fhall I.

Apo-

APOLOGIE FOR HIS RIVAL.

THE *Cucko* once (tis trew) in finging, did compare
   With *Prognes* fifter *Philomel, Pandions* daughter faire:
   And then the *Afine* graue, pronounc'd a fentence trew,
   For many arguments, of which fond Riual read thofe few.
The *Cucko* with fweet fongs faluts the yeerly Spring,
   Poore *Philomel* in tragic tunes of *Terens* wrongs doth fing.
Through tops of talleft trees the foaring *Cucko* flies,
   While *Philomel* in loweft fhrubs complains, difpairs, & dies.
The *Cuckoes* not's declare of humane life the date,   (peate.
   While hart-broke *Philomel* muft ftill her painefull plaints re-
The *Cucko* fings her name, no borrowed note nor ftrange,
   While *Philomel* for *Itis* blood, a thoufand tunes muft change.
The *Titling* doth attend the *Cucko* late and aire,
   And of her egs and Plumeles birds fhe taks continuall care,
None tends poore *Philomel*, for all her charms and chrils,   (thrils
   Yea if fhe fleip, the poynted thorne out-through her breift-bone
The *Cucko* fpends the Spring in mirth both eue and morne,
   And to the ielus heirar ftill portends the forked Horne.
At *Iunoes* fute great *Ioue* became a *Cucko* faire: (paire?
   Why fhuld the brood of *Grecian* Kings, with Gods aboue com-
Then *Phœbus* ftoope to *Pan*, be *Minerue* glad to yeeild
   Vnto th' inuennomd Spiders web, for thou muft loofe the feild:
And thou muft be content to weepe, and want reward,
   Since *Cuckoes* are in fuch accompt, and *Philomel* debard.
Thou to thy felfe complains, alone thou weepes and murns,
   Do fo poore foule till fortune change, whofe fauour goes by turns.

APPELLATION
TO THE LION.

The Lion fome time went abraode to fpy his pray,
And with the Fox he made the Affe cōpanions of his way,
Through wildfome wayles wayes, & foraine fells they fare,
To find fome food, which found, the Affe wold needs diuide
And thus triparts the pray, and fets his terce afide: (& fhare,
Yet died therefore; iuft punifhment of ignorance and pride.
But lo the fraudfull Fox did greeid and greife difgyfe,
And by the Afins miferie with wealth of wils was wyfe,
Now neither perrils paft, nor no examples new,
Can mooue the Afins of this age; O damn'd iudocil crew:
That long eaird beaft my Iudge hath made my riuall fleepe,
Fools concolor in fauours lap, while I poore wretch muft weepe.
Then *Lion* great of *Kings*, and *King* of *Lions* all,
To thee my Soueraigne and my Iudge, I do appeale and call:
Thou heares and fees my wrongs, thou muft dread Leige alone
Correct the *Cucko*, and detrude the Asine from his throne.
I like *Xantippus* Dogg, haue faund and followed thee,
And will thou fuffer mee in fight of *Salamin* to die.
It greeues my heart to fee thofe *Cuckoes* of the Spring, (fing.
Thofe tamed beafts, whom *Bion* haits, what flattering tunes they
I burft when I behold braue *Homers* Cloake fo bare,
When eu'ry foole & fimple fheepe the golden fleece doth weare
To thee alone I flie, in hope to find refuge:
Why fhould the leaud and lafie Affe to numered lyus be Iuge?
My Fortune and my Fate do both depend on thee,
My Spring expireth, fhall I fing, or fhall I filent bee?
    Set downe thy fentence heir, and quickly cure my care,
    Or let my wretched life take end twixt filence and difpare.

Epiftle

EPISTLE TO
HIS FRIEND.

Am fully perſwaded, that no man lyuing hath a more forgetfull minde of benefits receiued, then my ſelfe; and none more malitiouſly mindfull of ſmalleſt iniuries, then miſerable I: In the firſt a Melitides, *who could not number fiue:* In the laſt, a vindictiue Darius, *who leaſt hee ſhould forget the wrongs he receiued from the* Athenians, *cauſed his Paige when ſoeuer he ſate downe to his Table, ſing to him,* Sir remember the Athenians. Thy courtaſies, thy louing kindnes, thy hoſpitalitie, patrocinie in perels, and thy omnerited munificence are all forgotten, and thy leaſt eſcapes (Anonym friend) are here too much remembred, which both condems thy inconſtancie, and my vnkindnes: thy waueuring, and my weaknes. The Pythagorians make good to be finit, and euill infinit: ſo is humane waikenes redier to repay in greatest meaſure the ſmalleſt euill, then to repay in ſmalleſt meaſure the greatest good receiued: read then (   ) thy faults, and my follies: and while thou reads, mend the firſt in thy ſelfe, and pittie the laſt in

Thine old, and if thou will,
yet louing Frend,
CRAIGE.

E.

TO HIS ANONIM FREIND
and Miſtres *PALINODE*.

IN Annals old we read *Ioue* had but daughters two,
The one with *Ceres* he begat, *Proſerpine* hight, and ſo
Her for her beauties ſaik, proud *Pluto* Prince of hell,
   Amid the flowrie medowes ſpoild, and keepes vnto him fell:
The other *Helene* fayre in likeneſſe of a Swan,
He gat with *Læda*, and beguild poore *Tyndarus* her man.
Hir *Theſeus* tooke away, and had to *Athens* home,
And made her *Hymens* rupture long ere *Menelaus* come.
Thus *Ioue* no daughter had vnſpoyld at all you ſee,
Yet muſt *Pirithous* haue one to keepe his oath, or dee.
Braue *Theſeus* was his friend, his loue he would not haue:
Then muſt *Proſerpina* be ſpoild from *Plutoes* pitchie caue:
(For who can be content bright beautie ſhould be chaind,
Or in *Cymmerian* gloomy darke with *Dis* ſhould be detaind?)
Thus to the hells he haiſts, and is by *Cerber* ſlaine:
And *Theſeus* till *Alcides* came, in fetters did remaine:
O monument moſt rare of true and perfect loue,
Which neither beautie nor the hells could any way remoue.
Though *Tyndaris* was blaz'd the brighteſt that hath beene,
Pirithous would from her loue for *Theſeus* loue abſteene:
And when *Pirithous* tooke iourney towards hell,
Braue *Theſeus* would accompany his friend, as ſtories tell:
   But faith, nor truth on earth, nor friendſhip now is naine,
And *Pithias* now will looſe his life, or *Damon* come againe.
There is no loue allace vpon this mournefull molde,
Leaſt *Mydas*-like a man may turne each thing by tuch in golde.
                                      Falſe

POETICALL ESSAYES.

Falſe *Eriphile* now regards but greeid of gaine,
And will betray *Amphiaraus* to get a golden chaine.
The *Belidean* Dames in number fiue times ten,
(There is no *Hypermneſtra* now) will kill their maried men.
Falſe proud *Polinices* will *Theban* crowne poſſeſſe,
And baniſh poore *Eteocles* gainſt parents will expreſſe:
And proud *Plexirtus* too *Leonats* baſtard brother,
Makes *Tydeus* ſtriue with *Tolenor*, and one to kill the other.
Vrania Klaius ſturs with *Strephon* ſtill to ſtriue.
Nor can the Prince of *Macedon* find *Muſidor* online.
 Thus looke from ſex to ſex, no fayth nor truth remains,
Crow's flee but where the Carion lyes, & worldlings go for gains
I ſpeak not now allace, by ſpeculation vaine,
A practique in my perſone paſt, procurs my peereles paine:
For why, I ſom-time had a Miſtres and a Freind,
She fals falte frequent to that ſex: hee les woorth nor I weind:
She limping *Vulcan* ſtill admits in *Mauors* bed,
Hee like a ſubtill *Sinon* goes in *Damons* liuerie cled:
Shee *Pluto* black for me doth in her bed imbrace,
Hee but a caus hath caſt me off: O care contryuing caſe.
Was thou not once to mee *Pandora* deir and ſweit,
Till thou vntyed the balefull box with painefull plages repleit?
And was thou not againe a *Kallias* vnto mee?
But fooliſh *Alcibiad* I, to truſt ſo much in thee.
Then, Som-time Freind, farewel; farewell my late loſt Loue:
A *Lais* light, a *Sinon* fals, thus maks mee to remoue.
Betwix this doolefull deuce, how can my dayes indure,
Sence he hath playd the hypocrit, and ſhee the hatefull hoore?
And yet for kindnes old, I will conceyl your names, (ſhames:
And make your conſcience black, a Iudge to both your ſecret
And ſence both thou, and thou, haue thus contriu'd my fall,
Dis keeps my Dame, *Dis* katch my freind, & make me free of all.

E 2. *Sonet.*

SONET.

I Some time had a Miſtres, and a Freind;
Shee fair, hee good; and louely both to mee:
But both are wax'd vnwoorthier nor I weind:
Deceitfull ſhee, and moſt vnconſtant hee:
Thus for each lyne, I giue my ſelfe a lye,
That heretofore in to their praiſe I pend,
Hee, ſhee, and I, are alwayes chayng'd all three:
They firſt, I laſt; and thus our Loues muſt end.
Trew Friends allace, lyke blackeſt Swans are rare,
And fayreſt faices full of moſt deceat.
This cauſes mee alone for to regrat,
And from each eye to wring a bloodie teare:
And ſince no ſex beneath the Sunne is trew,
Falſe friend fareweell, faire facill Dame adew.

To his Calidonian
MISTRIS.

Hemiſtocles *after a great Victorie by nauall Battell, came to viſite the ſlaughtered bodyes of his Enemies, and found by the Sea ſide many Iewels and Chaynes ſcattered. Then ſaid he to his freind who then by chaunce followed him, Gather theſe ſpoyles, for thou art not* Themiſtocles . *This worthles Epiſtle like a looſe or neglected Iewell, though the wiſe and woorthy* Themiſtocles *ouerpas, I pray thee ſweete Miſtes peruſe and preſerue, leaſt it periſh; ſence too, and for thee, it is done: when I am abſent, or dead, it may breed thy delight, and make thee haplie remember thou once had*

A louing and kind man,

CRAIGE.

E 3.

TO HIS CALIDONIAN
MISTRIS.

WHEN I remember on that time, that place,
Where firſt I fix'd my fanſie on thy face,
The circumſtances how, why, where, and whan,
My Miſtres thou, and I became thy Man:
Whilſt I repeat that proces full of paine,
How firſt we met, and how we twind againe,
Our ſweete acquaintance, and our ſad depart,
It breedes a ſea of ſorrowes at my hart:
And yet for all theſe ſorrowes I ſuſteine,
With ſigh ſwolne hart, and teares bedewed eyne,
As I haue lou'd, ſo ſhall I loue thee ſtill
Vnto the death, hap either good or ill.
And now I ſweare by that true loue I owe thee,
By all the ſighs which day by day I blow thee:
By all the verſe and charming words I told thee,
By all the hopes I haue for to beholde thee:
By all the kiſſes ſweete which I haue reft thee,
And all the teares I ſpent ſince laſt I left thee:
That abſence helps (not hinders my deſire)
And ſets new force and Fagots to my fire:
Each thing that chance preſents and lets me ſee,
Brings arguments. and bids me thinke on thee.
For when they told me of that wrathfull flame,
Which from the high and holy heau'n downe came
On *Pauls* faire Church, and that cloud-threatning Steeple,
And how it flam'd in preſence of the people.
Then

POETICALL ESSAYES.

Then with my felfe thought I, this fire was quenfht,
But mine endures, and by no tears is drenfht:
And were not hope accreftis with defire,
I had long fince confum'd amid this fire.
  And when I viewd thofe walles of *Farnhame* fayre,
Where *Lamuel* with his Lady made repaire:
I layd me downe befide the ditch profound,
Where *Guineuer* difpairing Dame was dround,
And fell on fleep vpon that fatall brinke,
And ftill on thee fweete hart I dreame, I thinke.
And were it not, that by the tract of time
The well was full with earth, with ftone, and lime,
There had I drownd, and by my fatall fall
Made end with her of loue, and life, and all:
Yet halfe afham'd leaft curious eyes fhould finde me,
I went away, and left huge teaires behind me.
  And when I fpide thofe ftones on *Sarum* plaine,
Which *Merlin* by his Magicke brought, fome faine,
By night from farr *I-erne* to this land,
Where yet as oldeft Monuments they ftand:
And though they be but few for to behold,
Yet can they not (it is well knowne) be told.
Thofe I compard vnto my plaints and cryes,
Whofe totall fumme no numers can comprife.
  Olde *Woodftocks* wrackes to view I was defpos'd,
Where *Rofamond* by *Henrie* was inclos'd:
The circuits all and wildefome wayes I view,
The Laberinth, and *Cliffords* fatall Clew.
And where thofe time-worne monuments had beene,
Where nought remaines but ruines to be feene:
Yet in my hart moe wracks, moe wayes I fand,
Then can be made by any humane hand.
And all thefe wondrous wonders which I fee,
Makes me but wonder more and more on thee.

            E 4.   That

POETICALL ESSAYES.

That thou be well both day and night I pray,
And for thy health once I carrouſe each day:
From pype of Loame and for thy ſaike I ſouke,
The flegm-attractiue far-fett *Indian* ſmouke:
Which with my braine and ſtomach beares debate,
And like the lethall Aconite I hate,
That poyſning potion pleaſant ſeems to mee,
When I determe it muſt be drunke for thee.
    From *Venus* ſports I doo indeed abſtaine,
Nor am I now as I was woont ſo vaine:
Chaſt *Dians* laws I do adore for good,
Who kild her loue *Orion* in the flood.
    Drunke *Bacchus* maits I hold for none of mine,
I taſte no *Celtic* nor *Iberian* Wine:
Looke on my Lyns *Lyœum*, none they ſmell,
But *Helicons* poore ſtreams, where Muſes dwell.
    For all thoſe rare delights which *England* yeilds,
Of faces faire, of braue and fertill feilds:
For all the pleaſurs which our Court frequent,
Such as mans heart would wiſh, or witt inuent:
Yet I proteſt, I rather begg with thee,
Then be ſole King, where ſeau'n were wont to bee.
    But when my Freend thy berar ſpurd with pane,
The Poiſt to ſee this Chalkie ſhoare agane,
And brought thy ſymboll diſcolor of hew,
With commendations kind, but not anew,
I ask'd him how thou was? hee ſhooke his head.
What man (quoth I) and is my Miſtres dead?
No (anſwerd hee) but ſeik deir freend: Quoth I,
Thou know's I loue; I pray thee make no lye.
In faith but ſeik, and is no doubt err now,
As weell (ſayd hee) as ather I or yow.
This hee affirmd with ſolem oaths anew:
And yet allace I doubt if they be trew

Heare

POETICALL ESSAYES.

Here where the Peſt approacheth vs ſo narr,
To ſmoother breath before wee be aware:
For at the gates of our moſt royll King,
Corrupted Carions lie; O fearefull thing:
Yet feare I ſtill for thee, my loue is ſuch,
And for my ſelfe I feare not halfe ſo much:
And now I feare theſe fears ere it be long,
Will turne to Agues, and to Feuers ſtrong.
Long are my nights, and dolefull are my dayes:
Shott ſleeps, long waks; and wildſom are my wayes:
Sadd are my thoughts, ſowr ſighs; and ſalt my tearis:
My body thus els waik both wayn's and wearis.
For loſſe of *Calice*, *Marie* Englands Queene,
Had ſighs at hart, and teairs about her eyne,
When I am dead, caus rype my hart ſayd ſhee;
And in the ſame ſhall *Calice* writen bee,
Die when I will, thy name ſhall well be knawne,
Within my hart in bloods characters drawne.
But if (faire Dame) as yet on liff thou bee,
This Papyre then commends my loue to thee:
And if thy life by wrathfull weirds be loſt,
Chaſt *Laura* then thy *Petrarch* loues thy ghoſt:
And yet my hopes aſſures mee thou art weell,
And in theſe hopes a comfort hidd I feell.
This for the time ſweet hart, that thou may kno,
I leaue thy man, and loue but thee; and ſo,
Till by thy wreat I know thy further will,
I ſay no more, but ſigh, and ſeals my Bill.

            F.   *Sonet*

SONET.

FRom this *Abydos* where I duyne and die,
   And fore God know's againſt my hart remaine,
   I wreat with wo ſweet *Seſtian* Saint to thee,
   And blacke this Paper with the Inck of paine,
No waltering waues of *Neptuns* moone-mou'd maine:
Nor *Helleſponts* impetuous contrare tyde,
No Sea nor Flood, no ſtormie Wind nor Raine,
Are lets or barrs that from thy bounds I bide,
My wayes allace doth ielous *Argus* keepe,
And I am not acquent with *Mercur's* skill,
To lull aud bring his watching eyes aſleepe,
That I may wiſh, and thou may haue thy will:
    Yet till we meet, a conſtant *Hero* proue,
    And whill I liue thou art *Leanders* Loue.

CRAIGE.

To the Kings moſt
Royall Maieſtie.

1. SONET.

Kind *Attalus* in Annals old wee reid,
Was King of *Pergame* by the *Romans* ayde,
  Hee long time brookt the fame, but foraine feid,
  Which made thoſe noble *Romans* to be glad:
And yet becaus hee had no heyrs, 'tis ſayd
Hee to thoſe foreſayd *Romans* did reſigne,
  His Diadem and Crowne, and what he hade
  Hee gaue to them, that erſt made him a King.
Hade I been made no Poet S. but Prince
Of fertill bounds for *Parnaſe* bare and dry,
  Your Grace had gott my Crowne and all long ſince,
  For I laik heyrs, and none more kind then I.
    To vſe thee ſweet inchanting Poets vaine,
      You gaue mee Reuls, I giue you Ryms againe.

Sonet

2. SONET.

ANACREON two dayes two nights did watch,
   Till he return'd *Policrates* againe;
     Thefe Talents two which hee receiud, fond wratch,
     To wake for wealth, and pinch him felfe with paine.
But contrare wayes, I faikes foull am flaine:
I wake for want, and not for wealth allace:
My voyce is hoarfe with cryes; dry is my braine,
Yet get I not the fmalleft graine of grace.
A *Cythared* though poore, did fweetly fing,
Caus *Dionife* did promife him reward.
And thus to thee I wreat moft gratious King,
In hope thy Grace will once my greiffs regard:
     And by my Pen thy prayfes fhall be fpred,
     From ryfing Sunn to his Hefperean bed.

Non omnis moriar.

CRAIGE.

To the Author.

WHY thought fond *Grece* to build a folid fame,
On fleeing fhades of fables pafsing vaine?
Why did her felfe-deceauing fanfie dreame,
That none but fhee, the *Mufes* did maintaine?
Shee fayd, thefe facred Sifters did remaine
Confind within a *Craig* which there did lie,
That great *Apollo* felfe did not difdaine,
For that rough Palace, to renounce the skie:
That there a Well ftill drawne, but neuer dry,
Made Lay-men Poets eir they left the place:
But all were ta'ls, which Fame doth now bely,
And builds vp *Albions* glore, to their difgrace.
    Lo here the *CRAIGE*, whence flow's that facred Well,
    Where *Phœbus* raigns, where all the *Mufes* dwell.

Ro. Aytone.

47

46

THE POETICALL RECREATIONS OF Mr ALEXANDER CRAIG, of Rose-Craig, Scoto Britan.

Otium sine literis mors est, & vivi hominis Sepultura.

ABERDENE,
Printed by Edward Raban,
For David Melvill, 1623.

CVM PRIVILEGIO.

(P A G. 3.)

TO THE MOST
HOPEFVLL, VERTVOVS,
AND NOBLE LORD,
The VVyſe and Matchleſſe
MVSOPHILVS,
GEORGE,
EARLE OF ENYIE,
LORD GORDON, AND
BADYENOCHT, &c.

H E ſubtill Merchandes (moſt Honourable and hopefull Lord) before the Doores and Windowes of their Shoppes, hang out, and expone their worſt Wares, to ſignifie, that they haue better Stuffe of that ſame forte in the Shoppe to ſell: I haue committed to the Preſſe, vnder your Noble Protection and Patrocinie, theſe mine Ephemerid, and Miſcellanean RECREATIONS: Aſſuring your Honour, that

A 2   I haue

I haue better ftuffe (which is yet vnfeene) to prefent you. Accept of them with your accuftomed courtefie: For if you deny, I will fend them defperatlie through the world (like the *Lacedemonian* Baftards) to feeke an Habitation to themfelues. *Evaches*, the *Meffenian* King, confulted at *Delphos*, what event the Warres betwixt the *Spartans* and him fhould take: The anfwere was, If he facrifized a Virgine of his owne Kinred and Blood, the *Meffenians* fhould be victors. *Ariftodemus*, neareft of the Blood Royall, having but one Daughter, would needs facrifize her to the end forefaid. A Citizen farre in loue with the Virgine, (to faue her life) alleadged fhee was with childe vnto him. *Ariftodemus* killeth his Daughter in anger: And though fhe was a true Virgine, yet becaufe he facrificed her in wrath, the King *Evaches* was kild: *Ariftodemus*, his Succeffour, was likewife kild, and the *Meffenians* vtterlie over-throwne. I will not fweare with the Parafiticall *Ægyptians*, *By the lyfe of Pharao*: nor with the Barbarous *Perfians*, *Per Mithram*, which is, *By Phœbus:* nor with *Neftor*, *By Hercules*, becaufe hee loved him beft: But affuredlie, (Noble Lord) belieue the Affertion of an honeft Man, Thefe my RECREATIONS, the Libanotes and Oblations of my loue, are true Virgines, never received Impreffion till now, and in moft fincere loue and affection are facrifized to your Honour. Yea, as *Hercules* at his death left his Bow and Arrowes to *Philoctetes*, as the braveft Archer; So will I henceforth confecrate all my Songes and Poems to Thee: With this kinde Counfell, *Salem*, & *Menfam*, *ne prætereas*, keep the bonds of Friendfhip with the meaneft that loveth and followeth Thee. And for me, fince Thy Vertue hath won me, let Thy Vertue preferue mee ftill.

Thine owne faythfull
and freelie devoted,

Mr ALEXANDER CRAIG,
OF ROSE-CRAIG.

(PAG. 5.)

Ad eundem.

TO Thee, deare Lord, amidſt theſe drierie Tymes,
My dying Muſe vp-reares her drowſie Head.
To Thee ſhee runs, with rude vntutered Rymes,
And leaues the Bed where long ſhee lay as dead.
    A Countrey Mayde ſhee is, and yet Thou knowes her:
    And in Thine Armes to finde refuge ſhee throwes her.

Bee Thou the franke *MECOENAS* to maintaine her
Againſt the force and furie of her Foes.
If Thou defende, ſhee cares not who diſdaine her:
For ſhee muſt ſport in ſpyte of Fortunes Noſe.
    DEMOCRITS *Childe ſhee is, and I dare ſayd,*
    Smyle Thou on her, and ſhee ſhall make Thee glad.

(*PAG. 7.*)

TO THE
READERS.

Pray thee *Critik, Scratch-pate,* and *Find-fault,* suspende thy severe censure of mee, *Tecum habita, & noris quam sit tibi curta supellex.* And thou that vp-braidest mee with a volie of Volumes, which thou haſt read (though I confeſſe to ſmall vſe) remember this, *Plurima qui ſpondent, minimum præſtaſſe videmus.* And thou who (lyke CINADON) canſt not abyde a better Man in SPARTA than thy ſelfe; I wiſh thee (as CINADON, and his Confederates were) to bee ſtripped naked, and whipped to death in the Market place.

Conſilio perit ipſe ſuo conſultor iniquus.

A 4 But cour-

But Courteous and Gentle Reader, to thee alone I come, and betake mee; and with wyſe SENECA I ſay, *Apes debemus imitari, quæ ut vagantur, & ad mel faciendum flores idoneos carpunt, deinde quicquid attulere, diſponunt, ac per favos digerunt: Ita debemus quæcunque ex diverſa lectione congeſsimus ſeparare, melius enim diſtincta cernuntur: Deinde ad debitam facultatem ingenii in unum ſaporem varia illa libamenta confundere ut etiam ſi apparuerit, unde ſumptum eſt, aliud tamen quam unde ſumptum eſt, appareat.*

Reade then my RECREATIONS with Iudgement, and judge with Loue: And ſo fare-well.

Heartilie Fare-vvell.

M. ALEXANDER CRAIG.

THE MISERIE OF MAN.

HE Lyfe of Man is full of Griefe and Sorrow:
Firſt at our Birth we breathe, and next we mourne.
As Day to Night, and Night ſucceedes to Morrow,
Woe followes Woe, to Earth till wee returne.
    EVRIPIDES *did well and wyſelie ſay,*
    Mans Lyfe and Care are Twins, and borne one day.

The Shortnes of Lyfe.

ONe ſome-tyme ask'd DIOGENES, how long
   The woefull lyfe of wretched Man might laſt?
Hee to an Hill aſcendes, with vigour ſtrong,
Lookes round about, and ſtraight deſcendes als faſt:
   And ſo with ſilence gaue this Anſwere plaine,
   The Lyfe of Man is ſhort, and full of paine.

B   Contempt

Contempt of Fortune.

Mans weaker partes are thrall to Fortunes wrong;
The princelie part and portion is our owne:
And doeth alone to Vertue faire belong,
And is (alace) with our confent over-throwne.
 Let Fortune frowne, or fawne; for ſhee is blinde:
 Her power is nought againſt a Vertuous mynde.

POLEMOES REFORMATION.

VVHen drunke POLEMO came to heare the fpeaches
And Leſſons wiſe of ANAXAGORAS,
Of Temperance, and dyet good hee teaches,
To poliſh POLEM: And it came to pas,
 The Leſſon wyſe made him all Wine diſdaine,
 As whilſt hee liv'd, hee was not drunke againe.

POMPEYS MERCIE.

VVHen TIGRANES, the great ARMENIAN King,
With all his power by POMPEY was defeate,
His Royall Crowne and Realmes hee did reſigne,
And for his lyfe hee came in POMPEYS debt:
 But POMPEY ſayde, Keepe all, and ſtill enjoy them;
 I rather make great MONARCHS, than deſtroy them.

NEROES

NEROES CHANGE.

When *NERO* firſt the *ROMANES* did command,
A Man more meeke nor myld might no where bee:
Hee wiſh'd hee could not write, nor put his hand
To ſigne their Bils, who were condem'd to die.
  This laſted not: O Leſſon bad and evill!
  In Youth a Sainct, in Age to proue a Devill.

Difference betwixt a King, and a Tyrant.

Wyſe *ADRIAN* was oft-tymes wont to ſay,
Mercie with Men is deem'd a thing divine:
But chiefelie Kings, who beare chiefe rule and ſway,
To Clemencie and Mercie ſhould incline.
  A King will ſay, I may: and will not doe.
  A Tyrant ſayes, I dare: and then goes too.

The temperance of Epaminondas, King of Thebes.

A *THEBANE* kinde did ſome-time beg and pray,
EPAMINONDAS for his Royall Gueſt:
The King compear'd, and kept the Feaſting day:
Yet liv'd on Bread, and faſted from the Feaſt:
  Then ſayde, (good Friend) I came to thee indeede,
  As Man to eate, not as a Beaſt to feede.

LIBERAL-

(*PAG.* 12.)

LIBERALITIE OF PHOCION.

VVHen *PHILIPS* great vnconquered Sonne had ſende
To *PHOCION* Gifts, and Iewels of great worth;
Hee ſaw them all, and ſent them back in ende:
No Favours, but Refuſals, they brought foorth.
Then ſaid hee to the Legates, Doe not grieue:
I will not take, leſt I forget to giue.

OF THEMISTOCLES.

THEMISTOCLES was wife, and made a Ieſt:
His Sonne did guide his wyfe: his Wyfe bore ſway,
And power ov'r him: hee was in *ATHENS* beſt.
And then all *GRIECE* to *ATHENS* did obey.
Childe, Wyfe, Man, Citie, Countreyes great miſguided,
By weake Degrees, vndone, deſtroy'd, divided.

Nocumenta, Documenta.

SISAMNES was a *PERSIAN* Iudge, wee finde,
Corrupt, and falſe, and did foule Brybes in-bring:
His puniſhment was of a cruell kinde;
Hee was excoriate, by *CAMBISES* King:
But OTHANES, his Sonne, eſchew'd that ſinne,
And learn'd a Leſſon from his Fathers Skinne.

Man is

Man is in Honour, and from thence throwne downe:
Is hee not then excoriate, Skinleſſe, bare?
The Peaſant poore, the Baſe, and Countrey Clowne,
Liues more ſecure, no Downe-fall doeth hee feare.
> *Farre better not beene borne, than haue a Name*
> *Rolde in the bluſhing Rubrickes of blacke Shame.*

To the ignorant Iudge.

Whilſt *IGNORAMVS* on the Bench doth ſit,
   The N and L hee can command at will:
Which argues much, hee hath ſmall ſtore of wit;
Of C and A hee hath no kynde of ſkill:
> *Yet ſits a Iudge, as blinde as Bat or Owle.*
> *Greede PHALERATE, with Pride, muſt play the Foole.*

N. L. Non Liquet: C. Condemnare:
A. Abſolvere, vel Ampliare.

To a diſcredited Courteour.

The Snayle did once the Eagle faire intreate,
   That hee would teach and learne her how to flie;
Her Creeping low, her baſe obſcure eſtate,
Made her of Beaſts the baſeſt Beaſt to bee.
> *The Eagle ſaid, To flie is not thy kinde;*
> *Crawle on thy Wombe, and ſtriue not with the Winde.*

(*PAG.* 14.)

The Snayle at length preuailes with inſtant prayer,
(Wee conquer Heauen with lowde importune Cryes)
Betwixt his Clookes hee cleekes her through the Aire.
Shee on a Rocke, falles, dyes.   The Eagle wyfe
  Bids Snayles, FARE-WELL; *for henceforth hee'll forſweare them;*
  They ſhould not flie, that haue not wings to beare them.

ALIVD.

THe Forreſt Aſſe vndaunted did beholde
  A tamed Colt, fat, faire, and brauelie dreſt,
Did eate at eaſe, ſecure, and vncontrolde;
Of Aſſes all hee helde him then the beſt:
  But through the Fieldes as hee by chance did range,
  Within ſhort ſpace hee ſpyes a ſudden change.

A loathſome Loade was laide vpon his Backe;
A Cudgell ſtiffe his Maſter had in Hand:
And with each ſtep hee ſtrypes, and threates his wracke;
Till time the Beaſt could neyther ſtirre, nor ſtand:
  So hee who ſeem'd the happieſt as of late,
  His Maſter beates, and beares him at debate.

By this example anie man may ſee,
As in a Mirrour, or a Looking-Glaſſe,
How braue ſo er'e thoſe Beaſtes appeare to bee,
The greateſt Courteour, is the greateſt Aſſe:
  Fooles ſudden riſe, and headlongs fall from Glorie,
  Are Wyſe-mens Leſſons, and their laughing Storie.
                                        HERODIAS

HERODIAS AND SALOME.

IOHN *BAPTIST* tolde drunke *HEROD*, hee defilde
His Soule, who kept his Brother *PHILIPS* Wife;
HERODIAS taught *SALOME*, her Childe,
To daunce, and rob the Prophet of his lyfe:
    Thus twixt the Daughter, and the divelish Dame,
    GODS servant dies, to HERODS lasting shame.

But *HERODS* House was sack't, and swept away;
A sure Example to the comming Ages;
That such as hee, shall come to sad decay,
And reape of Lust, and Blood, the wofull Wages:
    For crying sinnes, ere King and Countrey mourne,
    Let HAMAN hang, let BAVDS and HARLOTS burne.

Tigellini Epitaphium, Qui sero & inhonesto exitu mortem sibi conscivit.

VVHo seem'd so sure, as hee who late departed?
    (Proude *TIGELLIN*) in his, and each mans eyes;
Yet vnawares decourted, and decarted,
To shift a Iurie his owne Burreau dies:
    For all his pryde, loe how it comes to passe;
    Hee liv'd a Tiger, and hee died an Asse.

TO PHILOCOSMVS.

THe Graffe-hopper hath wings, but cannot flie:
  The Wretch hath Wealth, no richer yet is hee.
MIDAS defir'd *APOLLO*, that hee would
Turne each thing (which his hand did touch) in Golde.
  Hee had his Wifh; the Mifers mynde was ferved;
  Meate touch'd by him, turn'd Golde: Thus MIDAS ftarved.

ALIVD.

HEe's good enough, if hee haue Goods anew,
  Thinks *PHILOCOSMVS* with himfelfe in vaine,
By Violence or Fraude, and Trickes vntrue,
(As Perjuries or Pupils) hee makes gaine.
  With Coyne, which hee (for felling CHRIST) did winne,
  Hee'll buy a Fielde, to burie Strangers in.

PHILOCOSMVS EPITAPH.

STay Pilgryme, ftay, if thou fo curious bee,
  As Pilgrymes are, what's heere inclof'd to kno:
Draw nearer then, and I fhall let thee fee;
Heere lyes a Thiefe, to Trueth and Vertue Foe;
  Belov'd of none, believ'd of none; who made
  His Golde his God, a Prey for DIS, lyes dead.

TO

TO CHREMES.

The God of Wealth, *PLVTVS* and *PLVTO* ſtroue,
  Whoſe man ſhould Godleſſe-guttiſh *CHREMES* bee.
A Reference was made to mightie *IOVE* ;
Who pleaſing both, gaue thus-wayes his Decree,
  Whilſt CHREMES liues, let him bee PLVTVS Man;
  But when hee dies, let PLVTO take him than.

Tranſlatio liberior.

LItigat, & multum Plutus Plutona *fatigat,*
    Cui ſervus Crhemes *dives inopſque foret*
Inque ſinu exultat nequam, quod Tartara terris
    Miſceat, & ſuperent Dæmona divitiæ:
Indicioque Iovis *cauſam ſubmittit uterque*
    Ille (nocens nulli) dividit Imperium.
Pluti *vivus erit, moriens* Plutona *ſequetur,*
    Quique dolo ditat, poſtea ditis erit.

Ad eundem.

The Partridge ſtores her Neſt with Eggs all ſtowne,
  Which ſhee ne're layde : But when the Birds are hatched,
The Mother true doth call away her owne :
All from the Thieviſh Step-dame are diſpatched.
  So Goods ill got, and heapt by Stealth together,
  And meanes vnjuſt, lyke IONAS Gowrd ſhall wither.

C   ALIVD

ALIVD.

Raw Meates make Stomackes ficke, and ftill doe lye,
Beftinking Breath, till they bee caft againe:
So Goodes ill got, by Craft, or Blood, will crye;
The Confcience ftill vnquiet muft remaine.
*Vnrighteoufneffe may builde the Houfe; but long
It fhall not ftand, till't finke for Sinne and Wrong.*

PANVRGVS.

Panurgus pryes in high and low Effaires;
Hee talkes of Foraine, and our Civill State:
But for his owne hee neyther countes nor cares;
That hee refers to Fortune, and his Fate.
*His neighbours faultes, ftraight in his Face hee'll finde,
But in a Bag hee hangs his owne behinde.*

MARGITES.

I Reade of one Margites, yet I kno
The Knaue is long fince dead: but fuch another,
As lewde a Lowne I feeme to fee. And fo
Margites liues, or then Margites Brother:
*Falfe, factious, fraudfull, neyther plowes, nor digs,
Robs Poore, treads Weake, from Rich hee begs, and thigs.*

To a

To a rude and barbarous Boore,
vvho vvronged the Author.

SOme rude, vnruelie, barbrous Boores there bee,
Chiefe Foes to PHŒBUS, and the MUSES nine;
Will counterfeite AURANTIUS prowde: for hee
Wrong'd SANAZAR, the Poët moſt divine:
Both Towne and Towre deſtroyde, in fearce despight,
Faire MERGELLINA, SANAZARS *Delight.*

Th'ov'r-partied Poët winked at the VVrong,
And his Revenge remitted to the LORD,
The GOD of HOSTES. Then newes were ſpread ere long,
AURANTIUS prowde was vanquiſht, kilde, and goard.
HEAVENS, grant all ſuch a ſudden ſhamefull ende,
That dare preſume a Poët to offende.

And let their Bodies bee embrewed ſtill,
Till Earth drinke vp their Blood, And loathe their ſtinke:
At STIX let CHARON grant them no good-will,
Till hundreth yeares they byde about that Brinke.
And when their Friends their Epitaph ſhall reade,
Let it heape Shame vpon their Childrens head.

The Authors Conſolation.

TAke Courage, CRAIG, though Thou be wrong'd too farre,
With Criminations of a curious Crew;
Whoſe murthering Mouthes, doe what they dow or dare,
To compaſſe thee with Scandales moſt vntrue.
With much a-doe firſt Paſsious are with-ſtood;
But in this point, let Patience doe thee good.

For ſince

For since their Mouth is but a Mint of Lyes,
To forge false Coyne, whose passage will bee stayde,
When it encounters with considering Eyes,
And in the Ballance of pure Trueth survayde.
    Looke to thy Wayes, and let the Wicked lye:
    Make Conscience good, continuall Feast to thee.

Apologie for Poets, against

OF all those Trees which VESTAES Wombe brings foorth,
    How fertile, faire, and braue so-e're they bee;
The famous Fig is helde of greatest worth,
And beares the best, and sweetest Fruit, wee see:
    And for this cause there is on Earth no Tree,
    Except the Fig, that scapes from Thunder free.

A Thunder strange is threatned now of new,
Gainst such as stood in favour once a-day:
Of Poëts yet the number is but few,
Whose Songs are sweet, lyke Figs, and last for aye:
    Whilst barren Birkes, Oakes, Firre, are throwne at vnder,
    Let Poëts bee, lyke Fig-trees, free from Thunder.

Barbare Musarum Phœbique inimice, quid obstat,
    Quin Musæ hostes sint, hostis Apollo tibi?
Insequitur vindicta nefas, mea penna merenti,
    Sera licet dederit verbera, sæva dabit.

                                               Amicus

*Amicus magis necessarius quam Aqua
& Ignis.*

WEll was it faide, A Friende that's kynde and true,
More needfull is, than eyther Fire or Water:
And there bee ftore of Stories olde, (of new
But few, or none, alace) to prove the Matter.
    DAMON *turnes* DEMON, *and Deceit hee loves*;
    And PYTHIAS, PYTHON, *poyfning Serpent proves.*

TO MVSOPHILVS.

BEloved Friende, I kindlie doe commende
  Thefe lyfeleffe Litures to Thy louelie Lookes:
For if a Poët may be trowde, they're penn'd
By him who's Thine, but Shiftes, Deceites, or Crookes:
    Who wifheth all thy Wifhes, but respect
    Of Friende or Foe, to take their full effect.

And when thofe Wifhes full effects haue found,
And Thy faire Hopes, which fraught with Hazardes beene,
With Iffues fweete, and true Contents are crown'd,
And Thou on top of Fortunes Wheele art feene,
    Bee not lyke Her, vnconftant, wavering, blinde;
    But to thy Friends (and honeft CRAIG*) bee kinde.*

A Coun-

A Counsell to his married Friend.

IF Thou with Fashiones of thy Wife offende,
Teach her with reason, or, (to ende the stryfe)
Learne to dissemble what thou canst not mende;
At small faults winke, if thou wouldst win thy Wyfe:
    Else of thine House thou mak'st a Prison strong;
    Thy rest vnrest, thy selfe a common Song.

To a libidinous Levi.

I See fonde Lust, with most vnlawfull Heate,
Doth melt thy Flesh, and burne thy Bones away:
'Tis shame to see a Sage, in such estate,
To preach the Trueth, and practise quite astray.
    With Tyme and Hunger Lust may bee with-stood:
    If not by those, an Halter would doe good.

To the Frontispice of Abakuk Bissets Booke, *Of the Olde Monuments of Scotland.*

TWixt Was, and Is, how various are the Ods!
What one Man doth, another doth vndoe:
One consecrates Religious Workes to Gods,
Another leaues sad Wrackes, and Ruines now.
    Thy Booke doth shew, that such, and such things were,
    But would to GOD that it could say, They are.

                                               VVhen I

When I pererre the South, North, Eaſt, and Weſt,
And marke (alace) each Monument amis;
Then I conferre Tymes preſent with the paſt;
I reade what was, but cannot ſee what is:
  I prayſe thy Booke with wonder, but am ſorie,
  To reade olde Ruines in a recent Storie.

TO THE COVRT OF PARLIAMENT 1621,
In Favours of the Subſidie deſired by His Majeſtie.

Giue Cæſar what is Cæſars; CHRIST did ſo;
Yet had no Coyne, till from a Fiſh hee found it,
By PETERS Angle: VVho dare then ſay No,
To render Tribute, if the Prince demand it?
  Who diſobeyes to pay a Tribute due,
  Is neyther CHRISTIAN, *nor a Subject true.*

To the Cauſdickes, who were made tributarie in the ſaid Court.

ARe wyſe Cauſidickes brought to ſuch a ſtraite,
At this great Court, as they are forc'd to yeelde,
And loſe the Freedome of their faire Eſtate,
And with their Tongues (chiefe Weapons) tyne the Fielde?
  Hence-foorth fare-well the force of Actes and Lawes:
  Who loſe their owne, ſhall ſeldome pleade my Cauſe.

C 4   TO HIS

(PAG. 24.)

To His Majesties Queſtors, for his Penſion.

BRaue BRUTUS begg'd a Loafe, to ſaue his Lyfe;
And from the Foes, which hee beſieg'd, receiv'd it.
Kynde Enemies forgetting former Stryfe,
Gaue Bread to hungrie BRUTUS, when hee crav'd it.
*I feare no Foe, and ſo ſuſpect no Wrong;
But ſeeke my Loafe, for which I ſerved long.*

ALIVD.

I Am no fayned *IEBVSITE*, for I
Haue travell'd farre, and haue true Cauſe to crye:
My Shooes are clowted, and my Cloathes are worne:
My Bread is mowl'd, my Bottell toome and torne.
*If I goe Home worſe than I came abroad,
Heere is no loue to Man, nor fcare of GOD.*

ALIVD.

OVr *QVESTORS* learn'd their Arithmeticke ill:
Three parts they know, the fourth they quite neglect:
They adde, ſubſtract, and multiplie at will:
In ſub-diviſion there is groſſe defect.
*Is Ignorance their fault? O no. What than?
The Chiragra: they will not, though they can.*

ALIVD

A L I V D.

ONce more one poore Petition I prefent;
  Marre not the Mufes, Mightie MARR, I pray:
Such as to Muficke haue a mynde full bent,
Will faue the facred Mufes from decay.
  The Dittie giues the Diapafon grace:
  Bee Friende to both; for now fits Tyme and Place.

Reply to a Dilatorie Anfwere, fent
by Sir Gedeon, &c. to the Author.

YOur Sub-Receiver fhew'd mee, you were forie,
  You could not fo difpatch mee as you would;
And tolde mee on, with ftambring Tongue, a Storie,
Scarfe vnder-ftood, when it was ten tymes tolde.
  This difference I put betwixt you two,
  Hee's fhort in Words, and you in Deedes are flow.

AD QVESTORES.

O What an Age is this, in which wee liue!
  Our Annuals are annumbred to our Stocke:
Wee dare not touch them, fhould wee ftarue, and grieue:
The Debitor detaines both Stocke and Brocke;
  And hath a Law to warrand his detaining,
  Which breedes our Wants, and barres vs from Complaining.

D   And

And which is worfe, beholde how Shepheards were
Abhominable t' ÆGYPTIANS in their Land:
Poore Penfioners muft ftand affrayde, afarre,
With heavie Heart, light Purfe, and emptie Hand.
 To want our Profites, and our Penfions too,
 VVhat more, or worfe, can Foes, or Tyrantes doe?

TO STATES-MEN.

THere was a Tyme when Thieves had leaue to fteale,
 And wreft their Wits to anie Wrong they can:
And were they not attatch'd, then all went well;
A cunning Thiefe was helde a fkilfull Man:
 But were hee found to haue a Fang, by Voces
 Of juft Affyfe, a Rope did ende the Proces.

I am no *SINDICKE*, worth a Pin, to fynde
With curious Eye th' Abufes of our State:
If anie bee, I am not of that mynde;
For I determe, no Dittaes to delate:
 But I pray GOD, *each Statef-man, Great and Small,*
 May take Example by his Fellowes Fall.

HYMERA olde, the *SIRACVSAN* Dame,
For *DIONISE*, the Tyrant proude, did pray:
Whom each man curft; (then Tyrants had no fhame:
The laft was worft) Thus farre with her I'll fay,
 Our Senate wyfe, LORD *bleffe from each mifhap;*
 Few fonnes haue Heads to fill their Fathers Cap.

ALIVD

ALIVD.

THe Royall Throne of *SALOMON* the Wyſe,
Was carv'd and cut with Lyons everie-where:
No Raven of rapt, nor Birde with craftie Cryes,
No greedie Wolves, nor Beaſts of Prey were there.
  Let Stateſ-men thus in ſhew proue Lyons graue;
  Not prone to prey, nor ſubtill to deceiue.

Mamertes Anſwere to a Paraſite.

ONe tolde *MAMERTES*, hee was happie thryſe,
Who had in *CORINTH* of true Friends ſuch ſtore.
MAMERTES to that Paraſite replyes,
If *FORTVNE* frowne, Friends ſhall bee found no more:
  Yea, to bee plaine, thoſe ſeeming Friends you ſee,
  Are Friends to my good Fortune, not to mee.

Of Timæa, Queene of Sparta.

TIMÆA faire, was *LACEDEMONS* Queene,
Yet ſhee defyl'd King *AGIS* Royall Bed;
Lay with a Stranger, erſt vnknowne, vnſeene;
Was oſtraciſm'd, and had from *ATHENS* fled.
  Shee bore a Sonne, the Seede of Sinne and Shame;
  And LEOTICHID was the Baſtards Name.

Yet *LEOTICHID* looked to bee crown'd,
When *AGIS* died. *TIMÆA*, foolifh Hoore,
Tolde, *ALCIBIAD* got him. Thus renown'd
AGESILA did *SPARTANS* Crowne procure.
VVomen are weake, and Veffels fonde, and frayle;
But hang the Hoore keepes neyther Tongue nor Tayle.

To the Cowfner.

THe Cowfner lookes with faire, but fraudfull, face,
   And Locuft-lyke a fting is in his Tayle:
(How Tragicall was fonde *PERILLVS* cafe,
In his Inventions who did fall and fayle ?)
   Let him alone lyke ABSOLON bee left,
   Twixt Heaven and Earth, that vfeth Fraude and Sheft.

To the Swearer.

THe wyfe *ÆGYPTIANS* punifh'd him who fware,
   With loffe of lyfe; The *GRECIANS* braue nor they
More mercifull, did crop the Swearers Eare;
Till falfe *LYSANDER* fcrap'd that Law away.
   Oathes ftryue with Wordes in number now, wee fee.
   The greateft Oathe preceeds the greateft Lie.

To the

To the Envyous.

ENVY doth creepe, where as it dare not goe,
And fees each thing, (lyke th' Eye) it felfe it fees not:
It feedes on Foode moft delicate; for loe,
It eates the owners Heart, from thence it flies not:
It brings the wretched Mafter to decay,
And ÆTNA-LIKE confumes in Fire away.

To the moft Noble, and Vertuous Lord,
SIR GEORGE HAY
OF KILFAWNES,
Great Chancellar of Scotland.

THe good fucceffe of *SYLLAES* great Effaires,
Made him to brag, that hee was Fortunes Chylde.
When Cæfars Pilote in a Storme fhed Teares,
And prayde for Windes more mercifull and mylde,
Feare not (faid Cæfar) make no more a-doe,
Thou carrieft Cæfar, and his Fortunes too.

AVGVSTVS wifh'd, the Heavens to him fhould giue,
With *SCIPIOES* Valour, *POMPEYS* Loue, but ftill
His owne good Fortune. Long tyme mayft Thou liue,
With Valour, Loue, and Fortune at Thy will.
Lyke SYLLA, Cæfar, and AVGVSTVS graue,
Let Fortune blinde, to Thy braue Mynde bee Slaue.

Ad Eundem.

WHo thinks dame Fortune blinde, and fpoylde of Eyes,
And fpyes our Peace, our State, hath little Skill:
For loe, King I A M E S, Good, Holie, Great and Wyfe,
Doth guide and rule her rowling Wheele at will.
Now good Men finde Preferment, Vertue Price:
Rods are the Fooles Rewards, and Strypes for Vice.

SATYRA VOLANS.

GOe, Swift-wing'd S A T Y R E, through all States, but feare,
Though thou a bafe and thankleffe Errand beare:
Goe thou Poft-hafte, & through all Hazards hye thee;
TRUETH is thy Warrand; Nip them that come nye thee;
Paffe King and Prince, with Prayfing, and with Praying:
And if to Court thou goe, make little Staying:
Yet tell thus much, to all, though it fhould wrong them,
There's but fmall Trueth and Honeftie among them:
And hee that's helde in moft Refpect, by all,
His Fellowes waite, and long to fee him fall.
                                          Tell Church,

Tell CHURCH, 'tis full of Shifme, vaine Pryde, and Greede;
They teach what's good, but doe no good in-deede.
Tell Noble-men, *They* are prowde Tyrants growne;
Ere they lacke Practife, they'll oppreffe their owne.
Tell fome Ignoble Nobles in their Faces,
They are not worthie of their Fathers Places.
Tell to the beft, *They* act but others Actions,
And vexe their Neighbours to beare out their Factions.
Tell Rich men, Riches would bee well employed;
Thofe that haue Much, haue manie to deftroy it.
Tell wretched CHREMES, His example heere,
Makes manie faft, where they haue got good Cheare:
The Traine retrainfh'd, the Table curt and fhort,
Sad Solitude, where I haue feene refort.
The Wrath of GOD confume that worthleffe Worme,
Who firft began this lewde and pinching Forme.
Hee lookes a Man fo hungrie in the Face,
As hee would eate him raw, and nere fay GRACE.
Tell fubtill Merchandes, *T*hey're perjur'd Exporters
Of needfull thinges; vnprofitable Importers
Of needleffe thinges, which men buy head-longes, rafh,
As Scalerigs, Wyne, Tobacko, and fuch Trafh.
Tell thofe who ftill attende Effaires of State,
They keepe no Place, nor Greatneffe, without Hate.
Tell, Knowledge wanting Zeale, is nothing worth;
And Zeale but Knowledge, many Shifme brings foorth.
Pray Iudges haue but two, not dowble, Eares;
Some fay, Their Hand, chiefe Organe, fees, groapes, heares.
Tell, Lawyers are the Children of Horfe-lieches,
Which crye, Giue, giue, and make great Gaine by Speaches:
Their chieffeft Sporte, is but to fow Diffention,
And builde their States by Crooks, Delayes, Contention.
Tell Clerkes and Writers, They are farre from ill:
Yet Scrybes of olde expon'd the Lawes at will.
Tell Phyficke-mongers, Drogs are growne vnfure,
And manie Doctors rather kill, than cure.

D 4   Tell th' Vfurer

(*PAG.* 32.)

Tell th' Vfurer, His Gaine for Money lent,
Is but maintainde by Actes of Parliament,
And Parables. It cannot bee with-ftood,
The Talent dowbled, was helde fervice good.
Tell, Zeale is blinde : Tell Loue is turn'd to Luft:
Tell fainting Age, it waftes : tell Flefh 'tis DUST.
Tell Youth, it takes in moft exceffiue meafure,
In Borthels lewde, and Taverns too much pleafure.
Tell Beautie braue, 'tis but admir'd a-while,
And fondlie prayf'd in Poëts franticke Stile.
Tell great Men, that, One Parafite, One Knaue,
Will make them lofe the trueft Friende they haue.
Nip Fortune to the quicke ; tell fhee is blinde.
Tell PITHIAS too, To DAMON hee's vnkinde.
Tell, Trueth hath left the Citie in a Grudge,
And in the Countrey finds but fmall Refuge.
Bid the Satyricke Find-fault Poët, Take him
To fome more Lucrous Trade: his Vane will wracke him.
Hee hath good Wits, and yet a Foole doth fpende them:
Fit to finde Faults, but moft vnfit to mende them.
Thus having runne, and rayl'd, till all admire Thee,
Fall on thy Face, beg Pardon, and retire thee.

AD LECTOREM CANDIDVM.

Multa pererravi, fed non erraſse videbor,
Errorum numeros, ſi numerare vacat.

SATYRVLA

SATYRVLA
IN PLEBEM.

Experience, long, and deare, hath made mee finde,
Nothing is more vnsure than Vulgare Minde.
All Commons are (Quicke-Silver-lyke) vnstable,
Fawning, and frowning, at each franticke Fable.
For Loue to day They'll crowne a Man a King,
Dethrone to morrow, for a naughtie thing.
Iust ARISTIDES, who rul'd ATHENS long,
Was ostracism'd, for being good: strange wrong.
THEMISTOCLES from GRECE made XERXES flie,
Who in exyle, amongst his Foes, must die.
To crowne SEIANVS Cæsar now they'r bent;
But in an houre hee is to Prison sent.
ANTIOCHVS in one day was saluted
A gracious Prince: a Tyrant straight reputed.
As blinde as HOMER was, in Iest and Scorne,
Hee could compare the Commons to the Corne:
Heere comes a puffe of Winde, on this side blowes it:
There comes another Blast, contrarelie throwes it.
To raging Billoes of the Waues vnruelie,
The Peoples nature is compared truelie.

(PAG. 34.)

Thofe Mouthes at firſt which did *OSANNA* crie,
Cryde, Crucifie, and let BARABBAS free.
The Mariner may as well wrap the Winde,
And in his Sayles, till his next Voyage binde,
As can a King, in anie modeſt Meaſure,
The Multitude command, and rule at pleaſure.
It is the LORD, who onlie May, Can, Will
The Windes, the Waues, and Peoples madneſſe ſtill.

GOD SAVE THE KING.

I. R.

Pronior in plebem, (ſi non ingrata fuiſſet)
Antea nullus erat, poſtea nullus erit.

The Authors Reſolution.

THe Nightingale, when ſhee hath ſtor'd her Neſt,
   With Feathers warme, feedes, ſleepes, & ſings no more:
Our Poëts ſo (who ſometyme ſung) take reſt,
Since they haue got their States inſtaur'd with Store.
   But I will ſing, even to the day I dye;
   Birds to themſelues make Mirth, and ſo ſhall I.

Roſipetræ

*Rosipetræ meæ ad Imitationem Psophidii
Arcadiensis descriptio.*

*A Ngulo in augusto terræ, fructusque ferenti
    Largos, Psophidius prædia parva colit:
Contentus parvo, minimaque cupidine fœlix
    Nil capit ille magis, nil cupit ille minus.*

ALTERA.

*P Arva domus, bene cultus ager, nec inepta supellex,
    Innumeras mihi fert parvula ripa Rosas:
Hic juga Parnassi, fontesque Heliconis, & umbræ,
    Sic habito, & mecum carmina blanda cano.*

Finis, quod Mr A^r Craig.

36

THE
PILGRIME
AND HEREMITE,
In forme of a Dialogue,

By Master *Alexander Craig.*

Imprinted in ABERDENE, *By* EDWARD
RABAN, *for David Melvill.* 1631.

TO THE RIGHT HONOV-
RABLE, WYSE, AND VER-
tuouſlie diſpoſed Gentleman,
WILLIAM FORBES of TOLQVHON.

RIGHT HONOVRABLE,

Aving collected the diſperſed, and long neglected Papers, of this ſubſequent Poëſie, the Poſthumes of a worthie Penne, for preſerving them from periſhing, for the Perfections of the Departed, maker of immortall memorie; who was one of the Faythfull, affectionate, (and re-affected) Favourers of the honourable Houſe of BAMFE, wherevnto Your ſelfe, and Yours, by a faythfull Affection, and affectionate Affinitie, are vnſeparably tied. And alſo, Sir, for the ſingular and ever bound duetie, wherevnto by many Obliedgements, and vnſpeakable Reſpects, I ever acknowledge my ſelfe to be vnterminably tied, to loue, ſerue, and honour, You and Yours, and to doe all that my poſsibilitie can performe, to the eternitie of Your Name, Houſe, and Honour. Herefore, Sir, I haue taken the boldnes, after the Author's expiring, to publiſh, and preſent, his Papers to Your Honours Hands, to paſſe vnder the Patrocinie and Protection of Your honourable Name. Receiue, therefore, Sir, this fatherles Orphane, vnder the Shield and Shadow of Your powerfull protection, & courteous acceptation: and

¶ 2   as hee

Epistle Dedicatorie.

as hee presenteth to Your view a wandring Pilgrime, *and a retired* Heremite, *both Despisers of the fleeting* Pleasures, *and flitting* Ritches *of this wretched World, whervpon most wretchedly so many doe doate: So, Sir, let the same call vs to mynd, what we are here, and what we should ayme to bee heereafter; that as wee are* Pilgrimes *on earth, wee may bee* Citizens *in Heaven; this being our way, but Aboue, our natiue Countrey; here our travell, there our rest; heere our race, there our prize; heere our fight, there our triumph; here our seed-time, there our harvest; and as wandring Pilgrimis here our Innes only, from whence we must remoue, but there our home, and mansion place, wherein we must remayne. In this estate then, Sir, let worldly things be but our* Viaticum, *which we should vse, as if we vsed them not: and let vs neyther be cloyed with their loue, nor clogged with their cares; but seeke those things that are aboue, & to temper the edge of our eager distractions, about many thinges with* Martha, *let vs with* Marie *consider that one thing which is necessarie; and requite, in some measure, that loue which CHRIST IESVS hath carried and kythed towards vs; not as this poore* Heremite *was with disdayne of her whom hee affected, but with mutuall tender affection, and a Christian care to keepe His Commandements; whereby we shall gayne to our selues, more than the greatest Conquerours, or busiest Worldlings, could ever acquire; even a glorious Kingdome, and a Crowne incorruptible. To the advancement whereof, Sir, both of you and yours, after manie and happie dayes heere, as my earnest Petition to GOD shall bee; so in all other thinges I haue vowed to remayne*

Your Honours, in all serviceable
and obsequious duetie,
ROBERT SKENE.

THE PILGRIME AND
HEREMITE,
In forme of a Dialogue.

WHen pale Ladie *LVNA*, with her lent light,
Through the dawning of the Day was driven to depart
And the cleare chriftall Sky banifhed the Night,
And the red morning rofe from the right airt;
Long ere the fond Childe, with Whip in his hand,
From his flight fleepe awoke, to lighten the Land;
   Twixt the Night and the Day,
   In my fleepe as I lay,
   Amidft my Dreame this fray
   And fairlie I fand:
Apparelled as a *Pilgryme*, with Staffe in mine hand,
Foorth the day as I went, vndriven bout a guyde,
Mee thought in a laigh Lay, a cleare Streame, a Strand,
A broade Bufh of Birke trees, by a Brooke fyde:
And hoping fome *Heremite* made there repare,
As faft as my feete might, forward I fare.
   Through a Wood as I fought,
   To a Bufh was I brought,
   Which Nature her felfe wrought,
   Withoutten airts lare.
Through the Wood as I went, halfe will of waine,
A Cell to my fharpe fight can fhortlie appeare:
A quyet and a colde Caue, a Cabine of ftone,
I drew me darne to the doore, fome din to heare.
And as I lent to my Lug, this well I heard,
How long fhall I loathed liue? I loue bout reward.
   And when I knew by the din,
   Some wight was therein,
   To waxe bolde I begin,
   And no perill fpar'd.
     A   As I

The Pilgrime and Heremite.

As I went through the floore of that colde Caue,
I well efpyed in the darke where the noyfe founded,
An hoarfe hoarie *Heremite*, grieved and graue,
Whofe boyling Breaſt nought but blacke baile abounded,
Whofe colour, countenance, and pale deadlie hew,
His whole hidden Harmes there and griefes foorth ſhew:
   Whose tumbling teares *bout ceafe, * *or*, without
   Lyke floods flowed over his face;
   With manie long lowde alace,
   And fad fighes anew.
Yet ſtoutlie hee ſtart vp, and ſtared in my face,
And craved how I there came? or who was my guyde?
By *Fortune*, quod I, thus fell the cafe,
Through the wild way as I went I wandered afyde,
And by a private plaine path I came to this Wood,
Wherein I wiſt well fome *Heremite* was hid.
   But fince I am heere brought,
   If that I offended ought,
   By the Blood that mee bought,
   I'll obey as yee bid.
A *Pilgryme*, quod hee, you feeme by your weede,
And a ſtrayed ſtranger, if I right weine:
But fince you are heere come, fo GOD mot mée fpéede,
Thou art welcome to fuch as you haue héere féene:
But yet of my treatment I trow yee ſhall tyre,
For neyther haue I Meate, Drinke, good Bed, nor Fyre.
   On raw Rootes is my Food,
   I drinke of the freſh Flood;
   On Fog and greene Graffe good,
   All night lyes my lyre.
Then helde I the *Heremite* with faire wordes anew,
And for his franke offring great thankes I him gaue:
And when I well tryde that his tale was all trew,
The caufe of his comming there ſhortlie I craue,
The caufe of my comming heere, *Pilgryme*, quod hee?
And with that the falt teares fell in his eye:
   Alace its for the loue of ane,
   For whofe fake thus I am ſlaine:
   A Martyr héere I remaine
   By fatall decrée.
           In faith

The Pilgrime and Heremite.

In faith, friend, quod I then, I faw by thy fong,
When at the colde Caue doore darned I ftood:
Some Sainct of the Shée fexe had wrought thee all this wrong,
And thou hadft long lived in loue, and yet vnlov'd:
And of the long letter this laft line I heard,
How long fhall I lothed liue? I loue *bout Reward,   *For bout
    Whereby I well knew,   *vnderftand*
    That thy Dame was vntrue;   without
    Thy pale and wan hew
    Foorth fhew thou waft fnar'd.
Alace! quod the *Heremite*, I lived once to loue;
But now drowned in Defpare, I fee my death dieft:
Though both Will and Wit would, I may not remoue,
I lye in the links of Loue fettered fo faft:
And all my Care-féeming-Swéets, are fo mixt with Sowrs,
That each moment almoft appeareth ten hours.
    Thus liue I héere alone,
    In this colde Caue of ftone,
    As next neighbour vnto none,
    But Trees, Fowls, and Flowrs.
And thus in my darke Den I mynde to remayne,
As bound Bead-man to Her that workes all my woe;
Till Death with his Dart come put mee from payne:
Elfe *Atropus* cutting quyte the Threed in two,
And on the greene growing Barke of each blooming Tree,
This Diton indorfed fhall well written bee:
    In forrow and fight flayne,
    For Her heere I remayne,
    Who lykes of another ane,
    Much more than of mee.
Fond *Heremite*, quod I then, thy loue would appeare
Too high to bée placed aboue thy degree:
And thy fond foolifh hope, frozen with feare,
And *Fortune*, thy *Olde Friend*, thy *New Enemie*.
For fhee whom thou beft loveft, as thy felfe fayes,
As reafonleffe, and ruethleffe, refpects thee nowayes.
    Thy fyle is her fight;
    Thy duill, her delight;
    And thy payne to defpight,
    Shee pleafantlie playes.
                    Whereby

The Pilgrime and Heremite.

Whereby it well ſeemes, thy labour is loſt,
And vnto thy graue thou'lt goe, ere thou get her.
Mad man! why mak'ſt thou thyne enemie thy hoſpe?
Die not a foole, man; for Gods ſake forget her.
For, put caſe, in hope to obtayne thy deſyres,
Thou die heere for want of Bed, Food, and Fyres:
   Then who ſhall bee ſeene,
   To louk thy dead Eine?
   And intombe thee, I weine,
   As cuſtome requyres?
Leaue, then, thy Heremitage, and this colde Caue,
And liue no more in loue, ſince thou art not lov'd:
But follow mee, and take part as I haue:
Companie and counſell may doe thee ſome good.
For *Don-Diëgo* had died in Deſart,
Wert not *Rodorico* did him there convert.
   Thus, it may fall ſo,
   That I thy *Rodorico*,
   May finde eaſe to thy woe,
   And heale thy hurt Heart.
Speake, Pilgrime, quod hee, of things that may bee,
Or that hath appearance, to take ſome effect:
For, ſuch is my faintneſſe, I want force to flee,
Loue, Fortune, Death, haue given ſuch a checke.
Betwixt Wit and Will there is great debate;
The one with the other ſtryving for the ſtate.
   Flee Loue, quod my Wit.
   Stay, ſayes my Will yet.
   So I byde; ſo I flit.
   So I loue: ſo I hate.
But where thou wouldſt ſeeme to ſalue all my ſore,
And by thy ſtrait ſtatutes to ſtay all my ſturt;
Meddle with that matter, good Pilgrime, no more,
Since all mine health hangeth on her that mee hurt.
The Coale that mee burnes to the bone, will I blow,
Though Liver, Lungs, and Lights, fly vp in a low,
   Since ſhee doeth decree it,
   That I die, ſo bee it;
   I long till I ſee it:
   Let Death bend his Bow.
          Vayne

The Pilgrime and Heremite.

Vayne wretch, quod I then, caſt off thy vowed Weeds,
And wander no more in this wilde Wilderneſſe:
It may bee thy Miſtres, that deare Dame, bee dead,
For whoſe ſwéete ſake daylie that dieſt in diſtreſſe:
Perchance before that thou her againe ſee,
By vote of the Wan-weirds, that buried ſhee bee.
   Or put caſe, thy Dame deare,
   Hath choſen a new Pheare,
   Thou wouldſt deſpare to ſee her,
   That ſo lightlies thee.
Or contrarywyſe, good Heremite, ſuppone
Thy Miſtres this moment hath good minde of thee;
And for thy long abſence maketh great moane,
And from her heart wiſheth her leile loue to ſee:
Saying in her ſelfe, Would God I wiſt where
My poore pyned Patient doeth make his repare.
   Wiſt I well, ſo I thryue,
   That hee were yet alyue,
   I ſhould bee no wights wyue
   For ten yeares, and maire.
Conceit with thy ſelfe, good Heremite, I pray,
If thy Dame bee dead, thou wéep'ſt but in vaine.
Thou art a ſtarke Stocke, heere ſtill for to ſtay,
And mourne for the loſſe that mendes not thy moane.
For if ſhee ſome other reſpect more than thee,
What grace canſt thou get, in duill heere to die?
   Or wouldſt thou thy trueth,
   Should reape reward of rueth?
   Why ſlipſt thou ſo with ſleuth,
   The thing that may bee?
Good Pilgrime, ſaide hee then, of theſe two I ſee,
As you ſeeme to conclude, the one muſt bee true:
Shee loathes, or ſhee loues: a mids may not bee,
As to my paines I may prooue by ſignes anew.
For my beloved Loue, my deare daintie Dame,
Deſpiſeth thoſe Elements which ſpell my poore Name.
   VVoe is mee, if I mint,
   To forge Floods from the Flint,
   My true travell ſhall bee tint,
   Such Friendſhip to frame.
           But

The Pilgrime and Heremite.

But you would fay, that Death, drierie Death!
Perhaps, hath abrogate my deare Dames dayes:
To looke for a long lyfe then muft I bee loath,
Whom each froward frowne elfe of Fortune affrayes.
And fince alyke for her loue I haue tane fuch payne,
I care not a cuit for her fake to bee flayne.
        I fhall not féeme for to fhrinke,
        Of Death, for her death, to drinke;
        Whofe fwéete Eyes, with a winke,
        May reviue mee agayne.
Let this then appleafe thee, good Pilgrime, I pray,
That no prefence, abfence, no diftance of place;
No fond toyes, no new frayes; no tyme, no delay;
No bad chance, no new change, nor contrarie cafe;
No, not the fierce flames that Fortune can fpit,
Shall make my firme fixed fayth or fancie to flit.
        Yea, let her fléete, let her flow;
        Let her doe what fhee dow,
        To gar my griefe aye grow,
        I fhall bee true yet.
Good Heremite, for trueth tolde I oft tymes haue heard,
The leileft in loue, commeth aye the worft fpéede:
And hee that deferues well to reape beft reward,
For firme fayth and friendfhip, fhall finde nought but feide.
Take tent to the tales tolde of true *Troyall* Knight,
And hee that hanged him felfe, if I reade right.
        Yea, though thy fute thou obtayne,
        With one word tint agayne;
        Short pleafure, long payne,
        With duile day and night.
But fince thou delighteft to liue ftill in loue,
Advyfe thee on this well, *Bee never too true.*
Though thou fweare and fay thy mynde fhall not moue,
For *Orphus*, take *Protus*, to change aye thy hew.
Was not great Ioue turn'd in a Showre, in a Fyre,
In a Swan, in a Bull, t'obtayne his defyre?
        For hee that loues lightlieft,
        Bee fure hee fhall fpeede beft:
        And hee that loues without reft,
        Shall furely get ill hyre.
                        Wherefore

The Pilgrime and Heremite.

Wherefore, in loue if that thou wouldſt come ſpeede,
Thou muſt flee fayth, bee facile, falſe, vntrue,
Ere thou prevayle right, ſo farre as I reide,
There muſt bee a ſympathie twixt her and you.
For I demand, How can right Concord bee,
Whyle you are true, and ſhee both falſe and flee?
      Shee lykes well another ſho,
      Then chooſe new, and change too:
      And if you well doe,
      Bee as falſe as ſhee,
Alace! quod the Heremite, too late I ſpye the right,
And wronged with woe, ſtill wrongly I frame.
I know that in loue, my Ladie proues but light:
And if that I were wyſe, I would doe the ſame.
But fayth and her remembrance martyres mee maire,
Than did her preſence perfect mee, when I was there.
      For whyles grieved, I greete;
      Whyles I mourne, till wee meete:
      And ſome tymes my poore ſprite
      Dies, drowned in deſpare:
And whyles in a rage I reckon with my fell,
And to and fro diſpute, to daſh my deſyre:
Halfe dead in Deſart, heere why ſhould I dwell,
And pyne with payne, wanting Bed, Food, and Fyre?
Why doe I loſe youths pryme, without all gayne?
Or why mourne I for her that kéepes Diſdayne?
      And when that I conclude,
      To burne Habite and Hood,
      Yet doe I not doe it,
      My Vow is ſo vayne.
Curſt bee that fond Vow, that ever it was made:
Curſt bee the firſt cauſe of my hidden payne:
And curſt bee falſe Fortune, that holds mee at feid:
And curſt bee the blinde Boy, that breedes all my baine:
Curſt bee the firſt houre, the tyme, and the place,
That fettred my fond Heart in her fayre Face.
      Curſt bee my wicked will:
      Quyte ſpoyling mee of Skill,
      And tooke mee captiue, till,
      That Groome voyde of grace.

The Pilgrime and Heremite.

Unsayde bee that bad word, *That Groome voyde of grace.*
What but her good graces can grieue mee so much?
For I may well saye, if Pittie had place,
Of all that on molde moues, there is none such.
Oh! had the tymes past in Prayer beene spent,
That rueth to my ruethlesse Loue had beene lent.
   And *Cupid*, I call on thee:
   Thou hear'st, and canst not see:
   Haue pittie on poore mee,
   And grant myne intent.
Dame *Nature*, sayth the wyse Clerke *Empedocles,*
Bestowes, good Heremite, her gifts here and there,
As shee well pleaseth, the best is but Claise.
Each man must bee content, hee gets no maire.
For sayth doeth not affect thy Mistres faire,
But Beautie, which doeth bring thee to despaire.
   Of pittie since no part
   Is hid in her hard heart,
   Yet let not the blacke dart
   Of duile thee devoure.
And deafe not the good Gods, with thy vayne Sute:
What they haue once done, they will not vndoe.
Loue's lyke a trim Tree, which beareth no Fruite,
But greene leaues, and blossoms, and flowrisheth too:
Oft gladning the Gardner, in hope of good gayne;
Yet reapes hee in Harvest no Fruit for his payne.
   Right so her fayre face,
   With gifts of sweet grace,
   Tint travell, alace,
   Bout fruit makes thee fayne.
Then sute, serue, pray, prayse, or doe what you can:
Loe, heere I fore-tell thee, thy labour is lost.
For by the great griefs thou thol'st now and than,
To haste thyne owne death, thou runnest the Post.
Though surges of sorrow full swift thee assayles,
Thy lawtie in loue, bout lucke, nought avayles,
   Though thou beat the Bush well,
   Yet thy foe, without fayle,
   Hints the Prey by the tayle,
   And prowdlie prevayles.
          Thou

The Pilgrime and Heremite.

The Pilgrime and Heremite.

The Pilgrime and Heremite.

The Pilgrime and Heremite.

The Pilgrime and Heremite.

The Pilgrime and Heremite.

The Pilgrime and Heremite.

The Pilgrime and Heremite.

The Pilgrime and Heremite

So by your fweete felfe I preaffe now to fpeake,
Whome by the god of Loue I pray, and befeike,
    Forget the fume of your force,
    On your Man haue remorfe;
    Left Death him and you divorce,
    For hee is fore ficke.

Or if a poore man's Plaint may pearce through your Eares;
If Loue anie Lordfhip in your Breaft may brooke;
Haue pittie on his Paffions, and falt tragicke Teares;
Who Libertie, and Lyfe both, hath loft with a Looke.
His Helpe muft bee had from Handes that him hurt:
For fterne muft hee ftay ftill, till you ftap his fturt.
    Then, choofe one of thefe twa,
    Your fworne Slaue for to flay,
    Or revert all his wae,
    Whome your Beautie hurt.

And then, with a fell Frowne, which had a full force
To over-rule the whole Worlde, with Eterne Might.
Whereby it well feemed fhee had no remorfe
Upon the poore Patient, pyned in fuch plight.
Faith, Pilgrime, quod fhee, thou raveft in a rage,
That feekeft by my fhame his ficke fore to fwage.
    For, in a word to conclude,
    I can doe him no good;
    Hee is reaft, by the Rood,
    Of all his wun Wage.

Though fometime the day drew, I dare not denye,
That hee in mine Heart had the moft fupreame place:
And fo, till the fond Fates his wealth did envye,
I ftill, with courtefie, confidred his cafe.
And truft mee, Pilgrime, his Paffions, and Paine,
Went as neare mine Heart, as ever did mine awne.
    Though his cafe now feeme ftrange,
    I will not my felfe cleange:
    His bad chance, and my change,
    Hath bred all his paine.

The Pilgrime and Heremite.

And as for my Loue, who lyes without releafe,
Affociate for my fake, with manie fad Song;
So am I payde in mine hand, with as carefull cafe,
For hee whom I beft loue, hath wrought mee great wrong.
And like as for his loue, hee reapes but difdaine,
The Loue whome I like beft, loathes mee againe.
   And as hee liues all alone,
   With manie great grievous groane,
   So to my felfe I bemoane,
   My hid piercing paine.

I flee to bee followed, and following, am fled:
I loue, and am loathed, and loath to bee lov'd.
Heere's a ftrange ftratageme, that my baile bred:
I frieze in the hote Flame, and frye in the Flood.
I lacke whome I beft loue, and choakt am with ftore:
Yea, haue fo much, that my mynde can craue no more.
   Thus goe thy wayes, whence thou came,
   And fhowe thy ficke Friende, his Dame
   Remaines yet the felfe fame,
   That fhee was before.

I will worke thee no wrong, that no wayes haft wyte,
But through the Fieldes on thy Feete friendlie doeft fare,
To feeke to thy ficke man fome Salue for his fyte,
And to cure by thy Craft his curft kindled Care:
Thou fhalt walke on thy way, and ftay on the Stréet,
And carrie him fhortlie his anfwere in Writ.
   And when fhee the Doore bard,
   I ftoode ftill yet vnfkard;
   And through a hole I heard
   This talke of the Sweete.

           Poliphila

The Pilgrime and Heremite

Poliphila, before Shee writ her An-
fvvere, difputeth vvith her ovvne
Defires, as followeth:

How hard it is, none knowes, fo well as I,
Unto a dolefull, and divided Mynde,
To make a well-joind Aunfwere, and Replye,
When all the chiefe and nobleft partes are pynde.
Then, Shall I bee to Crueltie inclynde?
Or pittie him that prayes, and pleades for Peace,
If this or that I fticke in contrare cafe?

I loue the Loue that lightlies mee againe;
And lightlie him that loues mee as his life:
Yea, for my loue with flaverie is flaine.
His lyfe's the Threed, my crueltie's the Knyfe.
How fhall I rid this ftrange and fatall ftryfe?
Yet beft it were, to looke, before I lope:
And not to quite Affurance true, for Hope.

O my divided Soule! what fhall I doe?
Whereon fhall nowe my Refolution reft?
Which is the beft Advife to yeelde vnto?
Of two Extreames, howe fhall I choofe the beft?
Come, Pithiane Prince: I praye, and I proteft:
Affift mee nowe, and make no more delay;
But guide mee well, in this my wilfome way.

Then, Heremite, that doeft in Defart dwell,
And buyft my loue, with deare and great expence;
With Toyle, and Tormentes, tedious for to tell;
Bee blythe, and let thy wonted Harmes goe hence:
Thou muft not die, while I may make defence.
Put then a point and period to thy paine:
Thy long-fought Loue and Ladie fhall bee thine.

Yet will I write difdainfullie to thee:
Thy loving Lines muft haue a colde Reply.
I will not feeme too credulous to bee,

C 2   With

The Pilgrime and Heremite.

With haſtie Faith, to truſt, before I trye,
But I avow, I ſhall not ſleepe, nor lye
In anie Bed, till I beholde thy Face,
And boldlie him whome I ſhould brooke, imbrace.

  Goe, loueleſſe Lines, vnto my Louer true,
Stay yet, leſt yee procure his farder paine.
God graunt nothing but Good heereof enſue.
Yet ſtay, for why? Yee will bee quite miſtane.
Goe yet: but yet yee ſhall not goe alane:
My ſelfe will followe, with convenient haſte.
God graunt my Voyage bee not waird in waſte.

Thus endeth her Diſputation.

And ſo, in a ſhort ſpace, that ſweete ſeemlie Sainct,
Preſentes mee, her Pilgrime, a baile-bearing Bill:
And as in the wilde way ſhee weind I ſhould want,
My Bag, and my Bottle, ſhee pleniſht at will.
A Ring from her Finger full faire did ſhee take:
And gaue mee, and prayde mee, good Newes to bring backe.
      And, having no more to ſay,
      But loath I ſhould long ſtay,
      Shee weeping went away,
      And not a word ſpake.

Then, when the blacke Night her fadde Mantle ſhew,
Ill Succeſſour, degenerate from the Day,
VVith the third Foote in hand, I throgh the thrang threw.
Though clad with the darke Clowdes, I went on my way.
And loath to detaine the Lecture too long,
I came to my ſicke Friende; and this was his Song.
      But, when I knew his voice,
      I kept my ſelfe full cloſe,
      To heare the Layes of his loſſe,
      The wilde woods among.

The Pilgrime and Heremite.

The Heremite his Complaint.

SO manie thinges before haue perfect Poets pende,
For to expreſſe their piercing paines, and cauſe their Cares
  bee kende,
That nought is left, alace, for moſt vnhappie mee,
In Skyes aboue, on earth beneath, nor in the glaſſie Sea.
No Metaphoricke Phraſe, no high Invention braue:
No Allegorie ſweete Conceit, no Theame ſublime and graue:
But all thinges elſe are ſaide, which I can write or ſay:
Thus in effect I wot not how my wracks for to bewray.
 And nothing doeth aggrege my griping griefe ſo much,
As that my ſkill ſhould be ſo ſmall, my ſorowes ſhould be ſuch.
Yet all thoſe Poets braue, which were, or yet ſhall bee,
Could I but vtter, as I feele, might all giue place to mee.
And thou whoſe mirth was leaſt, whoſe comfort was diſmaid;
Whoſe hope was vaine, whoſe faith was ſkorne, whoſe trueth
  was betraide.
Thou didſt declare thy duile, in braue and daintie dye:
Thou waſt vnhappie then, I graunt, but now vnhappie I.
 Thy Poemes did preſent vpon thy pleaſant Page,
Moe Sorrowes than thou ever felt into thy cunning age.
With coſtlie Nurix rare, Sidoniane Wares divine,
Thou litſt thy Lines, which makes thy Moanes miraculouſlie
  to ſhine.
My Paines, like Tagus Sandes, no numbers can bewray:
Or like Auroras tears, which ſhe for Memnon ſhéeds each day.
As Starres in froſtie Sky can not bee tolde which ſhynes;
So manie heaps of harms my hart without compaſſion pyns.
 Yea, would I preaſſe to tell the torments that I feele,
With travell tint then might I turne Ixions fatall wheele.
And to diſgorge theſe griefs which make mee ſigh and ſob,
Were for to weue a new Penelopeian webbe.
My Eyes like Fountaines might in bloodie Fornace frye,
Or like the Lidiane Tubs, whoſe doome is never to bee drye.
My hote and ſmoothred ſighes, no levill courſe can take:
But reſtleſſe round about my heart eſphearicke motion make.
 My Thoughtes are now of Bliſſe like ruine Ilion bare:
My ſhape, a reconfuſed maſſe, which flowriſht once ſo faire.
             My

The Pilgrime and Heremite.

My Ship, which fometimes faild in draiue of hope aright,
On Rockes full colde is rent, in blacke and ftormie night.
And I, forfaken Soule, a lyfeleffe lumpe of Lead,
Twixt wind and waue am caft, whereas no ftrength can ftand
    in ftead.
My Ventring was my Wracke; my high Defire, my Fall:
Which made the Naufrage of my Hurt, my Hope, my Hap,
    and all.
   Alace, alace, that I impoffiblie did preaffe,
Aboue my Fortunes for to flie, fo farre to my difgrace.
Difgrac'd with Loffe, with Shame, with Wracke, and end-
    leffe Wrong:
Thefe are the dolefull Ditties now, and fubjects of my Song.
Yet dare I not, alace, though I haue caufe, complaine:
Which makes me figh, and fob, and thus for loue am flaine.
But fince it is my weird, to fall, to waile, to weepe;
Then by my loffe let others learne a lower courfe to keepe.

Thus endeth the Heremite his Complaint.

And when I faw that his Song received a full ende,
I fhowde my felfe fhortlie, and kindlie did kythe.
And when that fore ficke man his true Bearer kende,
And faw the Face of his Friend, God knowes he was blythe.
Then fhowde I the blacke Bill, fubfcryv'd with his Name,
Well written with the hand of his owne deare Dame.
        And then, with a glad cheare,
        When Hope had ceaffed Feare,
        Hes read, that I might heare,
        The Will of the fame.

Her Anfwere, to the Heremite.

THy loving Lines I rafhlie did receiue,
   Wherein thy Trueth, thy State, thy Wracke, I fee:
But at mine handes no fuccour fhalt thou haue:
Though Friende to mee, I fhall bee Foe to thee.
       And fince thy death doeth on my doome depende,
       Liue loath'd, or die difgrac'd, and fo I ende.

       Thus fhee fhortly concludes.
                                      And

The Pilgrime and Heremite.

And when hee read thefe bad and noifome Newes,
Which did refrefh his Woes, his Hurtes, and Harmes:
Whiles red, whiles pale, hee chaunged manie hewes,
And fell downe, in dead-thraw, betwixt my weake Armes.
And when with my falt Teares I bath'd his pale Face,
His Sprites, and his Breath, came to their owne place.
    Hee cryde then, O Death, ftay
    Thy date, for this halfe day;
    That I in writ may bewray
    My high great Difgrace.

The Heremite his Teftament.

BUt now, and not till now, my Swan-lyke Song I fing;
And with each word my dying Eyes the bloodie Teares
    foorth bring.
Not that I loathe, alace, or fhrinke for to bee flaine:
For, what can be fo fwéet as death, which puts an end to pain?
My death fhall bee the Caufe, thy Honour and Renowne
Shal lofe the conquerd Diademe of Fames immortal Crown.
Yet fince it is thy Doome, that in difgrace I die,
Or loathed liue; the choife is hard whereas no mids may bee.
And yet of Evils twane, the beft muft aye bee tane:
So that I rather choofe to die, than liue in endleffe paine.
Long haue I lookt for joy, whence floods of forrow fpring:
The ende whereof, alace, muft bee my lateft Will to fing.
My Tones, are carefull Cryes; my Words are Plaints, alace:
Sad Sorrow muft the Singer bee, fince Pittie hath no place.
My Paines are like a Point, amidft a Circle fet:
Still in fuch nearneffe to my felfe, that no reliefe can get.
How can I hope for helpe, fince Heavens doe mee defpife?
And all the gods aboue are deav'd, with my Complaintes and
    Cryes.
Earths burden am I thus, whofe fighs infect the Aire,
With poifned breath, procéeding from an heart confum'd with
    Care,
For loe, the faithleffe Fates vnto this ftate mee calles:
By which the ftatelie Starres themfelues misfortune tholes.
What refteth then but Death? fince Death muft be the laft,
To put a period to my paine, for pleafures hope is paft.

The Pilgrime and Heremite.

Yet I atteſt the gods, ſince firſt our loue began,
I haue beene the lieleſt aye, and moſt affected man.
I loued thee, alace, thy Soliphermis ſworne:
O Poliphila falſe! my lawtie is forlorne.
My loue, woe's mee, therefore, ſtill thy diſdaine hath beene:
The moſt Extreams that ever were, or ſhall againe bee ſéene.
Thou firſt betrayde mine Heart, then falſifide thy Faith:
And where thou promiſde Lyfe, by Loue, thou haſt decreede
    my Death.
When that thy Cruelties I call before, and to
The Eyes of my Remembrance, I doubt what I ſhall doe.
Whiles doe I wiſh to liue, not to envye thy loue:
But that I might beholde my wracke, revenged from Aboue.
Or that ſuch wrongs as mine, if ſuch, or worſe, might bee,
Might make mee ſmile at thy Mishaps, as thou haſt done at
    mee.
Or then that ſometime thou, like that Minoniane Dame,
Mightſt loue, and loathed bee, and ſuffer ſuch like ſhame.
Or that the fatall Sparke, whereon thy Loines might lout,
And mounting much, might make thee pleade, for Peace thy
    time about.
Yet, whiles againe I thinke, might I my wiſh obtaine,
I could not but bee kinde to thee, for kindneſſe that hath
    beene.
Thus what I would, I wiſh: but wot not what I would.
Twixt Heate and Colde I frieze, I frye, and fearfull am, and
    bolde.
Yea, though I bee diſmaide, ſuch is my flaming Fyre,
That Neptunes Kingdome could not quench the Coales of
    my Deſyre.
Yet whiles I reade the Schrole of Torments which I thole,
Where no Miſchance is mixt to fill a grieved Martyres Roll.
And when I looke the Lines, wherein thy Helliſh Doome,
By thy Chyrographie ſent, That Death ſhould me conſume,
Thus I reſolue at ones, for to obey thy will,
Although my Lyfe the Ranſome bee, thy Furie to fulfill.
Since Contraries, wee ſee, are by Contraries cured:
Then, welcome, Death, to cut the Threed, which hath ſo
    long endured.
              For why?

The Pilgrime and Heremite

For why? my Prayers are but Curfes late and aire:
And I befeech the gods by night, to fee the Day no maire.
My wifhes are, that Hilles and Rockes fhould on mee fall,
To end my endleffe breath, my lyfe, my loue, and all.
Yet all thofe wifhes are but types, that I muft die:
Which revelations all at once, fhall now accomplifht bee.
Then loueleffe dame, adue, whom I haue helde fo deare:
And welcome, Death, to cut the Threede, which holdes my
              lyfe in weire.
And, Pilgryme, thou who took'ft thy way in manie airts,
For me prepare a burial Bed, for Bones, when Breath departs.
Yet recommend mine Heart, vnto my fometime-Sweet;
Who fhall, when I am dead and gone, for Grace and Guer-
              don greet.
And let that place bee nam'd, Strophonius Caue of care:
Where nought but woefull wandring wights, vndone with
              duill, repare.
And let this Caverne colde, wherein I dwelt, to die,
For Mifers, and vnhappie men, a matchleffe Manfion bee.
Let him whofe erring fteps fhould guide him heere to plaine,
Take paines to recollect my rolls, & fcattered Skrolls againe.
That thefe my Waylings now, and Sorrowes Children may
Extolde in after comming times, endure, and lieue for aye.
And that the wandring eyes, which reade my forrowing fongs,
When I am dead, may fay, that fhee caufeleffe hath wrought
              fuch wrongs.
The Mountaines high, whofe poynts doe pierce the afure
              Aire;
Whofe echoes lowd my Commerades make comfort to my
              Care:
Still mot your hights aryfe, with ftatelie tops and ftay,
To match the Alpes, that yee may bee as famous, faire as they.
Yee Valleyes louelie low, with fweete and levell lynes,
Where Natures workmanfhip and pryde in Floraes Mantle
              fhynes:
Greene mot yee grow for aye, and that no fpaits of raine,
No Snowie fhowres, no partching Sunne, your ftatelie broy-
              dering ftaine.
And thou, O bleffed Brooke, which didft accept my Teares;
And harbered thē within thy heart, fo manie loathfome yeares.

                           D   Vnto

The Pilgrime and Heremite.

Vnto the Ocean great, moſt ſwiftlie mot yee ſlide,
To pay thy debts, bout ſtop or ſtay of contrare ſtreame or tide.
Yee whiſling windes, likewiſe, which ſwiftlie did receiue,
My Cogiate Sighs, and burie them within your Boſome braue.
Doe thus much once for mee; Take one Sigh to my Dame:
And whiſpering ſweetlie, ſhow that Sainċt, thus haue I ſent the ſame.
And if ſhee doe refuſe, which out of doubt I dread,
The newes of *No*, ſhall bee a Spur, to haſte mee to my dead.
Yee braue and ſtatelie Trees, which circumcituate heere,
Still bloome, and bloſſome, with the change of yearlie changing cheare.
Though I did ryue your Ryndes, & brake your tender Barkes,
By painting Polyphilaes name to your immortall markes:
Agrieue not with your wounds, for I dare well avow,
That I more cruellie haue rent my tender Heart, than you.
But laſt, and by the laiue, thou Holline, graue and greene,
Wherein my Miſtreſſe name, and mine, moſt liuelie may bee ſeene,
I conſecrate to thee my Corpſe, when I am gone,
That by my loſſe I may enlarge thy thornie leaues eachone.
And when I ſhall conſume, and rot about thy roote,
Then ſhall thy Boughs and Branches bloome, and beare a fairer Fruit:
And as thou tak'ſt increaſe, ſo ſhall Her Name, and mine,
Vnto thy praiſe, my loſſe, her ſhame, in ſeemelie ſort aye ſhine.
Yee ſavage Citizens, which in this Forreſt bee,
That did exchange your Cruelties, in Courteſies to mee:
Well mot yee bee, poore Beaſtes, and that no ſhots of Lead,
No life-bereauing Bow, nor Bolt, procure nor haſte your dead.
And thou ſweete pyping Pan, ye Fawnes, and Satyres rare,
Which were amidſt my matchleſſe moanes, Companions of my care:
Ye Nymphes of Hilles & Dales, of Woods; of Vailes, of Floods;
I bid you all, alace, Good-night, and ſo my Muſe concludes.
For now the Herbinger of Death, muſt life and loue bereaue.
My Heart is faint, and loe, my Soule begins to take her leaue.
And ſo at point of Death, whoſe wiſht approach I feele,
To end my life, I write this laſt Ill-faring word, *Fare-well*.
So endeth the Teſtament of Stophonius.

The Pilgrime and Heremite

Thus the poore Heremite in midſt of his paine,
Began to repeate his faire Miſtres ſpeach;
Downe betwixt mine Armes fell, in dead thraw againe:
VVhen no Leid for his life, mee thought, could be Leach.
His Cognate Corpſe as Clay were, like the Lead;
Yea, healthleſſe and helpleſſe, were Heart, Hand, and Head.
    I began to bewaile,
    And eke for to raile,
    On her whoſe faith did faile,
    In ſuch time of neede.

Yet in the midſt of my moanes, downe lighted that Dame,
Companied with none, but her Palfray and Page:
And when ſhée ſaw her liele Loue lye dead ere ſhée came,
Her faire Face and rich Robes, ſhée rent in great rage.
And flatlings ſhée fell vpon his faint Face,
And great Seas of ſault Teares ſhée ſpent in ſhort ſpace,
    And ſéeing her Swéete ſlaine,
    No remead did remaine:
    Shee thus began to plaine,
    Her bad carefull caſe.

Polyphila her Complaint, and Teſtament.

O endleſſe Night of noyſe, which hath no Morrow!
O lowring Heavens, which harmes ſtill haue threat!
Ov'r mantling mee with ſable Clowds of Sorrow!
VVhereas no Starre doeth ſhine earlie nor late.
Although I ſkip from *Craig*, to ſeeke my Mate,
And from a glorious Garland to my Crowne,
I finde by death my daintie *Roſe* dung downe.

Yée ſwelling Seas, with waltering VVaues that roll,
To reſolute the weather-beaten Shoare:
They eb, they flow, and changing, Courſes tholl,
And dare tranſcende their bounded banks no more.
But I, alace, whom Duill doeth ſtill devoure,
I finde no entermiſſions to my Moanes,
But ere and late lament my grievous Groanes.

The Pilgrime and Heremite.

How can my wofull Heart, and weeping Eyes
Beholde the deareſt of my life bereaft?
How can my minde admit the leaſt ſurmyze,
Of anie Hope, that hath but Horrour left?
My Pilote now, by North, nor yet by Eaſt,
Eſpies no Calmes, but Mercie-wanting Stormes;
Pretending Death, in blacke and vglie Formes.

I grouelinges on the Ocean of my pride,
Did miſregard each true and loving Sute.
So manie ſude for favour on each ſide,
Which made my Seede to yeelde much barren Fruite.
Though I bewaile, as nowe, it bringes no buite.
Sighes, Teares, and Vowes, and all are waird in vaine:
Since nothing can redéeme thy life againe.

Aye mee, alace! Alace, and waile-away!
Deare Heart, poore Heart; what reſtes for thy behoue?
Since I procur'd thy death, by my delay,
And did miſtruſt my true and conſtant Loue:
Now ſhall my death, thy preſent death approue.
Though whilſt thou liv'd, to loue thee I was loath;
Yet I am thine beyonde the date of death.

Then let mee die, and bid Delight adue;
Since my delight is with thee dead and gone.
The comming Age ſhall ſay, thy Thiſbe true,
Was conſtant ſtill, and lov'd but thee alone.
Wee both ſhall lye vnder one Marble ſtone.
One Graue in ende, ſhall ende our fatall griefe;
Which yeeldes mee nowe, in point of death, reliefe.

Since yeſterday may not bee brought againe,
And Wronges may bee repented, not recall'd:
I will no more inveigh on Death in vaine,
But make all Womens cowrage to bee bolde:
And in the Tymes to come, it ſhall bee tolde;
Though thou till death didſt ſerue and honour mee,
I after death haue ſought, and followde thee,

And, Pilgrime, nowe, I praye, and I proteſt,
                                                    Before

The Pilgrime and Heremite.

Before I ende this laſt exequall Act,
Let mee bee bolde to make this ſmall Requeſt;
That for thy vmwhile Friende ſome paines thou take:
Firſt, In this place, a private Graue gar make;
And let vs lye interd conjunctlie there,
Where nought but Fawnes, and Satyres make repare.

Next, When thou comſt into my natiue Land,
Wherein my Loue, and Loueleſſe I was borne;
If anie of our Tragicke death demand,
With Pittie ſpeake, I praye, and not with Scorne.
This Practicke rare, which ſeldome was beforne,
Which when my deare and loving Friendes ſhall heare,
My Tragicke ende will coſt them manie a Teare.

     Thus endeth her Complaynt.

And ſo when that rare Pearle departed out of paine,
Vpon the colde dead Corpſe of her leile Loue,
Unto my elſe hurt Heart did heape Harmes againe,
And layde new weight on my braſt Breaſt aboue.
To ſee him and her gaſpe, ſtill nowriſht my care.
I wiſt not whom to helpe, him, or her there.
   While I ſtoode in this doubt,
   The Heremite lookt out,
   And gaue a faint ſhout,
   Twixt hope, and deſpare.

This is the Worldes moſt wondrous worthie Wight,
Moſt matchleſſe of all, that may on molde moue.
Halowed bee the Heavens, that ſhowde mee this ſight,
And lent mee this light, to looke on my leile loue.
Now am I glad, and vngriev'd, to Graue though I goe:
Thy travell and toyle doeth reward well my woe.
   For wilt thou belieue mee,
   My Maker miſchieue mee,
   If thou canſt agrieue mee,
   I ſtill loue thee ſo.

I come, quod the Cleare then, to cure all thy care,
Though the Faites had forſworne to fang thee my Feire.

The Pilgrime and Heremite.

Bee blythe then, my deare heart, and mourne thou no maire,
For Peace, faith the Proverbe, puts end to all weire.
Goe leaue then thy Hermitage, and thy cold Caue,
Where Wolfe, Lyon, wilde Beare, thy blood ftill doe craue,
   And with the good God's grace,
   Thou fhalt in a fhort fpace,
   For all thy loffe finde releafe,
   And firft Health receiue.

Then franklie the Frieke fuire, with her helpe and mine,
And to her Palfray hee paft, although with great paine:
And tooke on that fwéet Sainct, that méeke Jem divine;
That miracle which gods made, as next vnto naine.
Then blythlie the Bairne blent, and hyde haftie Hame,
Throgh fhéene Shawes, & donke Dailes, with his deare Dame.
   And fo with Adew dry,
   Through the Wood could they hye,
   As wee twind, they and I,
   I woke of my Dreame.

 Heere endeth the fatalitie of the loyall Lover Soliphernus, and
    of his fweete Ladie Polyphila.

The Poëme.

AS perfect Poets ere-tymes haue tane paine,
And fearch'd the Secrets of each high Engyne,
By bafe and lowlie Subjects to exclaime,
High Myfteries, both morall and divine:
Even fo into this worthleffe Worke of mine,
Which at Friends bidding boldlie I fet foorth;
Some things may féeme obfcure, though little worth.

 For as the Heremite leaues his deareft Dame,
And takes delight in colde Defart to dwell:
Syne of his Lot, and of himfelfe, thinkes fhame,
And ftill defpaires, and ftill doeth loathe him fell:
So wretched man, exchanging Heaven with Hell,
Forgetting GOD, in Darkneffe doeth remaine,
And ftill defpaires, to get Reliefe againe.
          And

The Pilgrime and Heremite.

And as the painfull Pilgryme, now and than,
With Arguments, and pithie reaſons ſtrong,
Would faine reduce the Heremite, if hée can,
And make him to beholde his woefull wrong:
And as the Woods, and ſavage Beaſtes among,
So with him bydes, and recomforts his Care:
Syne holds him vp, from dying in Deſpare.

And as in ende, hée mooues him for to wryte;
Syne ſhowes his Sutes vnto his Miſtres Eyes:
Wherein, yée ſée, ſhée tooke no ſmall delyte,
Becauſe in him ſome ſigne of Trueth ſhée ſies.
Shée cures his Cares, and all his ſicke Diſeaſe:
Yea, heales his hurt, and heartlie by the hand,
Shée home-ward leades him, to her natiue Land.

So ſinfull man, firſt by the helpe of Faith,
Deſpiſeth Sinne, repents, and ſore doeth pray,
That GOD in Mercie would avert His wrath,
And make His bred diſpleaſure to decay.
And when the ſicke converted would away,
From worldlie eaſe. with haſte hee maketh ſpeede:
Then comes the LORD, to helpe His owne at neede.

Hee cures our cares, Hee helpes vs to bee haile:
Hee makes our ſorie Soules for to rejoyce.
If wee in Him confyde, Hee will not faile,
To free vs from the force of all our Foes.
And at the laſt, with great diſgrace of thoſe,
That loving LORD, ſhall take vs by the Hand,
And with Him leads vs, to the *HOLIE LAND.*

FINIS.

Orpheus Fiddle.

THE AMOROSE

Songes, Sonets, and Elegies:

Of M. *ALEXANDER CRAIGE*, *Scoto-Britane.*

Imprinted at London by *William White*.
1606.

Prima velim teneris intendat amoribus ætas,
Et canat ad Cytharam nostra camena suam.

Molle meum Leuibus cor est penetrabile telis,
Et semper causa est cur ego semper amo.

Vitantur venti, pluuiæ, vitantur, et estus,
Non vitatur amor, mecum tumuletur oportet.

TO
THE MOST GODLY,
VERTVOVS, BEAVTIFVLL,
and accomplifhed *PRINCESSE*, meritorioufly dignified with all the Titles Religion, Vertue, Honor, Beautie can receiue, challenge, afforde, or deferue; *ANNA*, by diuine prouidence, of *Great Britane, France*, and *Ireland*, Queene: ALEXANDER CRAIGE wifheth all health, wealth, and royall felicitie.

Reat *Tamburlan* cloaked his fantafticall crueltie hee exercifed on Lazars and Leprous men, with a foolifhe kind of humanity, putting all he could find or heare of, to death, (as

Epistle to the Queene.

(as he said) to rid them from so painefull & miserable a life: Though my Poyems (incomparably bountifull, incomparablie beautifull, and so peerelesse Princesse) be painefull to me, and vnpleasant to the delicat Lector; shall I with *Tamburlan* destroy them? or like a cruell *Althea*, consume with fire the fatall Tree, kill mine owne *Meleager*, and so inhumanlie cut off mine owne birth? I gaue life to my Lines, and shall I now become their burreau? O liue my deformed Child, some other hand shall commit thee to *Phaeton* or *Deucalions* mercie, then mine: Though *Anaxagoras* resolued to die; yet for *Pericles* his Maisters sake he tooke courage, and

Epistle to the Queene.

& liued. Your royall God-mother poore *Rymes* hath saued your life: yet am I not like *Hercules*, who threw *Ionius* in the Sea, that by the violence of wind & waue the carkas might be caried to foraine shores, for propagation of his fame. I hunt not for fame; nor print I those Papers for prayses, but to pleasure your Princely eyes with varietie of my vaine inuentions. *Megabysus* going to visit *Apelles* in his worke-house, stoode still a long time without speaking one word, and then began to censure of *Apelles* works; of whom he receiued this rude & nipping checke: So long as thou held thy peace, thou seemedst a wise man; but now thou hast spoke,

A iii.

Epistle to the Queene.

spoke, and the worst Boy of my shoppe thinkes thee a foole. I am bold (diuine Ladie) to borrow thy blessed name, to beautifie my blotted Booke; and haue sent those Poems, like *Apelles* Pictures through the world: nor doe I care (since it is your Princely pleasure to protect them) the foolish iudgement of *Megabysus*. *Syrannes* the Persian Prince answered those (who seemed to woonder why his negotiations succeeded so il, whē his discourses were so wise) that he was onely maister of his Discourses, but Fortune mistris to the succes of his affaires. My Sonnets & Songes are (gracious Princesse) for the most part, full of complaints, sorrow, and lamentations:
The

Epistle to the Queene.

The reason is, I was maister of my Verses; but Fortune Mistris of my Rewards. When *Thetis* courted *Iupiter*, and when the *Lecedemonians* sende Legates to the *Athenians*, they put them not in minde of the good they had done them, but of the benefites they had receiued of them. Your Maiesties munificens, and frequent benefites bestowed vpon mee, haue headlong impelled mee to propine this worthlesse worke to your Royall view. Happie beyonde the measure of my merit shall I bee, if I can purchase this portion of your Princely approbation, as to accept and entertaine these triuiall toyes (where your Grace shall smell Flowes to refresh,

A iiii, Hearbes

Epiſtle to the Queene.

Hearbes to cure, and Weedes to be auoyded) in the loweſt degree of leaſt fauour. But howſoeuer, wiſhing your Highnes as many happie yeares, as there be wordes in my Verſes, and Verſes in my worthles Volume: I am

Your Maieſties moſt
obſequious Orator,

Alexander Craige,
Scoto-Britan.

Epistle generall to
Idea, Cynthia, Lithocardia, Kala, Erantina, Lais, Pandora, Penelopæ.

Zeuxis *painted a Childe bearing Vine clusters in his hand so perfectly, that the Fowles of the ayre were deceiued, & descended thereto in vaine: But angrie at his worke, he cry'd out, I haue painted the Clusters more liuely then the Child, and the burthen better then the bearer; for had the Child seemed as viue as the Vine Grapes, the Fowles had bin affraied at his face. I haue in these amorous* Sonets *and* Songes *matchles* Idea, *virtuous* Cynthia, *graue* Lithocardia, *sweete* Kala, *louely* Erantina, *lasciuious* Lais, *modest* Pandora, *liberall* Penelopæ, *painted my Loue; but haue (allasse) taken more paines on the Passions, then the Poyems; and more* worke

worke on my woes, then the Verſes. But had my Lines been as liuely as either they ſhould, or I wiſh they had been. No Momus *affraide at the beautie of my Verſes had preſum'd (to my diſgrace) to gather the Grapes of my Errors. Nor had I needed (which neceſsarily I muſt doe) to employ the Patrocinie of your protections. Were I an other* Hercules, *I could not cut off all the hiſsing heads of* Hydra: *& were I as perfect a painter as* Apelles, *ſome ſawſie Souter ſhall cenſure aboue the Shoo. But with* Agatharchus *(who did all in haſte) I humbly craue at all your handes (which with all reuerence, and analogike ſeruice I kiſſe) and looke you will excuſe*

Your louing, but rude
Zeuxis.

A. C. *Banſa-Britan.*

TO THE READER.

Myrnean Mæonides *vſed in his delicate Poems diuers Dialects, as* Ionic, Æolic, Attic, *and* Doric: *So haue I (O courteous Reader) in this; and but alaſse in this, imitate that renowned Helleniſt* Homer, *in vſing the* Scotiſh *and* Engliſh *Dialectes: the one as innated, I can not forget; the other as a ſtranger, I can not vpon the ſodaine acquire. The ſubtile Merchant placed* Æsop *in the middle betwixt* Cantor *and* Grammaticus, *that by the interpoſition of that deformed fabulator, the other two might appeare the fayrer. So haue I in middeſt of my modeſt Affections, committed to the Preſſe my vnchaſt Loue to* Lais, *that contraries by conttraries, and Vertue by Vice, more cleerely may ſhine. To each (courteous Reader) that will both of this & that mixtture of Ditties and Dialects, courteouſly cenſure, I am but end to the fatall end,*

A moſt louing Friend, in all poſsible imployment.

Craige.

To IDEA.

Any times from the Table of my Chamber (matchleſſe *Idea*) haue my deareſt Friends, both by them ſelues, and my Seruant (whom I ſometimes employed to write for mee) ſtole the inuentions of my wanton vaine, thoſe amorous Ditties, ſuch as they beſt liked: and for which hauing, thereby ſerued the humour of my paſſion, I cared no more; wherein their gaine and my loſſe were all one. But now, by printing my then ſcattered, and now lately collected Scrowles (the moſt and beſt part whereof, I can not finde) I haue thought good to eaſe my ſelfe, and ſatisfie (but with the firſt, your Ladiſhip) my friendes. The noble *Romans* were from all antiquitie, accuſtomed to leaue thoſe Kinges whom they had vanquiſhed, in the poſſeſsions of their kingdomes, that Kings by

To IDEA.

by them made slaues, might be instruments to vprayse the tropheis of their glorie. Thou knowest (Diuine *Idea*) I am thine by conquest; and yet thou allowest mee the seeming fruition of my libertie, while in deed I must pay the eternall tribute of vnfaigned Loue: For as *Carneades* the *Cyrenean* Philosopher said of *Chrysippus*; And *Chrysippus* were not, I could not bee; my beeing is by thy munificence. Take this in good part: and still I rest,

Idea's euer obleged and vnmanumissible slaue,

Ad Ideam.

O bona non tractanda homini bona digna rapina,
Cælicolum, superis o bona digna locis.

To CYNTHIA.

Ffend not, faire Dame; Though the Lines of my Picture change and varie. The World runnes on Wheeles, all things therein mooue without intermifsion: the folide Earth, the rockes of *Caucafus*, and the *Pyramids* of *Memphis;* both with publike, and their owne motion. Conftancie it felfe, is nothing but a languifhing and a wauering daunce. I am a *Pamphilus*, and can not fettle my obiect. And fince my Loue runnes ftaggering with a naturall drunkennes, I pray thee (vertuous *Cynthia*) with patience perufe thofe Poyems: And (as *Ariftippus* fayd to his man, who by the way was ouer burdened with too much money) carry what you may, and caft away the reft.

Your La. howfoeuer,
and wherefoeuer.

Ad Cynthiam.

Nil formæ natura tuæ, nihil aftra negarunt,
Vna fupercilij fi tibi dempta nota.

To LITHOCARDIA.

Feare to prefixe (Hono. Lady) to thefe few Poyems, a long Epiftle, leaft fome *Diogenes* fhould bid mee fhut the Portes of *Minda* ere the Towne runne out. Let mee this much kindly pray, & preuaile with your La. as to vouchfafe them fome place in the bench of your bibliothek. *Xerxes*, whofe Armies obumbrate all *Hellefpont*, was faine in a fmall Fifh-bote for fafetie of his life, to flie from *Greece*. So may you at fome idle howers deigne, and difcende to behold my rufticke Rymes, and kindly excufe his errours, who ere long, hath purpofe to prefent and pleafe you with fome better Poyem. Till when, and euer,

I am your La. owne,

Ad Lithocardiam.

Vt nulla e cunctis formofa eft fœmina tantum,
fic nulla est mifero tantum adamata mihi.

To KALA.

THese Poyems are, I confesse (sweete *Kala*) vnwoorthy thy presence, and so haue more neede of thy protection: But let (as *Cicero* writes in his Epistle to *Octauius*) Confession be a medicine for Errour. Twixt *Metellus Macedonicus* and *Scipio Africanus*, were mortall Warres: but when *Scipio* dyed, *Metellus* prayed the Citie-men to concurre, least their Walles should be ouerthrowen. Many louely iarres haue been amongst vs; but in my absence, those my Papers like Citizens of a good republike, shall all concurre to please and honor thee: And I both at home, & abrod, shall continue

Thine till death: *Craige*.

Et quanquam molli semper sis dedita amori,
Candida nulla magis, nulla proterua magis.

To LAIS.

Every man (as Pittacus *affirmeth*) hath some imperfection: *in mee Loue is most predominant.* But as Alcibiades *cut off his faire Dogs eares and tayle, & so droue him in the market place, that giuing this subiect of prattle to the people, they might not meddle with his other actions.* So haue I presumed to publish these my castrat Rimes vnder (ô lasciuious Lais) thy protection, that my chaster Verses may appeare lesse faulty. Antinonides *the Musitian, gaue order, that before or after him some bad Musitian should cloy and surfet his auditors.* So when the Lector shall be weary to ouerread these lubricke Lynes, hee shall with more alacrity consider and ouerlooke the rest. And thus were not hereby I minded to beautifie my other Poyems, I could gladly consent, that all those Lynes of Lais, were ouer whelmed in obliuion, I glory not (God knowes) in my frailty: and more for euitation, then imitation, are these Songes foorthsent to the view of the censnriug world. And thus nor crauing, nor carefull of thy acceptance, O Lais, I cease to serue, or more
to be Thine.

O miseri quorum gaudia crimen habent:

Dum furtiua dedit nigra munuscula nocte,
Me tenet, absentes alios suspirat amores.
B.

To ERANTINA.

IT is a wounderfull delight I take to liue in Loue; it is euer at my heart, and moſt in my mouth: and ſuch aſsiſtaunce it giueth to my life, that it ſeemes the beſt munition I haue found in this humane peregrination. The Diſciples of *Hegeſias*, hunger ſtarued them ſelues to death, incenſed therevnto with the perſwading diſcourſes of his leſſons, til the time King *Ptolomey* forbade him any longer to entertaine his Schoole with ſuch murtherous preceptes. Though I weare the howers of the day, and waſte the dayes of my life in Loue: I muſe, I roue, and walke: I enregiſter my humors and my paſsions. Let none be entiſed by my example: for I am borne to loue, and to die

Thy Louer.

O quid dura tuum ſic me contemnis amantem
Neglectumq; tuas deſpicis ante fores:
Frigida ſœnit Hyems, immitis et ingruit æther,
Excluſum pateris me tamen eſſe foris.

To PANDORA.

HE very fame Sonets which at fome time pleafed you (modeft *Pandora*) with much more courtefie and honour, then they, or I, any way deferued, to receiue and reade, I haue (but without alteration or change) heere placed and reduced in a folide bodie. When *Babilon* was befidged by *Darius*, the number of Women was fo great, the Captaine commaunded euery man to choofe one; which beeing accordingly performed, the reft were put to death, that their victuals might the longer endure. Hadft thou been there, and I Captaine of the *Babilonic*, armie, thou fhouldft been firft of all thy fexe felected to been faued. Pardon (peereleffe *Pandora*)

A ii.

dora) the perseuerance of my presumption, in still affecting thee: and for my sake peruse these Sonets, which may happily continue some dayes and yeares after mee: That since I could not be beloued being on-life, I may with desperat *Herostratus*, be famous after death: Till when (as *Socrates* sayd) as I may, I am

       Thy vnalterable man,

Ah nunquam potuj lachrymis, aut fletibus vllis,
Efficere vt nobis mitior ipsa fores:
Hoc nocuit misero seruifse fideliter vnj,
Hoc nocuit tanta semper amafse fide.

To PENELOPÆ.

Ntiochus in his youth, writ vehemently in prayſe of the *Academie;* but beeing old, hee chaunged copie, and writ as violently againſt it. While I am young, I muſt write of, and for Loue; and I muſt goe, becauſe I cannot ſtande ſtill: I am like the rowling Stone which neuer ſtayes, till it come to a lying place. As Infants repoſe in the rocked Cradell, ſo my ſpirit findes reſt in reſtleſſe Loue. *Alexander* diſdayned the *Corinthian* Ambaſſaders, who offered him the Freedome and Burgeoſie of their Citie: But when they tolde him that *Bacchus* and *Hercules* were likewiſe in their Regiſters, hee kindly thanked them, and accepted their offer. Doe

A iii. not

not (O vertuous *Penelopæ*) difdaine my fmall and poore propine. O be not afhamed to fee thy name in the bafe Chattons of my Poefie: Since better then *Bacchus*, and hardier then *Hercules* are in my Regifters. Thus, kifsing thy liberall hand, I hartily commende both mee and them to thy tuition.

Your La.

A. C.

Si qua videbuntur fcriptis temeraria noftris,
  hoc conftans veri pignus amoris erit:
Confilio regitur quifquis moderantius ardet,
  quiq; amor eft aliis fit furor ille mihi.

To the Queene her
moſt excellent Maieſtie.

APelles *man did all his Wits imploy*
  To paint the ſhape of Lædais *Daughter faire:*
But when he ſaw his worke prou'd naught, poore Boy,
He wept for woe, and tooke exceeding care:
Then deck'd he her with Iewels rich and rare:
Which when the braue Apelles *did behold.*
Paint on (quoth hee) poore Boy, and haue no feare,
When Beautie fayles, well done t'enrich with Gold,
I am (faire Princeſſe) like the Painters man,
As ignorant, as ſcant of ſkill as hee:
Yet will I ſtriue and doe the beſt I can,
To manifeſt my louing minde to thee.
    But to ſupply the weakneſſe of my ſkill,
      In place of Gold (great Lady) take goodwill.

Craige.

Amorous Songes
and Sonets.
TO IDEA.

IN Golden world, when *Saturne* did vpgiue
To *Pluto*, *Joue*, and *Neptune*, his Empire
They caſt their lots both how, & where to liue,
  Becauſe it was old *Saturns* owne deſire:
Joue ruld the Furnace farre aboue the Fire,
The ſtately Vault, beyond the ſtarrie round:
And *Neptune* gat the glaſsie Salt to hyre,
Then *Pluto* choofs'd the Helliſh blacke profound:
When *Cupid* ſpied they gaue him but the Ground;
Impatient wagg, went out to walke abrod,
And conquering theſe that were but lately cround,
He made him ſelfe ouer all thoſe Gods a God.
    Then *Loue* to thee, as to my Lord I yeeld,
    I feare to fight, where Gods haue fled the feeld.

Omnia vincit amor, et nos cedamus amorj.

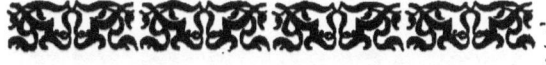

To IDEA.

Downe frō the Skies for to behold my Dame
Came Goddeſſes, and all the Gods aboue:
Ioue, Saturne, Mars, bright *Phœbus*, and with thame,
Rich *Iuno, Minerue*, and the Queene of Loue:
Her beauties fame, their mindes did ſo commoue,
They run, and tooke no reſt till they came thare,
Thus armies proud, approch't for to approue,
And giue their doome, that ſhe was matchles faire:
Loue like the reſt, would faine look'd on, & ſweare
Vnknit (faire Dame) this Craip, quoth he, & thou
Both Bagg and Bow a bonie while ſhalt beare,
Shoote where thou wilt, and I ſhall well allow:
   They change, & ſhe ſhot Loue, that he was faine
   To ſkarfe his eyes, and begge the Bow againe.

Cæcus amor ſuperos ſuperat, lithocardia amorem.

To LITHOCARDIA.

OF late the blind, and naked Archer Boy,
A libertine, out through the plains would play
With ayre-deuiding wings without conuoy:
Hee vaging went, and wift not where away.
Sad *Venus* wep't, and thus to mee can fay.
Didft thou behold my blind Babe any whare?
For hee is gone; O pittie ftrange eftray:
And he is fightles, fyndonles, and bare:
In *Craigs* and Rocks fuch Elu's doe make repare,
And fo perhaps hee harbers in thy hart.
It was too true, yet durft I not declare
His beeing there, for feare of further fmart.
    To want her Babe, braue *Venus* ftil doth murne,
    fhe drown's the world with teares, & yet I burne.

Hei mihi quod nullis amor eft medicabilis herbis.

To LITHOCARDIA.

Loue set his Bow, his Bag, and Bolts aside,
And went out through the watrie vaults of ayre
Dispos'd to play; he goes without a guyde,
And with the Winds he wauers heere and thare:
Till at the last a fleeting Castle faire
On smooth and glassie Seas hee doth espie:
Hee bords their Barke, the fishing craft to leare:
The poore men yeeldes, not daring to denie,
Hee hales their Hookes, and baites them by & by.
Then *Thetis* rose, and ask'd if Loue would burne
The liquid seat wherein her Lord did ly,
Disswading him from such a cruell turne.
   Feare not sayd Loue, I came to fish, thou sees,
   And left my flames in *Lithocardias* eyes.

O non humano nata puella toro.

To CYNTHIA.

THe Hobbie Haulke can catch at all no pray,
  Vnles aboue her ayme and marke she flie.
The Palme doth beare the brauer boughs some say
From neighbour trees, the higher that it bee.
So far'd of those my fansies fond and mee,
In hope of hap, I cannot cease to sore.
If loued, I liue: and if disdain'd, I die.
I pray, I prayse, I pleade, and I implore:
Proud *Cytherea* loued *Adonis* poore,
And *Cynthia* seru'd *Endimion* Sheepheard swane;
So though I be inglorious and obscure,
Yet may she loue her Poet and her Man.   (aire
Mount then braue thoughts through water, fire &
  And desp'rately pursue the sweete, proud, faire.

Blanditiis amor est, et succo mollior omni.

To PANDORA.

Since *Ioue* him felfe was fubiect vnto Loue,
And left the lift to catch a mortall pray.
   If *Neptune* did from glafsie Seas remoue,
   And would for Loue, afide the Scepter lay.
If *Pluto* loath'd his darke and pitchie Caue,
To fpoyle *Proferpine Ceres* Daughter faire.
If proude *Apollo Daphni* deare to haue,
Left *Phaeton* to rule his fyrie Chaire.
If fhaghhaird *Satyrs* mountaine-climing race,
Purfu'd *Ænonæ* through the *Phrygian* Woods.
If piping *Pan* from Muficke fweete did ceafe,
To hunt the *Naiad* Nymp's by bankes of Floods?
   What can I doe (fweet haart) but loue thee ftill?
   On whom nor Gods nor men can gaze their fill.

Iufsit amor, quis enim magno non cedat amorj,
In cignum, in pluuiam qui iubet ire Iouem.

To ERANTINA.

NOr there where as the yoaked reftles Horfe
   With *Phaeton* begins their wonted race,
and leads their Lord throughout the lift perforce
To circumgire the Earth into each place.
Nor there where as the hot and fyrie face,
The burning beames of *Phœbus* bright appeare,
When hee diuyds the day in equall fpace
With glorious rayes in his meridian Spheare.
Nor there, whereas *Apollo* proude, for feare
Our comming night, his lingering fhould controle
With fpeedie pace from our Horizon heare,
Is headlong hurl'd to view th'antarticke Pole.
   Nor no where els can any match at all
   be found to her; whofe vertues makes me thrall.

Tu mihi fola places.

To ERANTINA.

O Wounder to the world, whō woundering eyne
  Doe wounder still as on the rarest sight
Of Natures frame; yet come to common light,
Or Hemisphere, where our Horizon beene.
Sweete louely *Laura*, modest, chast, and cleene.
It seemes that Poet *Petrarche* tooke delight,
Thy spotles prayse in daintie lines to dight,
By Prophecies, before thy selfe was seene.
And now faire Dame, since thou art borne to bee
That Comet strange, and that prodigious Starre,
Whence life and death, and peace & bloody warre:
And calme and storme proceed, as pleaseth thee:
    Shine still, and still with sweete aspect infuse,
    Eternall theame, and matter to my Muse.

At mea cum multis placuisset musa puellis,
Huic vnj, dixj, noster inheret amor.

To IDEA.

THe chaſteſt Child will oft for mercie cry,
And bid the ſtriker ſtay and hold his hand:
Yea though he weepe, his teares he will vpdry
And kiſſe (ſuppoſe againſt his will) the wand,
With chiuering chin, but ſturring will he ſtand,
And patiently ſuppres his preſent paine:
Poore Babe he dare not but obey command,
And hold his peace, leaſt he be laſht againe.
Such is my ſtate, I faikles ſoule am ſlaine,
Nor can I get the ſmalleſt graunt of grace,
Nor dare I now, though I haue cauſe, complaine:
And though I durſt, my plaints wold haue no place
    Thus am I faine for feare of further wrong,
    Euen with the Babe to burſt, and hold my tong.

Non tamen audebæm tacitos operire dolores,
Ingenium metuens caſta puella tuum.

C.

To CINTHIA.

IT sometime chanst, as Stories tell by chanse,
That *Hercules* and *Hylas* were alone,
And seuerally they went apart to panse:
  But hee and hee, accompanied with none,
  Till *Hercules* to *Hylas* made his mone,
That hee for drouth was like to giue the Ghost.
Thus *Hylas* to *Ascanius* Flood is gone,
To draw a drinke, and lowting life hath lost.
So when mine eyes had spurd a speedie post,
To set the floods of fauour to their friend,
My burning heart, which drouth of comfort crost,
They dround them selues, & nothing els obteind:
  So Destanies my dolefull death concludes,
  By double force of Furious flames and floudes.

Uror, et heu nostro manat ab igne liqour.

To IDEA.

THe Lipper man, whofe voyce can not be hard,
With dolefull hoarfe vnpleafant tune wil cry,
And craue for loue of Iefus Chrift reward,
And alm's of fuch as chaunce for to paffe by:
But when (allace poore foule) he doth efpy
That no man heares, nor yet regards his voyce,
No longer then takes he delight to ly,
But claps his difh, and keepes his language clofe.
Right fo as curft, and carefull is my Croffe,
Suppofe the Fates haue not deform'd my fhape,
No words I vfe for to lament my lofe,
But make my Lines to be the Lippars Clap.
    Goe Sonet then and beg, I thee befeech,
    Some grace to him, whom feare deterres from
                                (fpeech.

Dicere quæ puduit fcribere iufsit amor.

To IDEA.

IN ſtately *Troy* which was by force of fire
Subdu'd in end, and turnd in embers cold,
Apollo's Church while *Priam* did empire,
   Was beautifull and braue for to behold:
In midſt whereof hung in a net of gold
A Cocatrice, that Spider, Bird, nor Flie,
To enter there, nor build durſt not be bold:
   That famous worke from filth was kept ſo frie.
The like (faire Dame) may well be thought of thee
For why, before thy beauties Altar hings,
Canceld with prid, both blood and birth I ſee,
   With cold diſdaine, which ſerue as certaine ſings,
      To warne a farre my fancie to refraine,
      And rather wrake then once reueale my paine.

Cor dolet gelidus torpet ſub pertore ſanguis,
   Me tamen oppreſsum dicere vetat amor.

To PANDORA.

I Panfe not on the gold of *Tagus* fand,
   Nor *Erithrean* braue and fhyniug fhells:
   Ilong not for the limits large of Land,
   Wherein the barbar newfound Nations dwels:
I bid not of thefe bounds whofe boofome fwells
With birth of braue and coftly Iewels rare,
Which with their Muske and Siuet fweeteft fmels
In faireft Chattons, fet perfume the ayre.
My pridles Hart fubdued with Loue and feare,
Seekes that thofe Songes the Heralds of my hart
Might mooue the fweet and flintie harted faire
Some fauour once, and pittie to impart:
   Els that vpon the Alter of her wreath,
   She would accept th'oblation of my death.

At fiue te regum Munera nulla volo.

To PENELOPE.

I Serue a Miſtris infinitely faire,
   And (which I more eſteeme) exceeding wiſe,
   In that, beyond the boundes of all compare:
    And this in her the wondering world enuies,
Thence doth of loue my reſtles rage arriſe,
Thence flowes the font of all the harmes I haue:
Her wit my heart, her beautie charm'd mine eyes,
To *Venus* thus and *Pallas* I am ſlaue:
If curious heades to know her name do craue,
Shee is a Lady *Rich*, it needes no more,
And wealthy *Iuno* wonted pride may leaue,
And gladly ſerue the Dame whom I adore:
    Rich, wiſe, and faire, to thee alone as thrall,
    I conſecrate loue, life, lines, thoughts, and all.

At mihi feruitium, et triſtis iam vita parætur,
Illaq; libertas priſtina furripitur.

To PENELOPE.

SHort is the day, but long (allace) to mee,
Who liue in loue, and am not loued againe:
My louely, faire, and loueles Saint I see,
Doth guild with gold her hid & coy difdaine.
thinkft thou faire dame, to buy my loue with gaine
Caufe thou art rich, I pray thee thinke not fo:
I am thy flaue, and for thy fake am flaine.
Nor can my Rim's reueale my inward woe.
Put now a poynt *Pænelopæ* I pray,
vnto this web fo oft retex'd by thee,
Pay loue with loue, and make no more delay:
O raine no more thy fhewers of gold on mee,
   One kiffe of thee would breed me more content
   Then make me king of *Crefus Lydian* rent.

To LITHOCARDIA.
By *Anagram*.

WHen Churches all of *Asia* les and more,
   By *Xerxes* great were burnt, & cast to ground
Of pittie hee *Dianais* Church forbore.
A peece of worke whose like could not be found:
And yet by fames report to be renound,
Herostratus did set the same on fire,
Which *Xerxes* great suppose a Monarch cround,
Did spare vnspoyld for all his proud Empire.
Right so, when as so many did conspire
To conquer mee a poore and Cuntrey Swaine,
My hardned hart withheld their hot desire,
And I till now, vnconquerd did remaine.
  That by my losse, I must enlarge thy fame,
  And slay my selfe to serue *a glorious Dame*.

Non ego seruitium Dominæ tam mite recuso,
Ah pereat si quis vincula et ipse times.

To LITHOCARDIA.

Anagram.

AS *Marigould* did in her Garden walke,
One day, O ten times happie was that day
I thitherward to fee my Saint, did ftalke:
Where *Floraes* Imp's ioy'd with her feet to play,
And loe vnfeene behind a Hedge I lay,
Where I beheld the Rofes blufh for fhame,
The Lillies were empald vpon the fpray,
The Violets were ftaynd about my Dame:
My Miftris fmild for to behold the game,
And fometimes pleafd vpon the graffe to fport,
Which canging hew's new cullors did acclaime,
For blythnes of fo fweete a Sainɛts refort,
 And from that walke while as away fhe went,
 They weepe with deaw, & I in teares lament.

Sprenit noftras galatea querelas.

To KALA.

FAire *Kala*, fairer then the Wooll moſt faire,
Of theſe my faire and ſiluer fleeced Sheepe
Which are committed to my careles care,
And vp and downe thoſe daintie Dales I keepe:
Faire Sheppeardeſſe, for thee alone I weepe.
None heares my plaints but bleating beaſts and I,
And for thy ſake I ſigh when I ſhould ſleepe,
And on thy name amid my dreames I crie.
Thē ſince thou know's the thraldome of my mind
And how my necke to beare thy yoke is worne:
Haue pittie once, and proue not ay vnkind,
And laugh no more thy ſhepheard ſwaine to ſcorne
    But if thou mind'ſt for to remead my mone,
    Let fanſies then, flocks, folds, and all, be one.

Tum miſtum cinerem communi onerare ſepulchro,
    Amborumq; vnus contegat oſſa lapis.

To LAIS.

What euer thou be that claimes or courts my deare
And in my abfence would fupply my place,
If courts thou, I pray thee to forbeare,
Rob not my right, and latelie granted grace:
For if it were, I friendly craue thy cafe,
And thou had credit as I fometime hade,
Were it not wrong, if I fhould proudlie preafe
To raue thy right? yes I may furely faide:
Be who thou wilt, I challenge thee therefore,
That with thy Daffings deauis my *Lais* care;
Ceafe from thy fute, and in to time forbeare,
Els we can be companions true no more.
      For put the cafe thou fpeed, thou gaines thefe
      A facill Dame, and of a friend a foe.   (two,

Cafta mane nec te lufus, nec munera vincant.

To LAIS.

EVen as a ventering Merchant skant of skill,
　Whom Fortunes frowne or fate hath forc'd to (fall
To recempence his former losse hee will
Within one Ship and Vessell venter all.
So haue I vsed my Stocke, though it be small:
My Hart I send halfe dround into dispaire
Vnto my Saint, whom euer serue I shall;
Shee is the Shipp, and it the ventered ware.
Oft hath my minde bin cloy'd with clouds of care
When contrar winds, with cold and stormie raine
would threat my losse; but now frō bounds of feare
My ventring thus, hath made me rich againe.
　Then shal my Muse triumph & mourne no more,
　　Since second windes haue brought my Shipp to
　　　　　　　　　　　　　　　　shore.

At nunc tota tua est, te solum candida secum,
Cogita et frustra credula turba sedet.

To PANDORA.

O Watchfull Bird proclaymer of the day,
 Withhold I pray, thy piercing notes from me:
Yet crow, and put the Pilgrime to his way,
And let the Worke-man rife to earne his fee:
Yea let the Lion fierce, be feard of thee,
To leaue his prey, and lodge him in his Caue:
And let the deepe Diuine from dreaming flie,
To looke his leaues within his clofe Conclaue:
Each man faue I, may fome remembrance haue,
That gone is night, and *Phofphor* draweth nie:
Beat not thy breaft for mee poore fleepeles flaue,
To whom the Fat's alternall reft denie:
   But if thou wouldft bring truce vnto my teares,
   Crow ftill for Mercie in my Miftris cares.

To PANDORA.

GO you o winds that blow from north to south,
Conuey my secret sighes vnto my sweet:
  Deliuer them from mine, vnto her mouth,
And make my commendations till we meet.
But if perhaps her proud aspiring sprit,
Will not accept nor yet rceiue the same,
The brest and bulwarke of her bosome beit:
Knock at her hart, and tell from whence you came,
Importune her, nor cease, nor shrinke, for shame:
Sport with her curl's of Amber cullour'd haire,
And when she sighs, immix your selues with thame
Giue her her owne, and thus beguile the *faire*.
Blow winds, flie sighs, where as my hart doth hant
  And secretly commend me to my sanct.

To PANDORA.

IN *Arcadie* fometime (as Sydne fay's,)
Demagoras a proud Lord did remaine,
In whom no thing I marke that merits prayfe,
   Sauc that he feru'd *Parthenia* fweet with paine:
But when he found fhe lou'd him not agane,
With leprocie he did infect her face,
Which cauf'd the conftant knight for to complane
But not to change his loue in any cafe:
Pandora faire his woofe infect'd allace
With leprocie of loathfome cold difdane,
Bred by my foe, to further my difgrace:
Yet neither fayth nor fancie fhall refrane:
    Yea, were her face deform'd as it is faire,
    I fhould ay ferue, though I fhould ay difpaire.

Fortuna potes inuita fecifse beatum,
    Quem velis.

To LITHOCARDIA.

A Very World may well be feene in mee,
My hot defires as flames of Fire do fhine,
My fighes are ayre, my teares the Ocean fea
My fteadfaft fayth, the folid Earth, & fyne,
My hope my heauen, my thoughts are ftars diuine
My iclofie the very pangues of Hell,
My fweete the Sainct, to whom I do propine
For facrifice my feruice and my fell.   (dwell
That hatefull Hagge, who neere my Dame doth
My riuall foe, my Loue the Sommer fweet,
My Spring-time, my deferts which fo excell:
And my Difpaires, the Winter cold and weet.
   But (O allace) no Harueft can I fee,
   Which fpoyls my yeares, & maks me thus to die

To ERANTINA.

WEll may I read as on a snowie sheet
  Of paper faire, my fortune in thy face,
Since at my sight thine eyes are both repleit,
With loueles looks presaging but disgrace:
And thou into my visage wann allace,
May see in sad characters of my care,
Since neither ruth nor pittie can haue place,
A boundles Booke, a volume of dispare.
Thus like a Glasse my face may well declare
My loue to thee, and with my loue my paine:
Thine show's againe (though it be matchles faire)
Thy hatefull heart and vndeseru'd disdaine.
  O antipathie strange to be susteind,
  I loue my foe, thou hats thy faithfull friend.

Vidi ego quæ veneris falleudo iura resesuit,
  Perfidiæ penas sæpe luisse graues.

D.

To IDEA.

THe Brethren three whose hot persut hath broght
  Death to them selues, & bondage to their land,
When as their foe before them fled, they thoght
The victorie was plac'd into their hand:
And yet his flight inferd no feare they fand,
For as they came, hee flew them one and one.
A *Parthian* forme, whose fight in flight doth stand,
For while they flie, their foes are kild anone.
Euen so may I, vnhappiest I complaine:
But pittie thus to serue a *Parthian* Dame,
Who shuns my sutes, and makes my fancie fane,
With hosts of harm's for to pursue the same.
  O sweet discord, O sweet concord agane,
  She flies to kill, I chase her to be tane.

To IDEA.

FAire louelie *Hæbæ* Queene of pleasant Youth,
Who bore braue *Nectar* to the Gods aboue:
Whose glansing beames like *Phœbus* in the south,
Do both bewitch and burne my brest with loue.
O thou that wars the woundring world for woorth
Whom Nature made to laugh her selfe to scorne,
More excellent then I can set thee foorth:
Whose like nor is, nor shall againe be borne.
My flowing Songs I consecrate to thee,
Good reason were, that they should all be thine.
Thy presence creats all those thoughts in mee,
Which mee immortall, and maks thee diuine:
   And such delight I haue with thee to stay,
   As twentie Moones do seeme but halfe a day.

Et tua quod superest temporis esse precor.

D ii.

To LITHOCARDIA.

THou who began by *Menalus* to mone,
   And lay alone for to lament thy loſſe
   Amid thoſe greene and grouie ſhads to grone
Where *Muſidorus* knew thee by thy voyce:
Thou haſt of me a comfort in thy croſſe,
With Princes proud if poore men may compare,
For why my cares ſuppoſe I keepe them cloſe,
Ouermatcheth thine, tho thy miſhaps were mare:
Thy thuartring thoughts were droūd in deepe diſ-
Mine haue no hope for to be brought to pas: (pare
Thy heart has hurt, and mine of blis is bare:
Thou chang'd thy ſhape, I am not what I was:
   In end thou ſped, I ware my worke in vaine,
   I loue allace, and am not loued againe.

Speq; timor dubia, ſpeſq; timore cadis.

To LAIS.

SEe *Deianira*, see how I am shent
 By that same Shirt which *Nessus* to thee gaue,
And thou againe to me by *Lychas* sent,
 I am inflam'd flesh, bons, and all I haue,
That *Ichthiophagic Æthiopian* slaue,
Who boyls his angled Fish by *Phœbus* beams
Vpon a Rock, no other stire may craue:
Nor Sun, nor Rocke, but these my gliding gleams.
Yet sweete thy sworne *Alcides* will not die,
There is no deadlie *Dipsas* in thy Sarke,
I languish but till *I* may meet with thee,
With quent Dialogs in the quiet darke:
 And so till time such happie time afford,
 My further will this bearer brings by word.

Sæpe greges inter requieuimus arbore terci,
Mistaq; cum folus perbuit herba torum.

D iii.

To PENELOPE.

THe *Perſian* King in danger to be dround,
Ask'd if no helpe in humane hands did ſtand.
The Skipper then caſt in the Salt profound,
Some *Perſians* braue, & brought the King to land.
Then *Xerxes* crowns the Skipper with his hand,
Who ſaues the King deſeru's (quoth he) a crowne:
But he atonce to kill him gaue command,
Die die, ſaid he, who did my *Perſians* drowne.
My Ladie faire, a *Xerxes* proud doth proue,
My worthles Verſe ſhe doth reward with gold:
But (O allace) ſhe lets me die for loue,
And now I rew that I haue bin ſo bold.
 As *Xerxes* crownd, and kild his man; right ſo
 Shee ſeemes a frind, and proues a mortall foe.

Credula res amor eſt . &c.

At IDEAS direction, thefe two Sonets were made.

1.

MOre then I am, accurfed mought I bee,
If er'e I did approch my deareft Dame:
But fuch a great refpect was ftill in mee,
As ay feare was equall to my flame:
Suppofe fome fots fpoyld of the fenfe of fhame,
Or feeling of my honeft Loue, will fay,
And publiklie to my difpraife proclame
That I delight in loathfome Luft as thay.
You facred pow'rs, I ftill inuoke and pray,
That all my fpeach turne poyfon in a clap,
If either I by word or writ bewray
One lufting thought her beautie to entrap,
   Let pale Enuie (faire Dame) admire and lie,
   With chaft defiers I ferue and honor thee.

D iiii.

To IDEA.

2

VVIth chaſt deſires I ſerue and honor thee
  Great Archi-miſtris of my rauiſht mind,
Moſt virtuous, wife, and faire, of all thy kind:
Whoſe leaſt command I vow to doe or die.
Chaſt was my Loue, yet is, and ay ſhall bee,
The prayſing Papers which I haue propin'd,
May well beare witnes how I am inclind,
And can (ye know) controull mee when I lie:
Phroneſis erring could eſpie no place,
Meete on this mould, but in thy breaſt to dwell,
A virtuous mind adorns a beauteous face;
And thou haſt both, and in them both excell:
   This maks my loue be chaſt, my paſsions ſtrange
   And I had rather chooſe to die then change.

Aſpice diuinas humano in corpore dotes
Nil mortalæ tibi fœmina digna polo es.

To CYNTHIA.

Hadſt thou been blacke, or yet had I been blind,
my muſe had ſlept, & none had known my mind
Or yet couldſt thou as thou art faire, be kind,
I had not thus with ſighs increaſt the wind:
But loe theſe frowning fauours which I find,
To which allace thou art too much inclind,
By which thy poore afflicted man is pind,
Haue broke the heart, which beautie firſt did bind:
Smile then faire dame, & ſometime ceaſe to frown
For ſmiles pleaſe mee, and do become thee beſt:
And ſince thou ſees how I am ſworne thine owne,
Smile ſtill on him who loues thee by the reſt,
   So neither ſhall I wiſh thee to be blacke,
   Nor curſe my eyes, the cauſers of my wrecke.

Nam ſi quem placidis facilis dignaris ocellis,
Nectaris huic fontes, ambroſiæq; fluunt.

To ERANTINA.

THe Tyrant *Nero* houering to behold
  The wrack of *Rome* on top of *Tarpe* hill,
He saw the rich, the poore, the young, the old,
Amid the flams in in present poynt to spill:
Yet woondering on that woonder, stood he still,
And (cruell man) would neither mend nor meene,
But tooke his pleasure to espie their ill,
And smild to see them smart before his eyne:
But had that man, that monstruous man yet beene
Reseru'd onlife by fatall Nimphs till now,
To view these flames which may in me be seene,
He would bewaile my poore estate I trow,
  whose boyling breast euen like mont *Ætna* burns
  When in his tomb the roaring monster turns.

To KALA.

THe *Perſian* Kings all waters did abiure,
Saue thoſe which flow'd frō faire *Choaſpes* flood:
From age to age this they obſeru'd as ſure,
As though no Waters els could do them good.
    This was a forme, no rather bondage ſtrange,
    which by no means theſe *Monarch's* braue would
                                (change.

I am as conſtant as a *Perſian* King,
And thou more deare then meat or drinke to mee:
For all th'entiſments beautie bright can bring,
With liſping toong, and ſoull entiſing eye:
    In ſpight of all theſe all as I began,
    I am thy true and neuer-changing man.

Thus will I ſurfet on thy beautie braue,
And *Lyzard*-like liue on thy looks diuiue:
In preſence abſence I am ſworne thy ſlaue,
And ſtill I would (were I a King) be thine:
    And for thy ſake, till life and breath endure,
    All other loue and ſeruice I abiure.

Tu quoq; iunge fidos fido cum coniuge amores,
Ipſe etenim et coniunx ipſe et amator ero.

To LAIS.

ALlace that abfence hath fuch force to foyll,
And to procure my euer pearceing paine,
Bereft of reft I toffe, I turne, I toyle,
Halfe in difpaire that we may meet againe:
Think on my vowes (& think they were not vaine)
My countenance, and each thing els I pray,
Which then I vf'd, when our goodnight was tane,
My inward wrack and woe for to bewray:
And when allone in clafped armes we lay,
With interchange of manie foulefooke kiffes:
Thinke how we fhed before the dawn of day,
With miriads of vnaccomplifht wifhes:
   Which with my felfe for lacke of prefens pind,
   I recommend vnto thy vertuous mind.

Sic mecum fixis herebas nixa lacertis,
Mutua cum placido trahebamus gaudia lufis.

To absent ERANTINA.

EVen as a man by darke that goes astray,
 Would faine behold and looke vnto the light:
Or as a Pilgrem erring from the way,
In wildsome wayes, would faine be set a right:
As Mariners in blacke and stormie night,
O'reset with Seas, strange winds, and stormie raine
Longs to behold the beames of *Phœbus* bright,
That after storme, the calme may come againe:
As he whom still the Iayler doth detaine
In bondage close, of freedome would be glade:
Right so shall I of presence be as faine,
To see the Sainct for whom my sighs are shade,
  Light, wished way, calme, freedome, should not bee
  So sweete to them, as *Presence* vnto mee.

To KALA.

Sore is my head and forie is my hart,
And yet for all th'emplafters I applie,
　No helpe hath Nature, nor no ayde brings Art,
Without, within, I burne, I fret, I frie:
A childifh thing when Care doth come to crie:
Yet this doth moſt my Feuer fell infect,
I hid my harms, and fo in filence die,
And thus my head muſt riue, my hart muſt breake.
But worſt of all, while vifage wan bewray,
What fecret fite my ficke foule doth affale,
How I or'edriue in deadly dooll the day,
And how this longfome Equinoct I vale:
　　　Shee cruell fhee that fhould my Surgeon bee,
　　　Allow's my loffe, and laughs, and lets me die.

Nec tamen vlla mea tangit te cura falutis.

To abſent IDEA.

Faire dame, for whō my mornfull muſe hath worne
To want thy ſight the black & ſable weede,
Whoſe houering haires diſheueld rent and torne,
May ſhow what baill thy abſence long can breed:
Looke if thou liſt my Rimes, and thou ſhalt reed
But coaleblack woes in coaleblack words brought
thy abſence long, hath made my cōfort deed, (forth
And makes my Verſes be ſo litle worth.
Shine then vpon my parched Sunburnd braine,
Chiefe ſtay of all my tempeſt-beaten ſtate:
Leaue not thy man diſconſolate againe,
Faire Goddes of my Fortune both and Fate:
    All earthly hopes for thee ſince I refuſe,
    Be thou my hope, my Miſtris and my Muſe.

Utq; ſupercilio ſpondes nutuq; loquaci,
Nonnihil ipſa meis mota venis precibus.

To ERANTINA.

OVt through the faire and famous *Scythian* land,
A Riuer runns vnto the Ocean mane:
Hight *Hypanis* with cleare and criftall ftrand,
Borderd about with Pine, Firre, Oake, and plane:
Whofe filuer ftreames as they delight the eye,
So none more fweet to either taft or fmell.
Yet *Exampeus* erre his Lord he fpies,
Maks him to ftinke like *Stigian* ftanks at Hell.
Eu'n fo faire Dame (whofe fhap doth fo excell)
Thy glorious rayes, thy fhining virtues rare,
No Poets pen, nor Rhetors tong can tell
So farre beyond the bounds of all compare:
    Yet are they fpoyld with poyfning cold difdaine
    And fuch as drink thy beauties floods are flaine.

Nil noftræ mouere preces verba irrita ventis,
Fudimus et vanas fcopulis impegimus vndas.

PANDORA refuseth his Letter,

THe faikles foule *Philoxenus* was flaine
  By courtes kind *Amphialus* the Knight,
   (Who for the faire *Cornithian* Queens difdaine
Borne to his forefaid friend had tane the flight:)
But when his Dog perceiu'd that forie fight,
He fawn'd vpon his maifters fatall foe:
Who then with hart and hand full of defpight,
Beats backe the Dog with manie bitter blo.
My deareft Dame and feemlie Sainct euen fo,
For whofe fweet fake I daylie die and dwins,
Hath flaine her flaue with all the wounds of woe,
And loaths allace, to looke vpon my Lins:
    That with the Dog my Ditties muft returne,
    And helpe their martird Maifter for to murne.

Quis Deus oppofuit noftris fua numina notis.

E.

To KALA.

TWixt Fortune, Loue, and moſt vnhappie mee,
　Behold a chaſe, a fatall threeſome Reele,
Shee leads vs both, ſuppoſe ſhee can not ſee,
And ſpurs the Poſt on her vnconſtant wheele:
I follow her, but while I preaſe to ſpeele
My bounds aboue, I faile, and ſo I fall:
Loue lifts me vp, and ſaies all ſhall be well,
In hope of hap my comfort I recall:
We iornie on, Loue is the laſt of all;
Hee on his winges, I on my thoughts do ſore:
I flie from him, ſuppoſe my ſpeed be ſmall;
Shee flies from mee, and woe is mee therefore.
　　　Thus am I ſtill twixt Loue and Fortune ſlaine,
　　　I neither take nor tarrie to be taine.

To LITHOCARDIA.

GOod cause hadst thou *Euarchus* to repent,
The reakles rashnes of thy bad decreit:
Thy crueltie did spring from good intent,
The grounds whereof were tedious to repeet:
Yet when thy Sonne fell downe before thy feet,
And made thine eyes confesse that he was thine,.
Thou wept for woe, yet could thou not retreat
The sentence said, but sigh'd and sorow'd fine:
So may it be that once those eyes diuine,
Which now disdaine and loath to looke so low,
As to behold these miseries of mine,
shal weepe whē they my constant trueth shal know
   And thou shalt sigh (though out of time) to see,
   By thy decret thine owne *Pirocles* die.

To LITHOCARDIA.

I Feare not *Loue* with blind and frowning face,
His Bow, his flame, nor sharpest hooked head:
A brauer Archer Death shall haue his place,
   And put a poynt to all my paine with speed:
And since it is my fate to be at feed
With her whom once I duelie did adore:
Yet fatall *Atrops* now shall cut the threed,
And breake the heart which she enioy'd of yore:
For fauors floods which I did oft implore,
Of *Letheis* Lake I time by time shall teast,
Her Marbel heart shal make me moorne no more
The buriall stone my dolor shall digeast:
Then farewell *she, auth, loue, hard-heart*, each one,
Come *Atrops, Lethe, Death,* and *Buriall stone.*

Nunc te tam formæ tangit decor iste superbæ,
Vt tua commorint tædia iniqua deos.

To inconstant LAIS.

HOw oft haſt thou with Siuet ſmelling breath,
told how thou loud'ſt me, loud'ſt me beſt of al?
And to repay my loue, my zeale, my fayth,
Said, to thy captiue thou waſt but a thrall:
And when I would for comfort on thee call,
Be true to mee deare to my ſoule, ſaid I,
Then ſweetly quheſpering would thou ſay, *I ſhall:*
And *echo*-like *deare to my ſoule*, replie:
But breach of fayth now ſeemes no fault to thee,
Old promiſes new periuries do proue.
Apes turſe the whelps they loue from tree to tree
And cruſh them to the death with too much loue.
    My too much loue I ſee hath chang'd thee ſo,
    That from a friend thou art become a foe.

Carminibus celebrata meis formoſa Neæra,
Aterius mauult eſse puella viri.

E iii.

To LAIS.

Sweet *Lais*, truſt me, I can loue no more,
And which is worſe, my Loue is turnd to hate:
Thou art vnkind, and woe is mee therefore,
Inconſtant fals and to my griefe ingrate,
It is too true *I* lou'd thee well of late,
And euen as true thou lou'dſt mee well againe:
I haue allace, no pleaſure to repeat
Our wiſhes and our vowes ſince all are vaine:
What reſolutions and what plots prophane
Wee two haue had in loue to liue and die,
The time, the place, the tokens giuen and tane;
Yf they could ſpeake, can thy accuſars bee:
  But ſince thou ſtill art falſe (I muſt confeſſe)
  Thy loue was lightlie won, and loſt for leſſe.

Ah crudele genus nec fidum fœmina nomen.

To ERANTINA.

Blind naked loue, who breeds thofe ftormy broyls
Which from my deare me to my dole debars:
To mee the pangs, to thee pertaine the fpoyls:
Thou taks aduantage of our ciuill warres,
I liue exild, but thou remains too neare,
Yet like a tirant fhee triumphs o're thee.
Her prefence maks thee more then blind I heare:
And abfence is farre worfe then death to mee,
Could I as thou, from ielous eyes be free,
Then fhould I be as blith as thou art blind:
I fhould not then difpaire, nor wifh to die,
Nor fhould my fighs increas the wauering wind.
    O rigor ftrange fince Loue muft ftill remaine,
    In prefence blind, and I in abfence flaine.

Vna dies tantum eſt, qua te non femina vidi,
Et fine iam videor feufibus efss meis.

E iiii.

To PENELOPE.

WHen ftately *Troy* by fubtill *Sinons* guile,
And *Grecian* force was brought to laft decay,
Uliſſes braue with faire and facund ftile,
Achilles Arm's obtaind, and went away:
In *Afrike* yet he was conftraind to ftay:
For when his friends did tafte of *Lotus* trie,
As *Homers* works do more at length bewray,
They green'd no more the *Greekiſh* foyle to fee.
So fares with mee, O moſt vnhapie mee,
Since I beheld thy faire and heauenlie hew,
The glorious rayes of thy all conquering eye,
My rendering heart and foule did fo fubdew,
    That for thy fake, whom euer ferue I fhall,
    I haue forgot my felfe, my foyle, and all.

TŌ IDEA.

MY Mufe fhal make thy boundles fame to flie
In bounds where yet thy felfe was neuer feene:
And were not for my Songs thy name had beene
Obfcurelie caft into the graue with thee:
But loe when cold and limping age fhall bee,
A figne of death, and when the graue fhall greene
And gape within her bofome to conteene
Her child, in fpight of Death thou fhalt not die:
For why, my Mufe, my reftles Mufe fhall eeke
Ten thoufand wings for to enlarge thy fame,
And eu'ry quill of eu'ry wing faire Dame,
to preach thy praife ten thoufand wayes fhal feeke
    Yet thou repayes my labors with difdaine,
    Thou liues by mee, and I by thee am flaine.

O ego non felix qui tam crudeliter amo,
    Nullaq; me redamat.

To frowning CINTHIA.

IF *Castor* shine, the Seaman hoyseth saile, (brace
With widkast womb the welcome winds t'em-
which gladly grasps the fare & prosperous gaile
And maks the Ship to run a fleeing race:
    But if *Orion* shine, the storme is nie,
    He lowes the Saile, which stood of late so hie

Such is my state, if *Castor*-like thou smile,
I onelie liue to serue and honour thee:
But if thou frowne, allace allace the while,
As at the sight of *Gorgons* head I die,
    As in thy lift so in thy looks diuine,
    Orion black, and *Castor* braue do shine.

Then since thou art th'*Orizon* of my loue,
Thine eyes the fatall starres which I adore:
With gracious blinks behold me from aboue,
Let me not sinke, safe bring me to thy shore.
    Or if thou loaths that I should liue, then frowne
    For die I, liue I, I am still thine owne.

Dicîte me Juuenem perijsse in amore mœq;
Vnita quod fuerit Cynthia causa necis.

To PANDORA.

Each thing allace, presents and lets mee see,
The rare *Idea* of my rarest Dame,
Deepe sunke into my soule the verie same,
Whose view doth still bewitch vnhappie mee,
The shining Sunne, her hart transpersing eye.
The morning red her braue and blushing shame,
Night absence, and day presence doth proclame,
foule wether frowns, & calme sweet smil's may bee
My scalding sighs tempestious winds, and raine:
But exhalations of my tragick teares,
In frost allace, her cold disdaine appeares;
In thaw, and fire, my melting heart agane:
    And thus each thing brings purpose to be pinde
    And to my thoughts cōmends the faire vnkind.

To PANDORA.

DEare to my foule, and wilt thou needs be gone,
   And leaue thy Man behind thee but a heart?
Is this the pittie which thou doft impart,
Disconfolat to let me die alone?
Thou haft two harts; mine, thine, and I haue none:
Heere fprings the surfe of my enfuing smart;
Yet play I pray the gentle Pyrats part,
And as thou lou's my life, yet leaue me one:
But brooke them both I gladlie grant and ftay,
How canft thou ride in raging raine and wind?
Yet thou muft goe, and woe is me away:
Then take my heart, and leaue me thine behind.
   I gaue thee mine, O then giue thine to mee,
   That mine and thine be one twix mee & thee.

Vna fides, vnus lectus, et vnus amor.

To LAIS.

I Haue compard my Miſtris many time
To Angels, Sun, Moone, Stars, & things aboue:
My Conſcience then condem'd me of a crime,
To things below when I conferd my Loue:
    But when I find her actions all are vane,
    I thinke my Rimes and Poyems all profane.

With perfect eyes her Pageants I eſpy,
To no thing now can I compare my Dame,
But *Theramenes* ſhoo; the reaſon why,
It feru'd each foote: and ſhe can do the ſame:
    She hears the futes of rich, poore, great, & ſmall,
    And has diſcretion to content vs all.

Si vitium leuitas, nulla puella bona eſt.

To PANDORA.

FAine would I goe, and faine would I abide,
Sweet *Hais agene,* and kiffe me erre I go,
Denie mee not fince there is none befide,
No teltale here, though thou wouldft giue me two:
Yet giue me one, if thou wilt giue no mo;
But one is none, then giue mee two or three,
Thy Balmie breath doth ftill bewitch me fo,
As I muft haue an other kiffe, or die,
Thy Rubent blufh now bids take leaue of thee:
Faine would I goe, and I would kiffe as faine,
Then giue me one, or change a kiffe with mee:
If neither giue nor change, take all againe:
    When thine & mine are thus conturb'd, I kno
    Thou canft but fmile, that I deceiu'd thee fo.

Mihi dulcia iunge
Ofcula, et in noftro molle quieffe finu.

To PENELOPE.

WHile fierce *Achilles* at the fiedge of *Troy*,
(the fatall Nimphs had fo decreed) was flaine
A fodaine ftrife arofe who fhould enioy
The Armes of that praife-worthie *Grecian:*
Aiax alleg'd he fhould the Arm's obtaine,
And by the fword to win and weare them vow'd,
Vliſſes faid, they fhould be his againe:
And he them gaind, if Stories may be trow'd,
But lo the fhield by Sea's was loofd, wee read,
And by a ftorme driu'n from *Vliſses* fight,
And rould to *Aiax* graue, though he was dead,
To fhow the world that he had greateft right:
  So when my tombe fhal end thofe teares of mine
  there fhalt thou figh & fay, I fhould been thine.

Tum flebit cum mi fenferit effe fidem.

To CINTHIA.

Oft haue I ment with Muficke, fleepe, & wine,
The foueraine cur's for fuperficiall cares,
For to reuiue this wounded heart of mine,
And free my felfe from forow, fighs, and teares:
Yet neither all, nor any one of thofe,
Haue force to end, or cure, or change my woes:
   My griefs are growne to fuch confufed force,
   No number refts for more, nor place for worfe.

If I had merit to be martird ftill,
And with the furie of thy frowns abus'd,
I could digeft thy gloomings with goodwill,
And neither looke nor craue to be excus'd:
I loue my Rod like *Mofes;* but if I
Perceiue it proue a Serpent, I muft flie.
   If thou wilt bind me ftill to be thine owne,
   Smile ftil (faire Dame) if not, I pray thee frowne.

Vincuntur molli pectora dura prece.

To LITHOCARDIA.

FAlse *Eriphile* sometime did betray
Facidic wife *Amphiaraus* her spouse,
(Who willing from the *Theban* warres to stay)
To hide himselfe secure at home he trow's:
Thus while his driftes *Adrastus* disallow's,
She (knowing that her husband should be slaine
At *Thebes*) for a golden chaine auow's
To tell *Adrastus* where he did remaine;
And thus reueald, he goes against his will,
But leaues *Alcmeon* to reuenge his wrack
On *Eriphile*, which he did fulfill,
When dolefull newes of fathers death came backe
    So since in loue thou art so vnloyall so long,
  Some strange *Alcmeon* must reuenge my wrong.

Quæq; prius nobis intulit illa ferat.

F.

To LAIS.

WHen *Cressid* went from *Troy* to *Calchs* tent,
    and *Greeks* with *Troians* were at skirmidg hot
Then *Diomed* did late and aire frequent
Her companie, and *Troil* was forgot:
Thou lay alone, such was allace thy lot,
And *Paris* brookt poore *Menela* thy Dame,
Shee twind in two the matrimoniall knot,
And tooke a stranger when thou went from hame.
Such is my case, if I may say for shame,
I florisht once; once there was none but I:
I once was lou'd, and I haue lost the same,
And as God liu's, I know not how nor why:
    So that my Sainct for falshood I am sure,
    May match the *Grecian* or the *Troian* whore.

Non sum ego qui fueram, mutat via longa puellas,
    Quantus in exiguo tempore fugit amor.

To KALA.

OFt haue I fworne; oft haft thou pray'd me too
  No more to loue, nor more to looke on thee:
Since looks and loue haue made fo much adoo
Twixt loueles thee, and vnbeloued mee:
Yet were I dam'd without redres to die,
I can not ceafe from feruing thee faire Dame:
Yea thou and all the woondering world fhall fee
The fayth, the force, the furie of my flame,
Moft like vnto the quefting Dogge am I,
Who ftill doth on his angry Maifter fawne,
While thou corrects, I kindly queft and cry,
And more thou threats, the more I am thine owne
    Thus loue or loath, or cherrifh mee or chide,
    Where once I bind, but any breach I bide.

Sit mihi panpertas tecum iucunda neæra.

To KALA.

WHen *Ædipus* did foolifhly refigne
    His Kingdome to his Sonnes, that he & he,
Aboue the *Thebans* yeare about fhould raigne,
And that his Crowne biparted fo fhould be.
Polinices firft raignd, but faith we fee,
He from the Crowne *Eteocles* debars:
Thus while they liue, they neuer can agree,
And after death, their burning bones made warrs.
My riuall foe againft all right enioyes
That Crowne & Kingdome which pertains to me
That proud vfurper worker of my noyes,
Shall find a foe, vnto the day I die,
    And were we dead, that are too long aliue,
    Our Afhes in th'exequial vrne would ftriue.

Riualem pofsum non ego ferre Jouem.

At the newes of IDEAS death,
Dialogue twixt the Poets Ghoſt
and Charon.

Ghoſt.

COme *Charon* come : *(Ch)* Who cals?
    (Gh.) a wandring Ghoſt,
By fortune led vnto the *Stygian* ſhore,
(Ch.) What ſeeks thou heere? *(Gh.)* a ſafe tranſport with poſt,
As thou haſt done to many mo before.   dore,
(C.) Who ſlew thee thus? *(G.)* euen ſhe whom I a-
Hath rould my name in ſcrowls of black diſgrace.
(Ch) What made her thus into thy griefe to glore?
(G.) *Loue* was my foe, & chang'd in wars my peace.
(C.) Go then aback, this Barke ſhall not imbrace
The ſmalleſt one whom *Loue* at ſead hath borne.
(Gh.) That ſhall I not, for lo before thy face,
I ſhall ou'r ſaile the flood and thou had ſworne:
    The Darts of *Loue* both Boat & Oares, ſhal bee,
    Sighs ſhall be winds, and Teares a *Styx* to mee.

F iii.

An other Dialogue to the same purpose.

Ghost.

COme *Charon* come. *(Ch.)* Who cals? *(Gh.)* a martyrd man,
Since Fame foorthtold the fairest faire was deid.
(Ch.) What seeks thou? *(Gh.)* Help to croce thy waters wan,
And I will pay thee for thy paines with speed.
(Ch.) Thou seems to be a quick & liuing leid,
And not a vmber, nor a palled Ghaist.
(Gh.) Feare not for that, since I for passage pleid,
But let mee haue thy helping hand with haist.
(C.) Though sage *Æneas* did o're-saile my streame
By *Sybils* helpe, none els must goe againe.
(G.) Then thinks thou *Charon*, to enioy my Dame
And stay my voyage from th' *Elesian* plaine?
(C.) Yes surely yes. *(G)* No *Charon* thou shalt lie
For *Loue* hath wings, and I haue learnd to flie.

Panditur ad nullas Janua nigra preces.

IDEA *after long ficknes, becommeth weil; and as he wept for her, he wifhes compenfation of her teares in his diftreffe.*

O Beautie doomb aftonifh'd Maruels chyld,
 The wanton obiect of my weeping eie,
Blith was my heart before I was beguyld,
And made to beare a feruile yoake by thee:
But now allace, though I by birth be free,
And not a flaue-borne *Mufcouite* by kind,
My Sainct fo Lords my heart, that now I fee,
There is no manumifsion to my mind.
Faire heauenly *Tigres*, be no more vnkind,
I wept for thee, when weerds did all confpire
Thy wrack; O then behold how I am pind:
Weepe thou for me, thy teares may quench my fire
 As I did thine, fo meene thou my eftate,
 And be not cald the worft of ills ingrate.

Sis ingrata licet fi modo bella manes.
F iiii.

To CYNTHIA.

PRoud *Zeuxis* gaue his Pictures all for nought,
Such was the loue he to his labors bore,
That by no gold nor price they could be bought,
And thus faue thanks poore man, he gaind no more
   I am as poore, and euen as proud as hee,
   For Loue nor Lines I craue no price from thee.

For if thou digne but with a gracious fmile,
To looke my Lines, and fpie how I am pind,
And with my toyes the fwift wingd time begile,
Then am I paide according to my minde:
   Joues oath was *Styx*, and *Phœbus Daphnes* haire;
   But from hencefoorth I by thy fmiles wil fweare.

To ERANTINA.

NO hart so hard, tho wrought of *Vulcans* steele,
　Or fearcely forg'd of Adamantine stone,
That doe endure or last so long so leele,
As mine, who loues thee most vnlouing one,
Whose purpose is and plot, as I suppone,
Most cruellie her captiue thrall to kill,
Who onely liues to loue but her alone:
Though she reward my true intent with ill:
Such is my state, I but abide her will,
Shee has the fatall stick into her sleeue,
And when she list her furie to fulfill,
Althea-like she may my breath bereaue:
　　Nor leue vnlou'd, I rather choose to die,
　　Then beat the fire, and burne the fatall tree.

Nam mea crudeles tetigerunt corda sagitte,
Atq; animam petijt vulneris asperitas.

To PANDORA.

Canſt thou haue eares, & wil not heare my plaint
Canſt thou haue eies, & wil not wipe my teares
Haſt thou a heart, and feeles not how I faint,
Debating twixt diſpairing hops and feares?
Canſt thou not ſee thoſe ſad and ciuill weairs
Which are within the kingdome of my heart,
Where Legions of perſuing pangs appeairs,
My vtter wrake and ruine to impart?
Heere burns the fire, there ſticks the deadly dart:
Here teares me droun, there ſmoky ſighs me ſmore
Here Beauty wounds, there riuals runs athwart,
And ielous eyes do pry into each pore:
    When al theſe al and thou my wrack contriues,
    I can not laſt, and I had twentie liues.

Perfida ſed duris genuit te montibus horrens,
    Cantaſus, hircaneq; admorunt vbera tigres.

Newyeares gift to PENELOPE.

THat *Colatine* did talke in *Tarquins* tent,
His Ladie *Lucrece* was moſt chaſt moſt faire,
Hee afterward had reaſon to repent,
Shee died a deemd adultres in diſpaire.
The *Lydian* King brought naked both and bare,
His wife before his friend for to be ſeene,
Which brought him ſelfe wee ſee into the ſnare,
For he was ſlaine, and *Giges* brookt his Queene.
Yet can not all theſe wracks forewarne my Muſe,
To hold her peace, but prayſe thee more & more:
I loue thee ſtill, and I will not refuſe,
Though ſmall allace, be my reward therefore.
   And ſo (faire Dame) for Newyears gift receaue
   My heart thine owne, my ſelfe to be thy ſlaue.

To PENELOPE.

WHen *Alexander* did fubdue and bring
  The coaftly Iles of *Inde* to his Empire,
Hee captiue tooke proud *Porus Indian* King,
And bid him aske what moft he did defire?
Nought faid braue *Porus* do I now require,
But that thou vfe me as a King fhould bee,
Thou fhalt haue friendly hoftage to thy hyre:
And for my fake I graunt thy fute (faid hee.)
Long with my pafsions haue I borne debate,
Oft haue I fought, and now haue loft the feeld,
It is my fortune for to be defeate.
I am thy Captiue, and faire Dame I yeeld:
  As *Macedo* was to the King of *Jnde*,
  If not mine, yet for thy caufe be kinde.

To LAIS.

WHen *Dionise* was shut from Regall seat,
    And quite depos'd from his Imperial throne
For tyrannies too tedious to repeate,
Which made oft times the *Siracusans* grone,
When he was thus disgrac'd, and left alone:
He could not cease to play the tyrant still,
He grew a pedant infants poore anone
He taught and quhipt to exercise his ill.
I with my Loue haue plaid the licher long,
And shee the loun with many moe then mee:
This custome vile, maks sinne to seeme no wrong,
And she must turne a common Whoore I see,
    Though both be bad, and each of both vnsure,
    I rather serue a tyrant then a whoore.

To abfent PANDORA.

Long fince hath *Cynthia* fhown her ful fac'd prid
And now compeirs with crefcent horns againe
Since at the banks of *Neptuns* flowing tide,
I tooke my leaue and fhew how I was flaine:
Allace allace, they haue not wept in vaine,
Who left vs annals of eternall date,
Condemning abfence for a cruell paine,
A foe to fayth, a vnfriend vnto fate:
A happy life had I in loue of late,
To ioy the fweete fruition of thy face,
Now from thy fight eftranged is my ftate.
Since all my life is darknes and difgrace:
   Yet midft my woes I wifh that well thou bee,
   And with the winds I fend thofe fighes to thee.

Nulla mihi fine te rident locæ, difplicet æquor,
Sordet terra, lenes ods cum retibus hamos.

To PENELOPE
ſeeke.

VVEre I as ſkild in Medecine as hee,
 Who did reſtore *Hippolits* health againe,
When he was torne with horſe; then ſhouldſt thou
I ſhould prepare emplaſters for thy paine: (ſee
 But ſince I am no *Æſculap* at all,
  I am thy Bondman, and thy Beadman thrall.

Phœbe faue, laus magna tibi tribuetur, in vno
 Corpore ſeruato reſtituiſſe duos.

Newyeares gift to IDEA.

THE *Locrian* King *Zaleucus* made a law,
  That each adultrar both his eyes fhould lofe,
But when his Sonne was faultie firft he faw,
That facred Kings haue hid and fecret foes,
Incontenent vnto the ftage he goes,
And from his Sonne one eye, one of his owne
He cauf'd pull out, and in the fight of thofe
A carefull King, a father kind was knowne.
In *Janus* Kalends faire and louely fweet,
Time out of minde hath been a cuftome old,
That friends their friends with mutual gifts fhould
To keep true kindnes from becōming cold. (greet
  Zaleucus-like thefe Lines are fent by mee,
  To keepe the law and kith my Loue to thee.

Da veniam merui nil ego, iufsit amor.

To CINTHIA.

Why loues thou more (faire dame) thy Dog then
   what can he do but (as the Scholer said (mee?
At *Xanthus* feaft) fhake cares and tayle on thee?
And I can do much more to make thee glade,
With tedious toyle and longfome labour made.
Hee can perhaps bring thee thy Gloue, or whyls
Thy Kirchiff when t'is either left or laide
Behind thy heeles with fweet and backaft fmyles:
But I, whom thou difdainefully exyles
From thy fweet bed, and thy moft fweet embrace;
Which fawning Currs with filthy feet defiles,
I could doe more, but I lack leaue allace:
    Fie Natures baftard, make no Dog thy Loue
    Leaft thou a Monfter, I a Martyr proue.

G.

To KALA.

I First receiud since did sweet Sainct vnfold
Thy louely Lines, the legats of thy mind,
And did with blith & ioy-swolne breast behold
How thou continew'd constant, true, and kind.
But when I did perceiue how thou wast pind,
Pind for the absence of thy loue-sick swaine,
My toong was doomb, my silent eyes were blind,
I read and mus'd, and mus'd and read againe:
And be thou iudge (deare heart) if I was faine
When I euolu'd from out the Paper whit,
That Symboll sweete transparent pure & plaine,
Wherein some time thou tooke so much delight:
   Yea thrise each day (faire Mistris) till we meet,
   I kis thy Symboll, and thy golden sheet.

Quisquis ad hanc vertit peregrinam littora puppim,
Ille mihi de te multa rogatus abit.

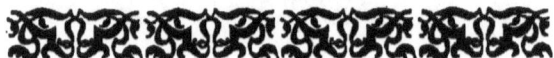

To KALA.

I Sweare (sweet *Kala*) by my flames, thy eyes,
O eyes; no eyes, but rather starres diuine:
Sweet *Dionean* twins into their skies,
  And by those kind alluring looks of thine,
I sweare by all our teares whils thine, whils mine,
Nor mine nor thine, but both combind in one:
By all the sighs blowne from the sacred shrine
Where *Craigs* true heart hath his heroick throne,
I sweare by all our secret vow's each one,
Made in the darke, and reconfirmd by day:
By all our kisses when we were allone,
And all the wishes when I went away:
    Let Weerds and Fortune do the worst they can
    I am in spight of *Misoes* Nose, thy man.

To KALA.

OHow I long to heare from thee againe,
  And vnderstand the tenor of thy state:
Thrife hath the Moone begun to wax and wane,
With spheirs and horns since I receiu'd thy wreat:
Then giue mee leaue (sweet Lady) to regrate,
Since thou may haue of traualing troups such store,
And I haue sent so many lines of late,
Thou art vnkind, and woe is mee therefore:
Each one that comes from thee, or from thy shore,
In hope of newes, I entertaine for thee:
Each Post I meet, each Horne I heare, yeelds more
Harmonious sounds, then musicke sweet to mee:
    But when my hopes proue naught with sory
    I sigh & say vnkind, vnkind, vnkind. (mind,

Tempora si numeres bene quæ numeramus amantes,
  Non venit ante suam nostra querela diem.

To CYNTHIA.

VVHen thofe which at *Ardea* did remaine
　With *Aracins* did many times contend
For Confind Lands, which neither could obtaine,
In many Battails, though much blood they fpend,
Yet that fometime the ftrife fhould take good end
Both they and thofe referre them felu's to *Rome*,
Imperious *Romans* parties both offend,
And to them felues the queftiond Lands affume.
Long warres heue been betwixt thy Maid & mee,
Yf fhee or I my loueficke heart fhould haue;
Shee thinks it hers, it was once mine, and wee
To end this ftrife, thy facred fentence craue.
　　Thou like thefe conquering *Romans* in this cafe
　　By fpoyling both, poffeyds my heart in peace.

Cynthia prima fuit Cynthia finis erit.

G iii.

To ERANTINA.

THe ielous eyes which watch my louing Dame,
And *Argus*-like to trap mee ftill attend,
They with my loffe allace, but fecke her fhame:
Which I befeech thee louing Lord defend.
O would to God my honeft courfe were kend,
Or that my breaft were made of Criftall cleare,
That triall might be tane what I intend:
And my true part in prefence might appeare.
But (O allace and weladay) I feare,
Thefe iarres fhall foone ingender fuch debate,
As fhall but doubt debarre mee from my deare,
And enterchange my wonted good eftate.
   O harmonie vnhappieft of all,
     Bad chance brings change, and change hath
       fram'd my fall.

Res eft folliciti plena timoris amor.

To ERANTINA.

DIsordered Haires the types of my disgrace,
  The testimonies of my seruile state:
Ou'ruaile my wanne and pale disfigured face,
And let my fauour answere to my fate:
For since I am th'vnhappiest hee, I waite
That Loue, or Fortunes enuie can assaile:
What resteth then? but still for to regrate,
Since word, nor writ, nor prayers can preuaile:
And since my deare disdainfullie doth deale
With hopeles mee, who was and is her owne,
My pearsing paines shall on my visage pale,
With hoarie, rough, & crumpled skin be knowne.
  And such as sees my furrowed face, shall say,
  The faire Vnkind is cause of my decay.

Illa dies fatum misero mihi dusit ab illa,
Pessima mutati cepit amoris hyems.

G iiii.

To ERANTINA.

Long haue I had long haires vpon my head,
Long haue I had hid harmes within my heart,
Yet none of thofe are powerfull for to plead
The fmalleft falue or foftning to my fmart.
Could I draw foorth the fharpe and golden dart,
Wherewith allace, I fecretlie am flaine:
Or put thofe black vnpouled locks apart,
For which the world accompts mee to be vaine:
Could I to flit as to be faft be faine,
Or thinke that foule that I haue thought too faire,
There fhould no harme into my heat remaine,
Nor fhould my head be ouerhung with haire.
    Sweet, if thou loues me, powll thofe locks I pray
    Yf not, cut life, loue, locks, and all away.

To PANDORA.

O What a world I suffer of extreames,
  Twixt hot desire and icie cold dispaire:
Most like the swift impetuous tyds of Theames,
Are those the ebs and flowings of my care:
I liue allace, a martire late and aire,
Coold with dispaire, and burnd with hot desire:
I see allace, and can not slip the snare,
In floods I frie, and freeze amid the fire:
In *Sestian* seas to *Hero* sweet I swim,
And faine would touch the simber of her goun,
Hoysf'd with desire vnto the clouds I clim,
But by dispaire *Leander*-like I drown:
    My *Dolphin* deare, let not *Arion* dee
    Saue mee vnsunke, and I shall sing to thee.

Quicquid conabor dicere uersus erit.

To PANDORA.

FAire *Sicil* fertill firft of Cruell Kings,
  When *Dionife* did all thy ftate ouerthrow,
And wrought fo many ftrange & monftrus things
And led fo long a life without all law:
Sad forrow was the *Syracufan* Song,
And all faue old *Hymera*, wifh'd him dead,
Shee wifh'd him weel, caufe many tyrants fprong:
And were hee gone, a worfer would fucceed.
It is my weird, and woe is me therefore,
To ferue and loue where recompence is none.
Oft haue I chang'd, and now can change no more
For badder ay fucceeds, when bad are gone.
  And this fweet hart maks me thy beadman thral,
  Leaft by thy loffe, in harder haps I fall.

Quando ego non timui graniora pericula veris.

To PANDORA.

When *Scythian* Lords long frō their lands had bein
Their ſlaues vſurp'd their abſent Maiſters place:
both wealth & wiues they breok'd before their eine
And did the ſame ſeuen yeares poſſes in peace:
They turning home, and ſeeing ſuch diſgrace,
fought with their ſeruants for their wealth & wiues
But by the men the maiſters gat the chaſe,
And hardly ſcap'd with hazard of their liues.
Then they conſult with neither ſwords nor glaues,
Nor open warres, to make their foes to yeeld,
with whips & wands they bat their randring ſlaues
And by the change of weapons wan the feeld.
  Since ſighs, nor teares, nor ditties can ſubdue thee
  I muſt (faire ſweet) with *Scythian* armes perſue thee

To IDEA.

I Put my hand by hazard in the hat
 Where many names did intermixtly lie,
 With her and her were you and this and that,
    A fortune blind, or niuie nake to trie:
And lo ſuch was my luckie lucke that I
Among ſo many, found thy Noble name,
And on my head, that thou and all may ſpie,
I well auow the wearing of the ſame:
It ſhall inferre no foyle vnto thy fame,
That thou art borne vpon ſo baſe a head:
A Begger find's a ſtone of curious frame,
And yet the ſtone remaines a ſtone indead.
    So thou art thou, and of more worth to mee,
    Deare Valentine, then thou waſt wont to bee.

To LITHOCARDIA.

GReat *Alexander* gaue a ſtraight command,
That euery Souldier in the Camp ſhould ſhaue
And that his face as haireles as his hand,
Both *Greeke* and *Perſian* time of warrs ſhould haue:
When Armes were put a part, he lent full leaue
To weare long beards; a ſign of fat-fed peace:
And thus in Greece a ſtranger might perceiue
The Countries ſtate into the Souldiers face.
I am content that cuſtome to imbrace;
I haue no beard to ſhow my peace with thee:
But thou wilt ſay, my hairs portend diſgrace,
And diſcontent is in my downcaſt eye:
   It is too true; but let me riſe or fall,
   Or ſinke or ſwim, I am thy ſeruient thrall.

Addimus his precibus lachrimas quoq; verba preantis,
  Perlegis, et lachrimas finge iudere meas.

To LAIS.

WHy loue I her that loues not mee againe?
   Why am I friendly to my fremmit foe?
Why doe I weare my wayting on in vaine,
In feruing her that hath deceiu'd mee fo?
Why did I thus my freedome fweet forgo,
To pleafure her that plagu's mee with difdaine?
Or wifh her weel that euer wrought my woe,
And would not figh fuppofe fhee faw me flaine:
O foolifh I, and haples I alone.
No then, O faythleffe and difloyall fhee,
Whofe try'd vntrueth thus maks me to complaine
And wifh before the fixed day to die:
   For now tint time and trauell maks me fure,
   I playd the foole, and fhe has playd the hoore.

Periuria ridet amantum,
Jupiter et ventos irrita ferre iubet.

To LAIS.

BRaue *Troilus* the *Troian* ſtout and true,
As more at length in *Chauſer* wee may find,
Dreamd that a faire White Bull, as did inſue,
Had ſpoyld his Loue, and left him hurt behind.
The *Phrygian* Nymphe *Ænonæ* dround in drerd,
When *Paris* towards *Grece* made ſaile from *Troy*,
In dreames foreſaw, as after did ſucceed,
Her Loue and foraine Ladie ſhould enioy.
When *Hecuba* the Wiſemen did imploy,
Her dreame of flaming Fire for to expone,
They ſhortly ſhew that *Paris* ſhould deſtroy
And ſet on fire faire *Ilion* ſticke and ſtone.
    Right ſo might I, if weerds had not withſtand,
    In dolefull dreames foreſeene the fall I fand.

Quid tuneam ignoto tuneo tamen omnia demens.

To IDEA.

LAſt yeare I drew (faire Dame) by very chance,
  Thy Noble name amongſt a number moe:
Glad was my ſoule to ſee the weirds aduance
The happy hazard of my fortune ſo:
    And proud thereof, vpon my pate I plac'd thee,
    With anagram's and Sonets ſweet I grac'd thee.

But now (wiſe Dame) behold a wonder ſtrange,
Which both I wiſh thee to beleeue and heare:
(I am ſo loath where once I chooſe, to change)
That in my heart thou harbours all this yeare:
    Then from a Hat I drew thee err I ſaw thee,
    Now from my hart it is my doome to draw thee.

Why ſhould I hazard what I haue ſo ſure,
Or ſcrape thy name into a ſcuruie Scrowle?
O thou art writ in blood's characters pure,
Within the center of my loueſick ſoule:
    Let others try a fortune blind and beare thee,
    Both on my head & in my heart I'le weare thee.

To KALA.

BLind Loue (allace) and Ielofie vndoo
That conftant heart which I bequeath to thee:
I loue theè moft, and am moft ielous too,
By this I liue, by that vndone I die:
Not that I thinke a fickle change can bee,
Where vertue dwels, but that mine owne vnworth
Is worfe then twentie riuall foes to mee:
My bafe eftate thefe baftard thoughts brings foorth
O were my moyane equall to my minde,
Or were my wealth as great as my goodwill,
Could I commaund the coftlie Iles of *Jnde*,
Thou fhouldft be weell, and I fhould feare no ill.
   Then Fortune, Fates, & all yee Gods aboue,
   Enlarge my luck, or els make les my loue.

Venit amor grauius quo ferius vrimur intus,
Vrimur, et fecum pectora vulnus habent.

H.

To PANDORA.

WHile gathering in the Muses garden flowrs,
   I made a Nosegay, which perfum'd the aire,
Whose smell shall sauour to times latest hours,
And shall for ay adorne thee cruell faire.
I laide mee downe vpon the grassie greene,
Where I beheld fruit's, flowr's, and hearbs anew,
Foorthspred by *Flora* glorious Sommers Queene,
Whereon the calme and gentle *Zephir* blew:
On haughtie hils, which Giant-like did threat
To pearse the heauens with their aspiring head,
Grew war-like Firs, strong Oaks, & Ceeders great,
Whose shaddie boughs the leauie groues ou'rspred
    Thus high and low I looked where I lay,
    Yet neither fruite nor flower was like my *Hay*.

To KALA.

WHen silent night had spred her pitchie vaile
On all the parts of *Vestais* fruitfull face.
And horned *Luna* pensiue sad and paile,
Was at thy presence darkned with disgrace;
Thinke (comely *Kala*) with what kind embrace
Wee shew the secrets of our sigh-swolne soule,
How strict a bond we ty'd in litle space:
Which none but heau'ns haue credit to controule.
Sweet Shippardes thinke on thy Loue-sick swane,
Whose life, whose all, doth on thy loue depend:
Let nought saue death, deuide vs two againe,
And let our loues euen with our liues take end.
    And when I cease for to be true to thee,
    Breath vanish in the winds aud let mee die.

Dij preter hoc iubeant vt euntibus ordine fatis,
  Jlla meos oculos comprimat, atq; suos.

H ii.

To his Riuall and L A I S.

AS thou art now, fo was I once in grace,
And thou waſt once difgrac't, as now am I.
O wonderous chaunce, o cruell contrarie cafe,
O ſtrange difcord, yet greeing harmonie.
I once was lou'd, thou loath'd; but now eſpie
How I am loath'd, and thou art lou'd alone:
In this the wheele of Fortune you may try:
I raignd, thou had no raigne; thou raignes againe,
Then happie thou, if fo thou might remaine:
But fayth thou muſt come downe there is no dout,
And thou muſt be a partner of my paine,
The nixt muſt needs haue place his time about:
  Els fortunes wheele fhould whirle about no more
  Nor *Lais* faire be fals, as of before.

Turpius eſt pulchra nam meretrice nihil.

Farewell to LAIS.

Thou fawns (faire nimph) for frindſhip at my hand
And ſayes, thou ſeeks no more of worldly blis:
But ſeid forgot that friendſhip true may ſtand,
And cryes met mercie if thou made amis.
But harke my heart, and truſt mee weel in this,
I can not loue a faigned friend; no no:
Since I am ſo acquaint with *Judas* kis,
Shape not (my ſweet) for to deceiue me ſo:
For *I* haue read in Stories old, of two,
Zethius and *Amphion* did diſcord,
Till time *Amphion* muſicke did forgo,
Which by his fellow was ſo much abhord:
    Thy ſute (my ſweet) is ſeaſond with ſuch ſals,
    We ſhall not friend ſo long as thou art fals.

Non amo te fateor quid enim ſimulare necefse eſt.

H iii.

A sparing farewell to KALA.

FOnd *Celuis* some time in a foolish vaine,
  Would needs applie emplasters to his foot,
And would as sick men doe, sigh, weepe, & plaine,
And make the world beleeue he had the Gout:
    And by this custome which he had, wee reed
    Dissembling *Celuis* tooke the Gout in deed.

How many broyls betwixt vs two haue beene,
Which I oft times of purpose would deuise,
That in that sort our loue should scape vnseene,
And vndeuulged in a darke disguise?
    But fayth that custome hath deceiu'd mee so,
    That in effect I am thy fremcast foe.

When first our Loue was in the pleasant prime,
Thou lou'dst mee well, I lou'd thee well againe:
But heere behold the strange effects of time,
My fire turns frost, thy loue turns cold disdaine:
Yet time may friend which made vs foes; til whan,
  I wish thee weell, but am no more thy man.

Namq; vbi non amor est vbi non miscentur amoris,
  Suauia nil lauti, nilq; leporis inest.

A wrathfull farewell to KALA.

THe whiteſt Siluer drawes the blackeſt ſkore,
  In greeneſt Graſſe the deadly Adder lowrs,
The faireſt Sunne doth breed the ſharpeſt ſhowrs,
The fowleſt Toads haue faireſt Stons in ſtore:
So fairſ'd of Loue, and woe is mee therefore.
In greeneſt Graſſe lies hid the ſtinging Adder,
In faireſt ſhining Sunne the fowleſt wadder,
A precious Pearle plac'd in a poyſning Pore:
Shall I ſupp ſweet mixt with ſo ſowre a ſals?
Or drinke the Gall out of a Siluer pot?
Or ſhall I caſt on libertie a knot?
Als faſt, als lows; als lowſe, als faſt, ay fals:
  No, I beſeech the Gods that rule aboue,
  They let me neuer leue, and euer I loue.

Durius in terris nihil eſt quod viuat amante,
Nec modo ſi ſapias quod minus eſse velis.

H iiii.

To PENELOPE.

WHen *Tyndaris* was broght from *Troy* againe
and princely *Pergam* leueld with the ground
And fatfed earth with *Phrygian* flesh was faine
Through shallow furrs faire fruit's for to refound,
The facund wife *Vlisses* most renound,
By fatall answers was foretold wee find,
That he should not in deadlie deep's be dround,
Although withheld with many contrar wind:
Yet that vnhappy and that bastard brat,
That Parricid which from a farre should come,
Telegonus whom he with *Circe* gat,
Should kill his father at his comming home:
    Though I haue past as many storm's as hee,
    The last is worst, and for thy loue I die.

Elegie to KALA.

REed this, and then no more,
    this fhalbe laft of all,
And fhould been firft, if now I could,
    my publifht Rymes recall,
But they are gone abrod
    vpon the winges of Fame:
Na, can the glyding Ocean waues
    put bounds vnto the fame:
The fpacious Continent,
    Nor yet the bordering mane,
Can neither hold the woes nor vowes
    of my vnquiet vane.
Nor prayers, nor the prayfe
    which I haue pend for thee,
Which makes me thus for to be pind,
    and thee fo proud to bee.
This then fhall be the laft,
    fince firft it can not bee;
For I haue waird alreadie els
    a world of words on thee:
But worlds *Democrit* faid,
    were infinite, and fo
                                         Thou

Thou looks to find infinites
    of worlds of words, or moe:
No no; my Poyems haue
    proclaymd thy prid, my paine,
And I am wo that I haue waird
    so many words in vaine.
For I haue dryd the braine
    of my inuention quit,
And neither conquered my desire,
    nor purchast thy delight.
Lo then how I was led
    with Loue, that Lordly elff,
That bred no pleasure vnto thee,
    nor profet to my selff:
But as *Phœneus* poore
    for Phisick sought in vaine,
And by his foe was cur'd, when as
    hee hop'd hee had been slaine.
So thy disdains haue cur'd
    my hurt and vlcerd hart,
And I am weell against thy will,
    but sense of old-felt smart.
To Sea with sweetest streams
    flows *Hypanis* the flood,

                                But

But *Exampeus* poyſning well,
    maks bad which erſt was good.
And thus vnlike it ſelfe
    grow's *Hypanis:* euen ſo
Thy coy diſdaine hath changd a friend,
    into a fremmed fo.
Thou ſawſt my dwining looks,
    my ſcalding ſighs and ſobs:
Thou ſawſt my tearefwolne eyes were full
    of liquid pearlie globs.
And yet, as *Nero* proud,
    when *Rome* was burnd, did grow
As glad as at a Comick ſport,
    and laugh to ſee the low.
So thou falſe Tyran, thou
    from turret of thy prid,
Thou ſmild at my miſhaps as proud,
    as braue as *Neptuns* brid.
But woorthy *Phocion*
    a Captaine braue and ſtout,
For theſe vnkind *Athenians*,
    fought fourtie Batels out,
And yet was ſlaine by them:
    and when he died, 'tis told

                        Hee

Hee pray'd his Sone for to forgiue
    his death, for kindnes old.
So though I be in poynt
    by thy difdaine to die,
My heart fhall charge my houering hand,
    to write no ill of thee:
For like *Themiftocles*,
    I rather drinke the Gall,
Then fight againft my once good friend,
    though now my loue be fmall.
Then fometime friend, farewell;
    this is my moft reuenge,
To thinke no good, to write no ill,
    but laft of all to change.

                                                                                      His

His Resolution of absence and farewell to *Lithocardia*.

FAire Dame adue, for whom I dayly die,
And quicke and dead a martyr still remaine:
Now must I flit o fairest, farre from thee,
And flie the force of vndeseru'd disdaine,
Since I haue weard my warbling Verse in vaine.
O Verse to be my sorows children borne,
Abortiue birth brought foorth with too much paine
And recompens'd too much with too much scorne:
Since Lines and I and all are all forlorne,
Faire Dame receiue this last enforst adew,
For I shall see, if Fates haue not forsworne,
If change of Nations natures can renew,
    If tract of time, if change of soyle or aire,
    May helpe thy Loue, or hinder my dispaire.

Quid loquor infœlix, an non per saxa per igne,
Quo me cunq; pedes ducunt mens ægra sequetur.

His Reconciliation to *Lithocardia* after abſence.

O *Lautia* poore was glad,
    when th'*Amazon* Queene of yore
Receiu'd a Noſegay from her hand,
    ſuppoſe ſhee ſmeld no more.
Cherillus heart was hoiſ'd
    to higheſt heauens hee thought,
When *Macedo* ouer lookt his Lines;
    ſuppoſe hee lik'd them nought.
So, if thou take my Verſe,
    a louing poore propine,
Which ouer-ſhadowed with thy ſight,
    throughout the world ſhall ſhine.
If thou the ſheet receiue,
    though thou vnfold no folds,
Yet ſhall thoſe hidden Lines be blith,
    whilſt thou their backs beholds:
And I poore hopeles ſoule,
    thy weell affected man,
Shall be as blith as *Cherill* was,
    or yet *Olautia* than.
                              Take

Take then my faultles Sheet,
    bedewd with mourning Inke,
And if thou wilt not view my Verſe,
    to know the thing I thinke;
Yet ſhall the Paper ſerue
    (O faire and matchles Dame)
To be a Bottom to thy Silke,
    or faſftie to thy Seame:
But leaſt my mourning Inke
    like *Niobe's* blacke tears,
Should blacke thy braue *Mineruik* worke,
    whilſt it thereto adhears,
Pine with thy ſnow-white hand
    the Verſe before thy view,
That they may not infect nor foyle
    the farſet Silks faire hew:
And thou ſhalt ſee no more
    ſet downe before thy face,
For to reueale my endles woe,
    but this one word *Allace*,
Allace, allace, allace,
    Allace, allace againe,
Ten thouſand times allace allace,
    can not expres my paine.
                                    Allace

Allace I am thine owne,
    na haue I hap to vew
Heraclits flood of change thereby,
    my nature to renew.
None knew of *Hercules*
    the poyfoning deadly fhafts,
But *Philoctetes;* none but I
    complains conceals thy crafts.
Though thou haft faild to mee,
    I am not falfe to thee:
I am thy Beadman day by day,
    and bondman till I die.
And would to God thou hadft
    rich *Amaltheas* horne,
To yeeld what fruites thou lift, though I
    liue lightlied and forlorne.
Æneas loft at *Troy*,
    Creufa faire his wife
And through and with ten thoufand *Greeks*
    hee made a defperat ftrife:
And rooming vp and downe,
    emboldned with difpaire,
Hee cryd aloud *Creufa* come,
    but could not find her there,
                            And

And ſtill he crid, till time
    her pallid ghoſt anone
Appeard, and gaue him certaine ſigns
    that ſhe was dead and gone.
So ſhall thy ſoule thy Ghoſt
    begin for to remoue,
And leaue to be within thy breſt,
    before I leaue to loue:
And when thy Ghoſt is gone,
    and paſt th'*Eliſian* lake,
No *Dido* ſhall complaine of mee,
    nor ſuffer for my ſake.
If *Romans* did returne
    in Arms of ſhining Steell
Our *Rubicon*, then were they deemd
    foes to the common weell:
But my returns to thee,
    are full of loue and peace,
As witneſſeth this iterat,
    and oft ſaid word Allace.
If I haue ſaid too much,
    let mee thy peace implore,
And my Epiloge with a ſigh
    I ſeale and ſay no more:
                 I.   Pro-

Protesting since thou knows
    how I am sworne thine owne,
And how thy Vertues by my Verse,
    throughout the world be known:
Thou wilt haue some remorse
    vpon my carefull case,
And let thy Courtasies conclude,
    my long long-cri'd Allace.

To LAIS.

THe faire faced Woman, and deformed Ape,
Hath Nature fram'd to want a taile wee see:
The fillie beaft with her vnfeemelie fhape,
Seems well content and pleaf'd that fo fhould bee:
    And yet the Woman ftriueth euen and morne,
    To haue a taile and ftill in Naturs fcorne.

But let it be (for to fupplie this want)
Each difcontented whore fhould haue one taile,
What reafon is't (fince Nature knew them skant)
A pockie Punck with pluralties fhould deale?
    This then is true, which I obferue as fure,
    A Beaft hath more difcretion, then a Whore.

Hac venit in thalamos dote fuperba tuos.

I ii.

His constant Resolution to
ERANTINA.

SHall abfence long, or diftance farr of place,
With lowring looks of frem'd vnfriendly foes?
Shall tract of time for les or longer fpace,
Haue any force to caufe mee change my choyfe?
No furelie no; I am not one of thofe:
I fhall be found no falce nor flitting friend,
My loue fhall laft as long as life fuppofe,
Luck be not fuch as fometime I haue feen'd:
But what remead, I may not mend, but meen'd,
And with your will I hold mee well content:
Though many thwartering things haue interueend
To interturb and ftay our true intent,
   Yet all thofe iarres fhall not my minde remoue
The day of death fhall be the date of loue.

Dum paris œnone poterit fpirare relicta,
Ad fontem xanthi verfa recurrat aqua.

Confirmation of his loue to
ERANTINA.

SHall abfence long bring change,
    or make my minde to moue?
Or yet fhall diftaunce farre of place,
    vnlock the linke of Loue?
Shall either this or that,
    yon, or the other thing,
Haue force to breake the blocke we band,
    before the *Paphian* King?
Thou art mine *Hero* ftill,
    and though the ftreams be ftark,
I through the waltering waues fhall fwim
    to thee but Boat or Barke.
I am not *Iafons* meat,
    Mædea to beguile?
My fayth is firme, this the caufe
    exponis mee exile.
Nor am I come by line
    of traytor *Troians* race,
I neuer thought no not by dreame,
    My *Dido* to difgrace.

Nor am I hee who brought
    the black faill for the white,
Leaft *Ariadne* kild his fyre,
    and if their wrack was white.
A *Pyramus* I am
    in deed, in thought, in word,
And fhould (wift I thou wert not weell)
    with blood imbrew my fword:
And if by Fames report
    thy pains I can perceaue
As *Hemon* did, fhall I giue
    the Ghoft abone the graue.
No that I looke to find
    fuch friendfhip on thy part,
Or promis kept which ay fhall be
    infhrind within my hart:
Or that I greeue for grace
    thy honor to degrade,
For if my Sainct be fafe and found,
    how can I but be glade.
In tears as *Biblus* did,
    though I confume away,
Who was huerted in a Well,
    as aunctent Writers fay.

                                                  And

And though I be refolued
    to loue thee tearme of life,
Yet muft I leaue thee for a while,
    Ulyfses left his wife.
My word fhall be my word,
    my kindnes fhall be knowne,
And with my oath I will no boure,
    for I am fworne thine owne.
And for thy fake I vow
    the Pilgrems weed to weare,
And when in wildfome wayes I walke,
    the Rod and Bag to beare:
And this my hoarie head
    vnrafed fhall remaine;
A tipe of my continuing trueth,
    till wee two meet againe.
And so with heauie hart,
    adue my deareft Dame,
In happie ftate long mayft thou liue,
    till I enuie the fame:
And would to God thy wealth
    were fuch as I would wifh.
So till the Gods our meetings grant,
    Thy fnowie hand I kis.
              I iiii.   To

To LAIS.

IF *Rodopæ* the loathsome Strumpet vile,
  Became to be a great *Ægyptian* Queene,
  Put not sweet heart thy hop's into exile,
Good luck may light vpon a life vncleene:
    Shee was a Queene, thou must an Emprice bee,
    For thou art thrise as great a whoore as shee.

Cui madidos minxit mentula multa finus.

His vnwilling Farewell to
PENELOPE.

A Frind fome time to *Thracian Cotys* fend,
In figne of loue, a veffell rich and rare:
But back againe before the bearer wend,
Hee brake the fame in peeces heere and there;
Not for contempt, but to preuent my care,
I brake this gift which thou haft brought, faid hee,
For if my feruants breake the fame, I fweare,
They fhould been bate, and I incenfed bee.
I *Cotys*-like (proud Dame, to eafe my paine,
And that thou be not forft to heare my cries)
Muft leaue to loue; nor fhall my Songs againe
Thy furfet breed, nor come before thine eyes:
   Not, that I loath, where I fo long did loue,
   Thou art vnkind, and I muft needs remoue.

His louing farewell to
PANDORA.

Deare to my soule once degne,
 those pafsions to perufe,
The Swan-like Dir'ges and the Songs,
 of this my deeing Mufe;
Which are *Minerua*-like,
 by beating of my braine,
Brought foorth to fhew the wondering world,
 my long fuppreffed paine:
For like the doomb borne fonne
 of that rich *Lydian* King,
Now at the imminent of death,
 with toong vntied I fing.
Had *Atis*-like my foe
 thy wedding day been flaine
By *Tydeus* fearce, then had I brook'd
 faire *Ifmene* allaine.
Or had thou been a man
 like her whom *Pheftne* bred,
Whom *Telethufa* promeft with
 Janthe faire to wed.

Then

Then had my riuall been
    as farr from thee as I,
Nor had he now, nor thou been iudge
    to my complaint and cry.
As *Tantalus* did cut
    poore *Pelops* corps a funder,
And made a banquet of his Sonne,
    vnro the Gods rare woonder:
Yet did they recollect
    his cutted Corps againe,
And *Tantall* they condemd to die
    In hunger ftaruing paine.
So cruell thou hes karu'd
    ten thoufand wayes my hart,
And thou indures obdurat ftill,
    and fenceles of my fmart:
Yet will the Gods, I hope,
    recure and purge my paine,
And punifh all thy cruelties,
    with cruelties againe.
Had I *Ixion*-like
    made vaunt of *Iunoes* fpoyle,
With patience then I fhould abide
    thy furie and this foyle.
                              But

But since it must be thus,
    from *Athens* I will flie,
With wise *Demosthenes*, and then
    in *Neptuns* asyll die.
Then cruell faire farewell,
    I may remaine no more,
I mind before wee meet againe,
    to see the *Celtik* shore.
But howsoeuer I err,
    or wheresoeuer I vaig,
In weell, in wo, in want, and wealth,
    thou shalt command poore *Crag:*
Yea might I make a Feast,
    As did *Democrits* sire,
To all the *Persian* troups, ou'r which
    great *Xerxes* bore empire.
Or were I begging bread
    like *Ithak Irus* poore,
Whom proud *Ulisses* with his fist
    feld dead into the floore.
Yea be I rich or poore,
    or poore and rich againe,
At hazards all I am thy man,
    and so shall ay remaine.

                                               Faire

Faire Homicid farewell,
    againſt my heart I goe,
And that al-maker knows I make
    a voyage full of woe:
But euen as *Araris*
    with ſilence ſweet doth ſlide,
And none perceiu's if vp or downe,
    or whither flows the tide.
So none ſaue thou ſhall know
    the caus of all my paine,
And none ſhall know wherefore I goe,
    Nor when I come againe.
And ſo till time wee meet,
    deare heart, whom I adore:
Farewell; yet giue me leaue to ſigh,
    and ſay, Farewell once more.

To

To his PANDORA,
from Englaud.

NOw while amid thofe daintie Douns & Dales
  with Shepheard Swains I fit vnknown to mee
Wee fweetly fing, and tell paftorall tales:
But my difcourfe and Songs-theame is of thee;
For otherwayes allace, how can it be.
Let *Venus* leaue her bleft abod aboue
To tempt my Loue, yet thou fweet foule fhalt fee
That I thy man, and thou fhalt die my loue.
No tract of time, nor fad eclipfe of place,
Nor abfence long, which fometime were due cures
To my difeafe, fhall make thy flaue to ceafe
From feruing thee till life or breath indures:
   And till wee meet, my ruftick mats and I,
    Through woods & plains, *Pandoras* prayfe fhal
                                     (cry.

To LAIS.

HArpaste poore, was blind of either eye,
Yet would fhee not beleeue that it was fo:
The roomes are darke wherein I dwell, fayd fhee,
Take mee abrod, and but a guyd I'le go:
   The wife was led abrod into the wind,
    And yet poore foule fhe ftill continued blind.

Thinks thou that change frō this to yonder place,
Can caus thy fhame and fcandall to decay?
No *Lais* no, I pray thee hold thy peace,
And put thefe fond opinions quite away:
   For while thy life, or yet my lins endure,
    The world fhall fay, thou art a fhameles whore.

Fœmina nulla bona est, vel ſi bona contigit vlla,
Neſcio quo caſu res mala facta bona eſt.

His faythfull feruice to IDEA.

MY wandring Verfe hath made thee known all- (whare
 Thou known by them, & they are known by
Thou, they, and I, a true relation beare: (mee:
As but the one, an other can not bee;
For if it chance by thy difdane I die,
My Songs fhal ceafe, and thou be known no more.
Thus by experience thou mayft plainly fee,
I them, thou mee, and they do thee decore.
Thou art that Dame whom I fhall ay adore
In fpight of Fortune and the frowning Fats,
Whofe fhining beautie makes my Songs to fore
In *Hyperbolik* loftie heigh conceits:
Thou, they, & I, throughout the world be known
   They mine, thou theirs, and laft I am thine own.

To my Honorable
good Lord and Maister (the true Mæcenas of my Muse) *George* Earle of *Dunbar*, Lord Barwick, high Tresurar of Scotland.

Am Noble (Mæcenas) *a spendthrift, vnwisely liberall; more prone to propine Presents, and make foolish Feastes, then to pay my Debts:* All my babling Bils are alreadie baptized, and nothing left, saue these *subsequent Songes; which to your Honor, in all duetifull loue and deuotion, I dedicate.* Philopæmen *did sometime leaue his companie, and comming aloue to a house where he was expresly looked for; his Hostes, who knew him not, and saw him so euill fauored a fellow, employed him to helpe her*
K. *Maydes*

Maydes to draw water, and mende the fire for Philopæmen. *The Gentlemen of his traine finding him busie at worke, enquired what he did? who answered, I pay the forfeyture of my vnhandsomnes.* I haue thought good (my Honorable good Lord and Maister) to giue these Songs the last place in my Booke: if any demaunde the cause, I answere with Philopæmen, *For their methodles and irregular vnhandsomnes.* If your Honor doe not protege and defende them, some Parasiticall Abdagasis *will seeke to kill* Asineus *and his brother vnder trust:* But be you a royall and seconde Artabanus, *who sayd to* Abdagasis, *(I can not cōsent to betray a man that trusteth to my protection; and since he hath giuen mee his hand, I will keepe the oath I haue made to him by my Gods:)* Doe herein (deare Lord) as you will encourage mee hereafter to vndertake a greater taske. I haue highly (I confesse) abused both time and talent in these amorose and idle toyes. But your Honor vpon the gracious acceptaunce hereof, may haplie ere-
long

long *fee mee recouer my eftate, and reedifie the decayed walles of my youth.* What I haue heere fet downe, is for your follace; and fo I befeech your Honor to accept from the Table of my Chamber, at your liberall charge and allowance, the . 5 . day of Nouember 1606.

*Your Honors owne man to the
laft article of expiration,*

Craige.

To the Reader.

MArie of *Vitezokia* beyonde *Iordane*, flying to *Ierufalem* when *Titus* and his *Romans* befiedged the fame, was enforced for hunger to kill her fucking Sonne, and hauing eaten the one halfe, the reft fhee referued. The Enemies fmelling the fent of that ezecrable meat, threatned to kill her, vnleffe they were fharers with her. Then fhee vncouered that part of her Sonne which fhe had left vneaten. At which fight they trembled, and horror fell vpon them. Then fayd *Marie*, this is truely my Sonne, & my doing; eate you of it, as I haue done; be you no more effeminate then a woman, nor more mercifull then a Mother. My *Poyems* and *Verfes* are (beloued Lector) the birth of my braine, & the ofspring of my ill aduentured

TO THE READER.

uentured youth. I haue thefe yeares bygone luxurioufly feafted and furfeited hereon, and haue with the *Vitczokian* Woman, couered this part of my Child till now: I pray thee with patience, take a part with the Parent; next time (God willing) thou fhalt fare better. But if any aske (how I prefumed to inuite my noble Maifter my Lord, my *Mecænas*, my all, to this foolifh and filthie Feaft of mine?) I anfwere: *Themiftocles* was animated to noble actions by beholding *Miltiades* trophies. And *Alexander* beholding *Achilles* Tombe, did greeuously figh with an honorable emulation. And his courteous welcomming of my vanities, will rauifh braue mindes from the boundles troubles of the world, and win them to the contemplation of Vertue. And fo his Honorable example in reading and refpecting Learning and the Learned, fhall pull donwe the *Babell* of ignoraunce. I confeffe (as *Plutarch*

K iii.   fpeaketh

TO THE READER.

speaketh of *Aristophanes* Poyems) my Verses are written for no moderat mans pleasure: yet since by his Honor they are countenanced, I beseech thee (good Reader) vse mee kindly; and for his sake, sit still with him, and take a part of my profane Feast. My Lord payeth for all, it costs thee nought saue thanks.

                Thine as thou behaues
                    thy selfe,

                      A. Craige.

ALEXIS to LESBIA.

COme be my Loue, and liue with mee,
And thou ſhalt all the folace ſee,
That glaſsie gulfs or earth can bring,
From *Veſta's* wealth, or *Neptuns* reigne.

For we ſhall on the Mountains go,
In ſhaddie Vmbers too and fro:
In Vallies low, and on the Bray,
And with thy feet the flowrs ſhall play.

And I ſhall make thee pleaſant Poſes,
Of Daſies Gilliflowrs and Roſes:
My Arms ſhalbe a Belt to thee:
Thine if thou wilt, the like to mee.

Of *Floraes* tapeſtrie thy Gowne,
Thy Cap ſhall be my Lawrell Crowne:
Which dreſt of *Daphne's* haire ſhall ſhine,
Whyls on my head and whyls on thine.

           And

And thou vpon thy rock ſhalt reſt,
And heare the Echoes from my breſt:
For I ſhall ſing in Sonets ſhill,
the charming numbers of my quill.

Yea wee with woond'ring eyes ſhall gaze
On many ſundrie curious maze:
And view the Architecture fare,
Of rich and ſtatelie buddings rare.

And we ſhall looke about and ſee,
The wrack of time before our ee:
The pendul ſtones, their builders ban,
Imploring help at hand of man.

And wee ſhall ſee the Riuers rin,
With delicat and daintie din:
And how my *Douern* night and day,
With ſweet Meanders ſlides away.

To pay her debts vnto the Sea,
And like a wanton *Nimph* doth flie
Through blooming banks with ſmiling face
Her Lord the Ocean to imbrace.
         And

And wee fhall fee the towrs of tree,
Halfe feeme to fwim, and halfe to flie:
Part in the Sea, part in the Aire,
And Eag'l heere, a *Dolphin* thaire.

Wee fhall behold *Nereid* Nymphs,
Make waters welcome from their lymps:
And euery houre into the day,
Fresh Floods and th' Ocean billowes play.

And we fhall heare the Roches ring,
While ftorme-prefageing *Mermayds* fing:
And on the Rocks the law's fhall roare,
Salut and refalut the Shoare.

And when *Apollo* taks his reft,
With wearie Horfes in the Weft:
And *Cynthia* begins to shine,
Thy Poets *Tugur* shall be thine.

Then shalt thou fee my homlie fare,
And what poore riches I haue thare:
And if thofe things can moue thy mind,
Come, come, and be no more vnkind.
Lifbia

LESBIA her anfwer to ALEXIS.

IF all were thine that there I fee,
Thou paynts to breed content to mee:
  Then thofe delights might moue my mind
To yeeld, and be no more vnkind.

Sith nought is thine that thou fets downe,
Saue Songs, thy felfe, thy Belt, thy Crowne,
Thy Tugure, and thy homely fare:
And that poore wealth which thou haft thare.

I might be compted moft accurft,
To dwell with thee, fuppofe I durft:
And men might thinke mee more then mad,
To leaue the better for the bad.

Yet leaft I fhould be deemd ingrate,
To loath thee for thy poore eftate,
Though Fortune be thy fremmit foe,
No reafon were I fhould be fo.

Thy Lines allure mee to be thine,
And thou fhalt fee it foone or fine:
The chriftall ftreams fhall backward moue,
Ere I forget thy faythfull loue.

                                A new

A new perswasion to LESBIA.

ONce more I pray thee be my Loue,
Come liue with mee, and thou shalt proue
All pleasures that a Poets vaine,
Can find on mould or in the mane.
Wilt thou vpon my *Parnas* walke,
And tread the Flowrs with leauie stalke,
Which bud on my biforked tops:
Bedew'd with sweet *Cactalian* drops.
On *Thithorea* wilt thou go,
Or *Hyampeus* too and fro?
Or wilt thou with *Pierid* Nimphs,
Drinke of these euer-flowing Limphs,
From *Hyppocrene* which diuall,
Or springs of *Aganippe* wall?
Wilt thou repose thee in the shade,
Which Nature hath diuinely made?
Apolloes Laurell thou shalt see,
And louely *Venus* Myrtle tree,
Alcides Popler full of state,
The Palme which thriues in spight of hate.
Minervaes Oliue, and the Mirr,
And of great *Mars* the warlike Firr:
                                    Which

Which Nature hath so well disposed,
And therewithall such walks inclosed,
As for rich Tapestrie shall serue,
From beames thy beautie to preserue:
The Gilliflowrs and Roses sweet,
Shall stoope their tops beneath thy feet:
The Vlolet and Primrose faire,
The Marigold with yellow haire:
Both Moli and the Balme shall smell,
With Miriads more then I can tell:
The louely Herald of the Spring,
The *Philomel* to thee shall sing,
Both Larke and Maues shall aboue.
Thy head their small recordars toone:
I'll make thee Garlands faire of Flowrs,
With Amadriads in their bowers,
With Myrtill boughs braue to behold,
And paint their leaues with spangs of gold,
Which I will checker all with frets
Of prettie pinks and Violets:
And when *Apolloes* Coach agaue
Giues way vnto *Dianaes* Wane:
Thy Poet on his pyping Reed,
Thy fansie with sweet Songs shall feed.

                                    Thon

Thou shalt want no content of mind,
Saue wealth, which feldome Poets find:
If pouertie hath power to moue,
Come, come fweet heart, and be my Loue.

A Letter to LESBIA, fhewing his difcontents.

OFt haue I pray'd thee be my Loue,
Come liue with mee, and thou shalt proue
All pleafures that a Poets vaine
Can find on mold, or in the mane:
Yet neither can my Loue (allace)
Nor my oblectaments haue place,
To moue thy hard and flintie hart,
Some pities portion to impart.
Difpeafure maks my Mufe be doomb,
And *Parnas* barren is become:
My Wels are dry, trite wayes my walks,
My Flow'rs do fade vpon their ftalks:
Trees lack both leaues, and Larks to fing:
Thofe Fruits thy falfet doth foorthbring,

Hadft

Hadſt thou not known that I was poore,
Then Luker might thy loue allure:
Why art thou of ſo churliſh kind,
To loue the moyan, not the mind?
Proud in her heart would *Phillis* bee,
To proue thy pediſeque, for mee:
Shee followeth mee, and yet I flie,
Purſew'd of her, and plagu'd of thee:
But wouldſt thou to thy ſeruile ſlaue,
Bequeath the credit which I craue?
Muſe, Birds, Hils, Wels, Trees, Flowrs, & Walks,
Would ſing, flow, floriſh on their ſtalks:
And I reuiu'd by thee (faire Dame)
My wonted courage would acclame.
Then let me know thy vtter will,
Vpon this Paper good or ill:
And ſo till I the ſame receaue,
I am thy well affected ſlaue.

Sonet

Sonet to LESBIA.

TIme and my thoughts Togither ſpurr the Poſt,
For once I thought to ſpend my time for gaine:
Yet while I thought this thought, the time was loſt
And left me there, to thinke my thought was vaine
And while I pauſe the poſting time to ſpend,
Time ſpends it ſelfe and mee: but how I muſe?
The more I muſe, the more I haſt my end.
*T*hus *T*ime doth mee, and I do *T*ime abuſe:
*T*hat *T*ime once tint can not returne againe.
A ſecret ſorrow doth poſſes my mind,
But leaſt the world ſhould know why I complaine
Deare to my ſoule I pray thee proue more kind.
   I dreame the darke, and driue in dooll the day,
   *T*hus waſt my time, and weare my ſelfe away.

LESBIA her anfwer.

DRiue not deare hart, in dooll the day,
Waſt not thy felfe nor Time away:
Doo not fo much as dreame by night,
Vnles thy Dreames be fhort and flight.
Though wauering wits in time will vaige,
Be thou thy felfe a conftant *Craige*.
And for thy Loue thou bears to mee,
I am thy debtor till I die.
What I haue hight hap good or ill,
But fraud or feare I fhall fulfill,
I am not of a churlifh kind,
To loue the moyane not the mind,
No contrar chaufe, nor fortune ftrange,
Shall make my fetled mind to change:
I am thine fworne, and I fhall feale
What I haue fayd; till when fareweale.

CODRVS Complaint and Farewell to *Ralatibia*.

A Shepheard poore with ſtore of pains oppreſt
Beneath the branches of a leauie tree,
With Lute in hand deliuered his vnreſt,
When none was nie but Satyrs, Fauns, and hee:
  And hauing tund his baſe and treble ſtring,
  Hee ſigh'd, hee ſob'd, and thus began to ſing.

Why am I baniſht from thoſe bleſſed bounds
Where I was wont with pleaſure to repaire?
What cruell doome my comfort ſo confounds,
And caſts mee in the confins of diſpaire?
What haue I done, ſayd, thought (allace the while)
  that can procure proſcription and exile?

I am condem'd, and no inditment heard:
There is no grace nor mercie in her eyes.
I plead for peace, and preſence is debard:
I loue, ſhe loath's; I follow, and ſhe flies:
  All modeſt means that may be, I haue vſ'd,
  My Songs, my ſelfe, my friends, are all refuſ'd.
         L.   Why

Why, was I borne to be the poynt of paine,
The fcorne of *T*ime, the obloquie of Fame?
My fellow Shepheards frollicke ouer the plaine,
*T*hey feed their flocks, & court the countrie Dame
   On Holidayes their Sonets fweet thy fing,
   And to their Loues their beft oblations bring.

But I exild from *Kalatibia's* eyes
By her decret, whom I fhall ay adore:
Muft facrifice, figh, tears, plaints, grons, and cryes:
But all in vaine, and woe is mee therefore:
   I long, I loue, I fry, I freeze, I pine,
   No punishment can be compard to mine.

Allace, allace, my flocks both ftarue and ftray,
quit macerat to want their maifters eye:
Which with *Licifcais* harmles Barke would ftay,
And turne againe from neighbour corns to mee:
   My litle Lambs, my faire and fertill Ewes,
   With fad reports their plaints for mee renewes.

What madnes mooues remorfles faire, thy mind,
Since neither plaints nor prayers can haue place?
Haft thou concluded ftill to kythe vnkind,
                                       And

And day by day delight in my difgrace?
  O bee it fo! if needs it muft be fo,
  For I am armd for euerie kind of woe.

Since I am thus profcrib'd, I pray thee take
(Faire *Kalatibia*) this inforc'd farewealc.
Since Fortune, Loue, and weerds, auow my wrake,
To whom fhall I (defpifed foule) appeale?
  O loue no more, nor leue no more a thrall,
  Die *Codrus* die, end loue and life and all.

But Pufillanyme poore and hartles man,
Why wouldft thou die to pleafe fo proud a Dame?
Though thou be banisht for a while, what than,
Shee's not fo cruell but shee may reclame?
  Yet flie, be gone; let good or bad befall thee.
  And care no more, fuppofe she neuer recall thee

And thus poore foule, from out the Groue he goes,
And leaues (allace) both Lines and Lute behind:
Which I (the true Secretar to his woes,
And fellow of his fortuns) did foorth find:
  And for his fake I figh, fing, fay, & show them
  that cruel fhe, whō they concern may know thē.
            L ii.   *Codrus*

CODRVS his reconciliation to his heart, after he hath abiured KALATIBIA.

POore wandring hart, which like the prodig child
  From reasons rule hath run so long astray,
Misled by *Loue*, with fancies fond beguild:
And now returnd with torne and rent array,
    my halfe and better part since thou art come,
    with true remorse most kindly welcome home.

Laciuious looks of life bewitching eye,
Inconstant oath's of most vnsetled mind,
You fals inflections of a *Iudas* knee,
You worthles vowes which vanish with the wind,
    Dispatch your selfe, and let mee liue in peace,
    Within my hart thou haue no dwelling place.

Come sit thee downe (deare hart) wee'l haue a feast
My fond Conceits I for a Calfe will kill:
I am thy Oast, and thou shalt be my guest,
Repenting Teares will furnish Wine at will:
    Our Musick Sighs : and if I were more able,
    Fayth thou should find a banquet for thy table.
                                                with

With hartie draughts will wee to drinke begin,
Vnto the brim let reaſonn fill each bowll:
I'll lock the gate, and *Loue* ſhall not looke in,
That our contract may knit without controull,
    In ſureſt ſort let vs betroth our ſelfe,
    And band gainſt Beautie, and the blinded elfe.

Sigh ſorie hart, and I will weepe with thee,
Let no eclipſe diuide vs two againe:
Let Reaſon hencefoorth guyd and ruler bee,
And waſt no more the ſwift wingd Time in vaine
    And while my teares can intertaine thy feaſt,
    Repenting heart thou art a pleaſing Ghueſt.

Now ſetlet heart ſecure and free from feare,
Though all the earth ſhould ſinke in ſeas of Loue,
Fleet in the Arke, ſit ſtill in Reaſons chare,
And to the world giue verdits from aboue,
    The life of Wiſedome in Experience lies:
    Then let thine owne misfortuns mak thee wiſe.

Fœmineos poſt hac diſce cauere dolos.

FINIS.

To the Author.

L Oue now refolu'd to work fo rare a wonder,
As to make *Rocks* bereauers, Stones a Streame,
Straight to a *Craig* of *Caledon* hee came:
Whofe yet vndaunted prid hee gan to ponder.
Haue I (faid hee) the Earth's deepe Center vnder,
Made *Phlegeton* his floods to feare my flame?
Did I the mightie Trident bearer tame,
And threatned too, the thrower of the thunder?
And fhall one onely *Craig* withftand my dart,
With that his Arrow to his eare he drew,
which through the yeelding air loud whiftling flew
And turnd his hardnes to a humane Hart:
From out whofe wound, witnes you Nymph's but names
Great Floods gufh out of fweet Castalian ftreames.

I. M.

Cragio suo.

INgenij si verna seges primoribus annis,
  in tam laudandum luxuriauit opus:
Quos fructus sperare iubes cum forttibus annis,
  Iudicij accedit lima seuera tui.

     Robertus Aytonus.

De Alexandro Rupœo populari,
 familiari et amico suo qui supra
  plebem vulgus et populum.

THreicij quisquis credit modulamine vatis
 saxa, feras, scopulos refsilijsse locis:
Orphea *crediderit rediuiuum carmine* Rupis
 Arctoæ *tumulo refsilijsse suo.*

    Arthurus Gordonus.